WRITING ACROSS CONTEXTS

WRITING ACROSS CONTEXTS

Transfer, Composition, and Sites of Writing

**KATHLEEN BLAKE YANCEY,
LIANE ROBERTSON,
AND KARA TACZAK**

UTAH STATE UNIVERSITY PRESS
Logan

© 2014 by the University Press of Colorado

Published by Utah State University Press
An imprint of University Press of Colorado
5589 Arapahoe Avenue, Suite 206C
Boulder, Colorado 80303

Portions of Chapter 4 appeared in an earlier version as "Notes toward Prior Knowledge and Its Role in Transfer," *Composition Forum* 26 (Fall 2012).

 The University Press of Colorado is a proud member of the Association of American University Presses.

The University Press of Colorado is a cooperative publishing enterprise supported, in part, by Adams State University, Colorado State University, Fort Lewis College, Metropolitan State University of Denver, Regis University, University of Colorado, University of Northern Colorado, Utah State University, and Western State Colorado University.

Cover design by Daniel Pratt

ISBN: 978-0-87421-937-1 (paper)
ISBN: 978-0-87421-938-8 (e-book)

Library of Congress Cataloging-in-Publication Data
Yancey, Kathleen Blake, 1950–
  Writing across contexts : transfer, composition, and sites of writing / Kathleen Blake Yancey, Florida State University ; Liane Robertson, William Paterson University ; Kara Taczak, University of Denver.
    pages cm
  ISBN 978-0-87421-937-1 (paperback) — ISBN 978-0-87421-938-8 (ebook)
  1. English language—Rhetoric—Study and teaching (Higher) 2. Report writing—Study and teaching (Higher) 3. Interdisciplinary approach in education. I. Robertson, Liane. II. Taczak, Kara. III. Title.
  PE1404.Y38 2014
  808'.0420711—dc23

                          2013048379

Cover illustration © Shutterstock/Hitdelight

CONTENTS

ACKNOWLEDGMENTS

Informed in part by a CCCC (Conference on College Composition and Communication) research grant awarded to Kathleen in 2006—"'The Things They Carried': A Synthesis of Research on Transfer in College Composition"—this collaboration began in 2007 when we first discussed our shared interest in researching transfer, especially through curricular design and classroom pedagogy. In 2009 Kara and Liane chose areas related to transfer for their respective dissertations at Florida State University, each directed by Kathleen, and for several years now we have continued to collaborate and share our continued transfer-related research in numerous publications and conference presentations. However, we wouldn't have been able to complete this project without the support of those around us, and for that we'd like to thank a number of people and institutions.

We owe a debt of gratitude to our FSU students, especially those who participated in the two studies we report on here, but also to the students who gave anecdotal feedback from our Teaching for Transfer (TFT) course pilot efforts and course iterations after that. They helped us understand where and how their learning was taking place. These students, many in their first semester at college, demonstrated as much commitment to learning as we have to teaching and researching, and we thank them for sharing their input and experiences.

Liane and Kara wish to thank the Florida State University English Department, and the Graduate Program in Rhetoric and Composition, for their funding of our graduate studies. We are grateful for the years of support that made possible our research studies and our scholarly inquiry into the question of transfer.

Thanks also to the First-Year Composition Program at FSU: to Deborah Coxwell-Teague, who helped ensure scheduling of our TFT course and who encouraged our studies; and to the graduate teaching assistants who allowed us access to their classrooms and materials so we could complete our research. And thanks also to Emily Dowd and Tamara Francis for their assistance with the CCCC research grant.

We also thank the colleagues who provided responses to our research—especially Kristie Fleckenstein, Linda Adler-Kassner, Ruth Outland, Jennifer O'Malley, and Jessie Moore. Likewise, we thank colleagues at the Elon University Research Seminar on "Critical Transitions: Writing and the Question of Transfer"; thinking with them throughout the life of the seminar has been extraordinarily helpful. We also thank Elizabeth Wardle for her assistance with our *Composition Forum* article; the Conference on College Composition and Communication for its 2006–2007 research grant; and the Council of Writing Program Administrators (CWPA) for its 2010 WPA Research Grant to Liane and Kara supporting this research. Thanks too to our current institutions for their continuing support: Florida State University, William Paterson University of New Jersey, and the University of Denver.

We have shared our research at several institutions and venues, and we thank them as well: Doug Hesse and the University of Denver; Paul Anderson and Miami University of Ohio; Mary Sheridan and the University of Wyoming; Gwen Gorzelsky, Kevin Roozen, and the Qualitative Research Network; the Conference on College Composition and Communication; The Council of Writing Program Administrators; the International Writing across the Curriculum Conference; and the Critical Transitions: Writing and the Question of Transfer Conference.

Special thanks as well to the reviewers of this book for their readings and response, the latter of which helped shape the final manuscript, and to Michael Spooner at Utah State University Press for encouraging this project from the beginning and shepherding us through the editorial and publication processes.

Not least, we thank our families, colleagues, and friends—including David Yancey, Genevieve Yancey, Sui Wong, Matthew Yancey, Kelly Yancey; Elizabeth Robertson, Douglas Robertson, Beth Robertson, Rich Robertson, Andy Colwell, and Richard Ellis; and Terry Taczak, Suzie Taczak, David Taczak, and Joey Taczak—all who continue to support us in work and in life.

WRITING ACROSS CONTEXTS

1

THE CONTENT OF COMPOSITION, REFLECTIVE PRACTICE, AND THE TRANSFER OF KNOWLEDGE AND PRACTICE IN COMPOSITION

Once you understand that writing is all about context you understand how to shape it to whatever the need is. And once you understand that different genres are meant to do different things for different audiences you know more about writing that works for whatever context you're writing in.

— Clay

Since the formation of the field of composition studies in the latter half of the twentieth century, writing faculty have worked to develop writing courses that will help students succeed; indeed, in Joe Harris's (1996) invocation of the 1966 Dartmouth Conference mantra, composition is, famously, a teaching subject. Thus, in the 1950s, during a period of productivity in linguistics, we tapped insights from linguistics—style or coherence, for example—to enrich our classrooms. In the 1960s and 1970s, researching what became known as the composing process, we began putting at the center of our writing classes process pedagogies that have since transformed the curricular and pedagogical landscape.[1] And in the 1980s and 1990s, we had a new sense of the writing called for in school—what we began calling academic argumentative writing—that was on its way to being fully ensconced in the classroom, notwithstanding the Elbow/Bartholomae debates about the relative merits of personal and academic writing.

If we fast-forward to 2013, however, we find that the landscape in composition has changed yet again. The academic argumentative writing that so influenced the teaching of composition is now regarded as only one variety of writing, if that (see, for example, Wardle's 2009 "Mutt Genres," among others). Likewise, scholars in the field have raised questions about our motives for teaching (Hawk 2007) and about the efficacy of what are now familiar approaches (Fulkerson

DOI: 10.7330/9780874219388.c001

2005). Just as important, the classroom research that distinguished the field in the 1970s and 1980s is again flourishing, especially research projects explicitly designed to investigate what has become known as the "transfer question." Put briefly, this question asks how we can support students' transfer of knowledge and practice in writing; that is, how we can help students develop writing knowledge and practices that they can draw upon, use, and repurpose for new writing tasks in new settings. In this moment in composition, teachers and scholars are especially questioning two earlier assumptions about writing: (1) that there is a generalized genre called academic writing and (2) that we are teaching as effectively as we might. Moreover, we have a sense of how to move forward: regarding genre, for instance, the singular writing practice described as academic writing is being replaced by a pluralized sense of both genres and practices that themselves participate in larger systems or ecologies of writing. Likewise regarding the teaching of such a pluralized set of practices and genres: curricula designed explicitly to support transfer are being created and researched. And as we will report here, various research projects (e.g., Wardle 2007) seek to document the effect of these new curricular designs as well as the rationale accounting for their impact.[2]

As *Writing across Contexts* demonstrates, we too are participating in this new field of inquiry, and our interest in how we can support students' transfer of writing knowledge and practice has been specifically motivated by three sources: (1) our experiences with portfolios; (2) our interest in the role of content in the teaching of composition; and (3) our understanding—and that of higher education's more generally—of the importance of helping students understand the logic and theory underlying practice if we want students to practice well.

A first source motivating our interest in transfer is our experience with portfolios of writing. Linking portfolios to writing curricula, especially when portfolios include texts outside the writing classroom (Yancey 1998, 2013), has been useful pedagogically, of course, but it has also helped put a very specific face on the transfer question. Through what we see within the frame of the portfolio—the set of portfolio texts and the student narration—we have been able to ask new questions about how students write in different settings and about how they understand writing. Looking at the multiple texts inside one portfolio, for instance, we can be prompted to observe—indeed, learn from the student—how he or she has made a successful transition from high school to college, while looking at another makes us wonder what else we might have done to support such a transition. Similarly, when exhibits in a portfolio include writing from other college classes, we ask other questions, chief among them why some students are able to make use of what they seemed to have learned in first-year composition to complete writing tasks elsewhere, while other students are not. Through the portfolio reflective text, what Yancey has called a reflection-in-presentation (Yancey 1998), students tell us in their own words what they have learned about writing, how they understand writing, and how they write now. In this context, we often ask other questions. How is it that students, drawing on previous writing knowledge, are able to recontextualize it for new situations? When students cannot do so, can we see why not, and given what we see, are there adjustments we should make to the curriculum?

A second source we have drawn upon in our thinking about the transfer of knowledge and practice in writing is the recent discussion in composition studies about what might be the best content for a composition curriculum. Forwarded by CCCC in 2006,[3] this discussion about the relationship of content and composition has sparked vigorous debates. Such content, some say, can be anything as long as the focus on writing is maintained. Michael Donnelly (2006) argues: "There is no 'must' content; the only thing(s) that really matters is what students are _doing_ — i.e., reading, thinking, responding, writing, receiving (feedback), and re-writing. When these things are primary, and whatever other content remains secondary, we have a writing course." Given this view, it's perhaps not surprising that many institutions—including many elite institutions like those in the Ivy League, as well as public institutions like Florida State University—provide additional evidence of this approach in the terms of their numerous theme-based approaches to first-year composition. Students in these FYC courses find themselves studying and writing about topics of interest to faculty, from medical narratives and video games to comic books and British history.[4] However, a competing theory of the role of content in any writing situation, including in FYC, is provided in Anne Beaufort's (2007) model of writing expertise—including its five overlapping domains: writing process knowledge; rhetorical knowledge; genre knowledge; discourse community knowledge; and content knowledge. In this model of writing expertise, content knowledge is not arbitrary, random, or insignificant, but rather is one of five domains that expert writers draw upon as they compose any given text. Such a model of writing thus invites us to consider whether and how this domain of content might be designed for FYC. Put as a more specific question, is it the case that all content supports students' transfer similarly, or is some content more useful than other content in assisting students with transfer?

A third source for us in our thinking about transfer in writing is recent discourse in higher education about the role of theory in assisting students with general learning. In fields like the scholarship of teaching and learning, and with the leadership of scholar teachers like Mary Hubar and Pat Hutchings, faculty in higher education are creating new ways of enhancing practice, especially in contexts where we incorporate theory *into* the practice as a mechanism for supporting students' development of practice. In other words, we are coming to understand that if we want students to practice "better," in fields ranging from chemistry to history and even in medicine, we need to help them understand the theory explaining the practice, the logic underlying it, so that it makes sense to them. Toward that end, for instance, advocates of "signature pedagogy" have created a tagline summarizing this approach: invoking "the core characteristics of a discipline to help students think like a biologist, a creative writer, or a sociologist." Here they emphasize the key expression *think like*. When applied to FYC, we began to consider how we might help students *think like* writers, in particular through the use of reflection. Including reflection in writing classes by now, of course, is ubiquitous, but its use is often narrow and procedural rather than theoretical and substantive. Students are often—perhaps typically—asked to provide an account of process or to compose a "reflective argument"[5] in which they cite their own work as evidence that they have met program outcomes. They are not asked to engage in another kind of reflection, what we might call big-picture thinking, in which they consider how writing in one setting is both different from and similar to the writing in another, or where they theorize writing so as to create a framework for future writing situations. We wondered, then, what difference, if any, it could make if we asked students to engage in a reiterative reflective practice, based both in their own experience and in a reflective curriculum, where the goal isn't to document writing processes or argue that program outcomes have been met, but rather to develop a theory of writing that can be used to frame writing tasks both in the FYC course and in other areas of writing.

What we present here, then, is our inquiry into the transfer question, an inquiry focused on the role a curriculum integrating composition content, systematic reflection, and the theory/practice relationship could play in assisting students with the transfer of writing knowledge and practice. More specifically, our research into how a curriculum *designed* to support students' transfer of writing knowledge and practice might function demonstrates our central claim: that a very specific composition course we designed to foster transfer in writing, what we call a Teaching for

Transfer (TFT) course, assists students in transferring writing knowledge and practice in ways other kinds of composition courses do not.

This research has two dimensions. First, the project developed the course content of the TFT course, one that is composition-specific, located in key terms students think with, write with, and reflect with reiteratively during the semester. The content is likewise reflection-rich, i.e., informed by readings in reflection and animated by students' use of the key vocabulary to create a theory of writing. Second, to inquire into the efficacy of this course, and more particularly into the role that this specific content of composition might play in fostering transfer of writing knowledge and practice, we studied the effect of composition content on students' transferring of writing knowledge and practice in three FYC classes. Each class offered a distinctive composition content: the TFT class focused on composition as content; an Expressivist composition class addressed voice and authorial agency; and a cultural studies, media-inflected composition class invited students to think about their place in an increasingly differentiated and mediated world. In reviewing these three classes and in interviewing students—as they completed FYC and again when they moved into and completed another semester of university courses, what we refer to as the post-composition term—we found that the reflective TFT composition curriculum we describe and analyze here supports students' transfer of writing knowledge and practice in ways (1) that the other courses did not and (2) that have thus far not been documented in the literature. In summary, the content of this course and its reflective practice provide a unique set of resources for students to call upon as they encounter new writing tasks.

As we conducted this research, we also encountered what we call a surprising finding. Although our study wasn't designed to explore the role prior knowledge plays in students' transfer, we found that prior knowledge—of various kinds—plays a decisive if not determining role in students' successful transfer of writing knowledge and practice. Based on our work with students, we have developed a model of students' *use* of prior knowledge as they encounter new writing tasks, located in three practices: first, an *assemblage* model in which students graft new composing knowledge onto earlier understandings of composition; second, a more successful *remix* model in which students integrate prior and new writing knowledge; and third, a *critical incident* model where students encounter an obstacle that helps them retheorize writing in general and their own agency as writers in particular.

In the rest of this chapter we provide considerable information as background for our study—indeed, one very helpful reviewer encouraged us to alert readers to how considerable and complex our discussion of this background is. It develops in layers, moving from the most general to the composition-specific. The first layer involves the concept of transfer itself: our chronological review of contrasting definitions of transfer and summary of current theories of transfer, noting areas of agreement as well as questions, especially those with relevance for the transfer of writing knowledge and practice. The second layer involves research on composition curricula generally, particularly where the research has implications for students' transfer: although not all the studies we report were designed to trace transfer, they all nonetheless provide empirical evidence of the efficacy of transfer, and thus demonstrate ways that our curricula have, and have not, historically supported students' transfer of writing knowledge and practice. The third layer also involves research on composition, in this case students' writing activities outside of school: research shows that what students learn about composing outside of school—in terms of practices, textuality, and their own abilities—can influence what happens inside school, in some cases dramatically. And the fourth and final layer involves the experiences of two of the more famous students who have made visible the challenges of transfer, McCarthy's (1987) Dave and Beaufort's (2007) Tim; their experiences help us forecast some of the issues to which our study responds.

LAYER ONE: DEFINITIONS OF TRANSFER: EARLY THINKING

What we mean by transfer, and how much—if any—transfer of writing knowledge and practice might be possible is a subject of some contention in higher education and in writing studies. At the heart of the contention is the issue of generalizability: is the activity in question—for example, writing—one where generalizability from one iteration of a practice to another is possible? Perhaps not surprisingly, as scholars have pursued this question, our understanding of what is and is not possible has become more sophisticated.

A conceptual background for transfer has been provided by psychology and education, and in terms of teaching for transfer, research in both fields has shifted from concluding that transfer is accidental (and thus not very teach-able) to promoting the teaching of transfer through very specific kinds of practices. Early transfer research in the fields of psychology and education (Thorndike and Woodworth 1901; Prather 1971; Detterman and Sternberg 1993), for example, focused on specific situations in which instances of transfer occurred. Conducted in research environments and measuring subjects' ability to replicate specific behavior from one context to another, results of this research suggested that transfer was merely serendipitous. Given our current research paradigms, however, which are more contextual and situated, such research is now discounted, in large part because earlier research traced evidence of transfer in highly controlled situations that were very unlike the situations in life requiring transfer. We now understand that research into transfer, to be helpful, will need to include contexts more authentic and complex than those simulated in a laboratory.

A conceptual breakthrough occurred in 1992 when David Perkins and Gavriel Salomon—often thought of as the godfathers of transfer—suggested an alternate approach: they argued that researchers should consider the *conditions* and *contexts* under which and where transfer might occur. They also redefined transfer according to three subsets: near versus far transfer, or how closely related a new situation is to the original; high-road (or mindful) transfer involving knowledge abstracted and applied to another context, versus low-road (or reflexive) transfer involving knowledge triggered by something similar in another context; and positive transfer (performance improvement) versus negative transfer (performance interference) in another context. Two points here are particularly important. One: the claim is that teaching for transfer is possible; indeed, if we want students to transfer, we have to teach *for* it. Two: given the complexity of transfer and the conditions under which it does or does not occur, Perkins and Salomon suggest deliberately teaching for transfer through *hugging* (using approximations) and *bridging* (using abstraction to make connections) as strategies to maximize transfer (Perkins and Salomon 1992, 7).

Definitions of Transfer Keyed to Tasks, Individuals, and Activities

Despite this breakthrough, scholars and researchers are still at odds about two issues: (1) how to conceptualize transfer and (2) how to develop a language for it congruent with what it involves. Thus, one difficulty some have with the word transfer is with what it suggests, that is, the sense that transfer could be understood as merely a mechanical application of skills from one situation to another. Such a conception of transfer, of course, is problematic given that the exercise itself, especially in the case of "high-road" transfer, is neither directly applied nor mechanical in its application. In other words, the historical definition of transfer can be seen as incongruent with what it is that we think transfer involves or requires, that is, with an adapted or new use of prior knowledge and practice. And at some level, this difficulty is rooted in how we conceptualize and define transfer, as Elizabeth Wardle suggests:

> Is transfer the act of an individual taking something she knows from one setting or task and applying it successfully in another setting or task? Is transfer the act of transformation, in which an individual takes something he knows and is able to repurpose or transform it for use in another setting or task that is similar or not quite the same? Is transfer found in the individual, in the task, in the setting—or in some combination of all three? And if transfer is found in the combination of individual, task, and setting, how do we understand and explain it? How do we teach for it, study it, and engage in it ourselves? (Wardle 2007, 66)

Based on questions like these, and drawing on the scholarship of Tuomi-Gröhn and Engeström (2003), Wardle outlines three conceptions or constructions of transfer located in different units of analysis—(1) tasks, (2) individuals, and (3) activity—although as we will see, there is overlap or interaction among them.

The first of these, what Wardle identifies as *task conceptions of transfer*, "theorize transfer as the transition of knowledge used in one task to solve another task" (Wardle 2007, 67). To support transfer of knowledge and practice, then, efforts located in this perspective focus on the design of tasks useful in the "training of basic mental functions . . . thought to have general effects that [will] transfer to new situations" (Tuomi-Gröhn and Engeström 2003, 19; quoted in Wardle 2007, 67). The second conception of transfer addresses *an individual's disposition*, specifically a disposition to search for situations where previously learned knowledge and practice can be used, in part through reflective practice. Here, as Wardle observes, "the focus is on an individual's 'disposition'; the goal of schooling, according to this view, is to teach students 'learned intelligent behavior' that will help them seek out and/or create situations in which what they have learned will transfer" (Tuomi-Gröhn and Engeström 2003, 24; quoted in Wardle 2007, 67). In this conceptualization of transfer, attention is given to helping a student develop a learner's disposition, but ultimately it is the individual who is responsible for transfer.

In addition to task and dispositional conceptions of transfer, however, we have a third conception, this one targeting context and the one primarily of interest to many compositionists (e.g., Donahue 2012). This third perspective intends to highlight *the learner inside of an environment so as to look at the interaction between the two*. In addition, it includes three versions: situated, sociocultural, and activity-based. The first, a notion of *situated* transfer, attends to "patterns of participatory processes across situations" (Tuomi-Gröhn and Engeström 2003, 25; quoted in Wardle

2007). Such processes come into play when an individual perceives the need to enact prior learning; terms to describe such an approach include *productivity* and *participation*. The second perspective, the *sociocultural* transfer, also influenced by Tuomi-Gröhn and Engeström, "shifts the emphasis from individual learners to interactions between people" who are engaged in the tasks (67). Wardle and Jessie Moore (2012) believe the work of another scholar theorizing transfer is helpful here: working in something of the same tradition, King Beach (2003) identifies *generalization* as the key term for the same perspective. According to Moore, King Beach, in "Consequential Transitions: A Developmental View of Knowledge Propagation through Social Organizations,"

> critiques the notion of transfer and instead examines generalization as knowledge propagation, suggesting that generalization is informed by social organization and acknowledges change by both the individual and the organization. Generalization as propagation further emphasizes associations across social organizations as active constructions, not just the application of knowledge to a new task. Beach extends his discussion by introducing the concept of consequential transition, which he explains as follows: "Transition, then, is the concept we use to understand how knowledge is generalized, or propagated, across social space and time. A transition is *consequential* when it is consciously reflected on, struggled with, and shifts the individual's sense of self or social position. Thus, consequential transitions link identity with knowledge propagation. (42)"[6] (Moore 2012)

What is particularly interesting here is Beach's rationale for identifying generalization as a more appropriate description of a transfer interaction. As Wardle explains, in Beach's view earlier conceptions of transfer point to a vague sense of learning, "which is difficult to isolate in studies and thus of little use to researchers even though we know such learning happens constantly" (Wardle 2007). But generalization in Beach's formation allows us to conceptualize transfer as "our ability to use prior knowledge in new ways and in new situations." It thus

> includes classical interpretations of transfer—carrying and applying knowledge across tasks—but goes beyond them to examine individuals *and* their social organizations, the ways that individuals construct associations among social organizations, associations that can be continuous and constant or distinctive and contradictory (41). Generalization, according to Beach, happens through transition." (68)

Building on this model, some writing researchers—and teachers—conceptualize transfer as requiring both the crossing of a boundary, otherwise known as a transition, *and* a willingness to engage in the new terms and practices the new context may require (e.g., Reiff and Bawarshi 2011; Brent 2012).

And last but not least, the activity-based perspective on transfer takes the ecosystem itself as the beginning lens, focusing "more explicitly on interactions between individual learners and contexts but expand[ing] the basis of transfer from the actions of individuals to the systematic activity of collective organizations" (Wardle 2007, 68). In this model, a key expression is not transfer, but rather "expansive learning," and for two reasons. First, transfer in its historical definitions, as we have seen, tends to isolate the individual from the system; and second, with a new expression there is less likelihood of confusion regarding the concept and the focus.

Transfer through the Lens of Bourdieu

In her most recent work on the conceptual problem of the ways we define transfer and the language we create to describe it, Elizabeth Wardle nominates yet another term, *repurposing*. In introducing her guest-edited fall 2012 special issue of *Composition Forum* focused on transfer, Wardle theorizes transfer as *repurposing*, contextualizing it through the conceptual lenses of Bourdieu's habitus and doxa:

> In this introduction to the special "transfer" issue of *Composition Forum*, I would like to offer some preliminary thinking about ways to expand our consideration of this phenomenon, which I will describe from here on out as "creative repurposing for expansive learning," or "repurposing," in brief (Prior and Shipka; Roozen). I argue for understanding repurposing as the result of particular dispositions that are embodied not only by individuals but also by what Pierre Bourdieu calls "fields" and the interactions between the two. In doing so, I focus primarily (but not exclusively) on the dispositions of educational systems. In sketching out my initial thoughts on dispositions, I draw on Bourdieu's discussions of "habitus" and "doxa." I suggest that to move forward in our consideration of repurposing and expansive learning, we might look beyond one task, one setting, or one individual to consider the habitus of the educational systems that encourage particular dispositions in individuals. I will suggest that creative repurposing is one consequence of what I will call "problem-exploring dispositions," while "answer-getting dispositions" discourage such repurposing. (Wardle 2012)

What is interesting about this conceptualization of transfer is threefold. First, Wardle brings insights from composition studies and cultural theory together to provide another way of understanding transfer. Second, the expression itself—*creative repurposing for expansive learning*—taps a common practice of writers in the 21st century—that is, the repurposing of texts for new rhetorical situations and/or media. Her use of the word repurposing is particularly appropriate for research on transfer in composition. And third, Bourdieu's notion of habitus corresponds roughly to dispositions, but in this case makes them available for institutions as well as for individuals.

Of notable interest to Wardle in this conception of transfer is the role that the educational system as habitus plays in shaping the dispositions of students, which, as indicated above, she categorizes into two types, problem-exploring dispositions and problem-solving dispositions. The first, problem-exploring dispositions

> incline a person toward curiosity, reflection, consideration of multiple possibilities, a willingness to engage in a recursive process of trial and error, and toward a recognition that more than one solution can "work." Answer-getting dispositions [in contrast] seek right answers quickly and are averse to open consideration of multiple possibilities. The first disposition is appropriate for solving ill-structured problems, while the second seems connected to well-structured problems often found in the field of education. (Wardle 2012)

In other words, a concern here is that, regardless of our best efforts, students are less likely to develop problem-exploring dispositions because the institutional habitus rewards only students' answer-getting practices, which practices exclude awareness:

> What emerges for me from this discussion is not only that both individuals and fields inhabit dispositions, but how institutional habitus creates and recreates orthodox discourse and attempts to push the social world to the status of doxa—beyond question or even recognizable as anything other than natural and inevitable. Individual dispositions toward finding and answering and moving on, rather than asking questions and exploring problems, might be directly linked to dispositions of fields or educational habitus that have a vested interest in maintaining dominant structures, beliefs, and practices (doxa). (Wardle 2012)

Such concerns, of course, seem to be particularly important given the US and state governments' continued emphasis on testing, one that consistently rewards problem-answering as the highest value.

As this quick review of the history of transfer suggests, for nearly 100 years researchers in higher education have theorized and retheorized transfer, during which time models of transfer have become both more contextualized and more inclusive of various factors, identifying participants, systems, and interactions between them that may all play a role. Likewise, in this process we have shifted from a simulation-informed notion of transfer to a highly contextualized one located in a new set of terms, among them generalizability and repurposing. As important for composition studies—although we appreciate the complexity of transfer as a phenomenon and the difficulty it therefore poses for learners and teachers—our interest in transfer continues for two reasons. First, education as an institution is predicated on the assumption that transfer of knowledge and practice is possible, and we take the role of education in supporting students as a first priority. Second, researchers and teachers alike believe that if we have a better understanding of transfer as phenomenon and practice, we are more likely to design curriculum and pedagogy effectively by creating tasks, support structures, and environments that do the best job assisting students with their transfer of knowledge and practice, regardless of how difficult that may be.

LAYER TWO: STUDENTS' TRANSFER OF KNOWLEDGE AND PRACTICE IN WRITING: WHAT EMPIRICAL EVIDENCE SUGGESTS

Sometimes informed by research on transfer generally and sometimes operating from other perspectives, research in writing studies has for many years inquired into how well, or not, our writing curricula support students and how our students use what they learn in our classes. Thus, despite the fact that some of this research was not designed to look specifically into transfer, the research reports often include findings bearing on the transfer question, precisely because they focus on the same concerns and employ similar methodologies. Some of this research has resulted from institutional interest in transition points (e.g., high school to college); some is an unexpected benefit of other kinds of studies (e.g., assessment studies; curricular studies); and some derives from research inquiring into the relationship between students' non-curricular literacies and their school-sponsored writing. In sum, we have empirical evidence showing that students do transfer knowledge and practice of writing. And as we explain, a general review of this research, including location, disposition, and institution, demonstrates evidence of such transfer in five dimensions: (1) the high school to college transition; (2) the introduction of writing process to students; (3) the rhetorical stance of the novice as a necessary beginning; (4) the interaction between students' academic and non-academic literate lives; and (5) the role of time—past and future—as influence and motivator.

From High School to College: Problems of Process, Conceptualization, and Language

Most studies of high school and college composers focus on either one or the other, but information about what students might bring with them from high school to college, in terms of writing practice and knowledge, can be helpful to curriculum designers. We know, for instance, that most high school students do not develop elaborate composing processes (Scherff and Piazza 2005; Applebee and Langer 2009, 2011; Denecker 2013). We also know from Pew research studies that while students write frequently and voluminously outside of school—texts, emails, Facebook posts, and blogs, etc.—they do not identify those activities as writing, which they attach to school and find tedious, but rather as *communicating* (Lenhart et al. 2008). But these students do bring to college what the school culture has emphasized: a test-based writing practice keyed to creating texts with simple beginning-middle-end structures, a central claim, and some forms of evidence, producing what is often called the five-paragraph theme, and what one of our Florida State students, invoking the Florida state test, called "FCAT-writing."[7]

One of the reasons we might be interested in what students bring to college in terms of writing knowledge and practice, of course, is that prior knowledge influences new learning. Transfer and prior knowledge, in the language of the National Research Council volume *How People Learn* (Bransford, Pellegrino, and Donovan 2000, 53), are interdependent: all "new learning involves transfer based on previous learning." Not all such prior learning is efficacious, however; prior knowledge can function in one of three ways. First, as suggested above in our discussion of task-conceptions of transfer, an individual's prior knowledge can match the demands of a new task, in which case a composer draws from and builds on that prior knowledge. We might see this use of prior knowledge when a first-year composition student thinks in terms of audience, purpose, and genre when taking up a first-term college writing task. Second, an individual's prior knowledge might be a bad match for, or at odds with, a new writing situation. We see this in students who believe that correct syntax and punctuation are the most important features of any text. And third, an individual's prior knowledge—located in a community context—might be at odds with the requirements of a given writing situation. For example, this writing classroom situation, in part, seems to have motivated the Vander Lei and kyburz (2005) edited collection that documents the difficulty some FYC students experience as a function of their religious beliefs coming into conflict with the goals of higher education.[8] As this brief review suggests, we know that college students, like all of us, call on prior knowledge as they encounter new writing demands, and the significant points here are: students actively use their prior knowledge; and while some prior knowledge provides help for new writing situations, other prior knowledge does not and can even present hurdles.

The Role of Students' Prior Knowledge Writing

The interest in how first-year students use prior knowledge in composing has not been taken up by composition scholars until very recently. Just in the last four years, Mary Jo Reiff and Anis Bawarshi have undertaken this task. For example, "Tracing Discursive Resources: How Students Use Prior Genre Knowledge to Negotiate New Writing Contexts in First-Year Composition" provides a compilation of this research, conducted at the University of Washington and the University of Tennessee. Centering on if and how students' understanding and use of genre facilitates their transition from high school to college writing situations, the Reiff and Bawarshi (2011) study identified two kinds of students entering FYC: first, what they call *boundary guarders*, "those students who were more likely to draw on whole genres with certainty, regardless of task," and second, what they call *boundary crossers*, "those students who were more likely to question their genre knowledge and to break this knowledge down into useful strategies and repurpose it" (314). In creating these student prototypes, the researchers drew on document-based interviews focused on students' use of genre knowledge as they entered their first term of composition: first, as they composed a "preliminary" essay, and second, as they completed the first assignment of the term.

> Specifically, we asked students to report on what they thought each writing task was asking them to do and then to report on what prior genres they were reminded of and drew on for each task. As students had their papers in front of them, we were able to point to various rhetorical conventions and ask about how they learned to use those conventions or why they made the choices that they made, enabling connections between discursive patterns and prior knowledge of genres. (319)

Based on this study, Reiff and Bawarshi (2011) identify two kinds of boundary guarding students, with the most important expression being what they call "not talk," what these researchers describe as language used by students describing "their written work (and writing process) by exploring what genres it is not" (325).

> The first, what might be called "strict" boundary guarding, includes students who report no "not talk" (in terms of genres or strategies) and who seem to maintain known genres regardless of task. The second kind of boundary guarding is less strict in that students report some strategy-related "not talk" and some modification of known genres by way of adding strategies to known genres. (329)

These students, in other words, work to maintain the boundary marking their prior knowledge, at most adding to the schema only the strategies they seek to preserve. By way of contrast, the boundary-crossing student accepts noviceship, at least implicitly, often as a consequence of struggling to meet the demands of a new writing task. Therefore, this writer seems to experience multiple kinds of flux—such as "uncertainty about task, descriptions of writing according to what genre it is not, and the breakdown and repurposing of whole genres" that may be useful to students entering new contexts in FYC (Reiff and Bawarshi 2011, 329).

What's interesting here goes beyond the prototypes themselves and extends to how those prototypes might change given other contexts. Moreover, this study raises intriguing questions, such as: How do students draw on prior knowledge in FYC? How does that impact their success in writing? What happens when students move on to a second term and take up writing tasks outside of first-year composition? Do they call on the prior knowledge they created in FYC, or do they default to strategies they learned in high school? Likewise, assuming that we recognize boundary-guarders and boundary-crossers as prototypes in a FYC class, what difference might both curriculum and pedagogy make? In other words, what might we do *inside our curriculum* to motivate those students exhibiting a boundary-guarding approach to take up a boundary-crossing one? And once students have boundary-crossed, what happens then? How can we support boundary-crossers and help them become more confident and competent composers?[9]

The Transfer of Process

In the 1960s, the field of rhetoric and composition began a well-documented shift from what's been called current-traditional approaches to process-based approaches, approaches that Richard Fulkerson (2005) surmises we are still using today, although it's fair to note that those processes can be very different one to the next. One important question we might raise, given the ubiquity of our "process pedagogy" over several decades, is whether or not the research shows that students transfer process. If transfer is possible, one would expect that students would be transferring some process of writing; if it's not, then our teaching of process would lead to a student adoption of process that was only temporary. Similarly, low-road transfer, the use of practices in multiple contexts without conceptual understanding or reflection, presents another issue to consider: no one argues that low-road transfer isn't occurring. Regardless of new situations, college students draw on their vocabularies, employ syntax, and create texts that have beginnings, middles, and endings, although it's worth noting that different genres will call for different diction, sentence structures, and rhetorical organizations. Thus, the issue that typically concerns compositionists is not the set of seemingly rudimentary practices associated with low-road transfer, but rather those associated with high-road transfer—the capacity to compose rhetorically, for a purpose in a given genre and for a specific audience—when two occasions are "paradoxical," both similar and different. And not least, fundamental to transfer is a set of occasions for writing that provides a scaffold for writing development. Put differently, if transfer of knowledge and practice is to be successful, students need to have future occasions to which they can bring their knowledge of composing and composing practices. Such occasions can be provided more systemically—thus contributing a helpful repetition—through a vertical curriculum supporting student development from the first year of college into general education and beyond into the major (Miles et al. 2008).

The research suggests that students do *develop* a writing process and they do *use* and adapt it as they move beyond FYC. Here, two studies are particularly illustrative. Conducted at the University of California at Irvine (UCI), Jarratt et al.'s (2005) study, constituted of interviews with 35 upper-level students in diverse majors, looked into the knowledge students transferred from FYC into other writing contexts. In their interviews, students spoke of two forms of transfer: (1) the *idea* of writing process and (2) its *practice*. More specifically, students reported that in their first-year composition course they learned about writing as process, about writing as a mode of learning, and about ways to develop their own multi-draft composing process, a process they adapted over time and occasion:

> The UCI undergraduates in our study demonstrated a sophisticated understanding of, or at least familiarity with, their writing processes. The majority reported engaging in pre-writing, drafting, and revision, techniques they learned from their lower-level writing classes. When asked an open-ended question about their approach to writing, students referred to a range of strategies: "cloud and visual diagrams, the use of arrows to organize ideas, brainstorming, and free-writing exercises." Even those who eschewed a formal process and instead preferred "just to start writing" spoke of composing as a process. . . . A cognitive sciences major describes a . . . recursive and process-oriented approach to his writing: "Usually what I do is I will write and I will read through it and then I will write some more and then I will read the whole thing over again, and then if I remember something that I haven't put down, I will work it in. I have never written down an outline, I don't know why. I am writing and revising the whole time." Though these students may not produce discrete drafts for revision, they still view their writings as works-in-progress rather than finished products. (Jarratt et al. 2005, 3–4)

Jarratt and her colleagues were especially impressed with the students' "acceptance of beliefs that we, writing studies specialists, have long held. They understand that writing, or more specifically, the process of writing, leads to the construction of knowledge" (5). At the same time, while the students could point to or describe writing practices, they often struggled to find language that would facilitate their descriptions, especially in regard to "modes of development" and "academic genres"—a point not unlike that made previously by Reiff and Bawarshi:

> While the students we interviewed were articulate about writing process and disciplinary differences, many of them lacked a basic vocabulary well accepted across disciplines for modes of development and academic genres. If students don't remember, or can't reproduce the terminology for common academic writing practices, can they be said to have "learned" them? In a practice-based field, the case can be made for tacit knowledge, mobilized within various contexts and in response to situated invitations to write. On the other hand, one could make the case that any continuity of learning across the highly fragmented and long-term process of university education must rest in a shared language carried from setting to setting. This sample of students did not convince us that we have succeeded in cultivating a pedagogical memory of writing terminology. (Jarratt et al. 2005, 8–9)

A key question here, then, is how a shared language might facilitate students' progression across "various contexts"; another is what role such a vocabulary might play in fostering transfer of knowledge and practice in writing.

Like the UCI study, the Hilgers, Hussey, and Stitt-Bergh (1999) University of Hawaii project intended to explore the efficacy of its writing across the curriculum program; in its results, we see ways that students carry forward what they too have learned in earlier contexts. In their study, Hilgers, Hussey, and Stitt-Bergh set out to answer two questions: (1) How does disciplinarity affect students' understanding of writing tasks? (2) What do students nearing completion of the university's writing-intensive (WI) requirements report that they know about writing? This study involved two sets of interviews with 34 students, the first interview providing a chance to get to know the student, the second to explore with the student the impact of the writing experience provided by the University of Hawaii. Interestingly, this study also showed that students develop and carry forward an elaborated writing process they value, and that they struggle with a language to describe this activity. For example, Hilgers, Hussey, and Stitt-Bergh (1999) report that

> None of the students viewed writing as a linear process in which they regurgitated facts or recorded their thoughts on paper. None of them

described writing as merely drafting and revising. Instead, students viewed "writing" as a set of problems to be solved and goals to be reached. In solving problems and seeking goals, they backtracked, changed tactics, and engaged multiple sources of information and advice. (334)

The writing processes that students engaged in varied, to be sure, but most of the writing processes that students described were "social": 59% them "talked with their classmates or friends about their focal assignment and/or received feedback from them on written drafts," even when not encouraged by their instructors. Students had a language to draw on to describe writing process activities—drafting and revising, for instance—but when trying to describe genres and disciplinary writing, students exhibited what the researchers refer to as an "unaware[ness]":

> Our interviewees, while confident in their facility with certain genres, seemed unaware that their understanding of genres was limited by the contexts of a specific classroom, a "controlled circumstance." Further, the difficulties interviewees experienced in discovering appropriate inquiry processes and in solving content problems suggested that they had an essentially superficial understanding of genres: they were versed in format and stylistic conventions; they knew that the writing in their major was different from other writing they had done; but they in general lacked an understanding of the underlying values and epistemologies that different genres, or even a particular genre, represented. (Hilgers, Hussey, and Stitt-Bergh 1999, 347–48)

It's good news, from a curricular and pedagogical perspective, that there's a match between what we *teach*—writing process—and what students say that they *know* and *practice*; students develop composing processes in first-year composition, and they take those processes—and an understanding of their value—with them into other composing situations. Such a match suggests, per Perkins and Salomon (1992), that we can teach for transfer. This research recommends four areas of focus for our teaching of composition: on contexts of writing; on language or vocabulary of writing; on genres themselves; and on the "underlying values and epistemologies that different genres, or even a particular genre," represent (Hilgers, Hussey, and Stitt-Bergh 1999, 347–48).

The Rhetorical Stance of Noviceship

There's a good deal of research showing how important it is that students beginning college inhabit the role of a novice. In this section, we report on two strands of that research—longitudinal studies, and studies of the impact of Advanced Placement on college writers—both of which speak to the need for students to begin as *new* writers when they enter college.

Like Jarratt et al. (2005, 2008) and Hilgers, Hussey, and Stitt-Bergh (1999), Nancy Sommers and Laura Saltz did not intend to study transfer of knowledge and practice; their intent, as Sommers and Saltz (2004) explain, was to conduct a longitudinal study investigating students' experience of the writing curriculum at Harvard University. But perhaps not surprisingly, what they find is transfer-related. The early writing courses that Harvard students take are rich with scholarly and academic texts and the reading of them; readings provide the material for writing. Thus, as part of their study, Sommers and Saltz document and address ways that students seek to make sense of an overwhelming amount of material they must read in order to write. What Sommers and Saltz also find, however, is that as important as learning how to read is, even more important is the student's *disposition* toward the material itself and its uses.[10] This finding has two components. First, the first-year student must willingly adopt the stance of a novice in a new world, one that demands more of his or her writing than was asked in high school, and a stance fraught (admittedly) with uncertainty and ambiguity. Second, the student cannot write from a position of expertise, but must write *into* such expertise: students need to immerse themselves in the material, get a sense of the parameters of their subjects, familiarize themselves with the kinds of questions asked of different sets of evidence, and have a stake in the answers before they can articulate analytical theses (Sommers and Saltz 2004, 134–35). Students who were not successful in adopting this novice-as-expert stance, according to the study, did not fare as well as those that did; that is, they may have earned good grades and a Harvard degree, but they did not learn to "participate in the world of ideas," or as one student put it, to both "give and get" as a participant in a larger conversation (141).

Other studies, like Lee Ann Carroll's (2002) longitudinal study at Pepperdine, have reported similar results. Examining the ways that students navigate the college's writing curriculum, Carroll's research pointed to two moments especially important for rhetorical noviceship, first as students move into college, and second as they move into their majors. Interestingly, this model of college writing development corresponds to the model of curriculum Thaiss and Zawacki (2006) articulate in *Engaged Writers and Dynamic Disciplines*. In this study of the writing across the curriculum program at George Mason, and based on multiple data sources (e.g., faculty interviews, student interviews), Thaiss and Zawacki hypothesize three tiers of activity supporting a college writer's development: a beginning tier where writers search for disciplinarity and for a set of rules that will govern their writing; a second tier where, since the rules aren't clear, there seems to be only inconsistency; and a third tier where differences are associated with disciplinarity (109–10). Between each tier, of course, is a site of transition and thus an opportunity for transfer, and the two points of noviceship seem, like those plotted by Carroll, to occur at two entry levels: the college and the major.[11]

A second kind of study, focused on a somewhat different aspect of college writing, points to the importance of noviceship from the perspective of students who try, in some formal curricular way, to bypass it. Hansen et al.'s (2004) research on the efficacy of Advanced Placement, for example, speaks to the need for students to understand college writing—paraphrasing Moffett (1968)—as a *new* universe of discourse where they are novices: "our results show that students who score a 3 on the AP exam and do not take a first-year writing course are likely to suffer real consequences in sophomore courses that require writing assignments" (Hansen et al. 2004, 40). In this case, the AP students exempting FYC believe that college writing can be "delivered" in high school, but the Hansen et al. data suggest otherwise, that in fact being a college writer requires learning how to write college writing in college settings. More generally, as these studies document, success in college writing contexts requires (1) that students begin as novices and (yet) become novices again, especially as they begin the major, and (2) that they write their way into expertise from taking a position of expertise.

LAYER THREE: THE ROLE OF WRITING OUTSIDE SCHOOL

At the same time students write *in* college they are writing *outside* of college, sometimes as a function of a college assignment, other times on their own—as part of a job or for personal reasons. Moreover, in the case of transfer of writing knowledge and practice, these other writing sites, even when linked to curriculum, function differentially, sometimes with an extra set of writing demands and challenges, other times as an opportunity for concurrent transfer. Nora Bacon (1999), for instance, focuses on the kinds of transfer involved in community service learning, where the service is linked to a course but whose writing requirements do not precisely mirror those of the classroom. Bacon observes that successful writing in this setting involves extra writing factors such as "social involvement." Based on her work with students writing in this kind of setting, she raises several questions about the complex nature of transfer of knowledge and practice to a non-academic setting even when that setting *is* directly linked to the academic setting:

What exactly is the relationship between the knowledge students develop in school and the knowledge they need in other settings? Do the skills and knowledge we value here have value in the community and the workplace as well? Do students learn them well enough to make use of them? Do they transfer automatically, or with effort, or not at all? (Bacon 1999, 53)

Students engage in writing outside of school as well, and such writing can provide for an often-invisible concurrent transfer that is sometimes helpful, sometimes not. Matt Davis (2012) documents the experience of Natascha, a self-sponsored blogger whose very successful experience with blogging presents an obstacle to her completion of a fairly standard review of literature for a college assignment. In part, this may be because Natascha isn't just any blogger: she created, administers and writes a book review blog attracting over 2,500 members and, at the time, over half a million page views. Given this experience, and when asked to write a review of the literature for a longer project, Natascha enthusiastically perceives a connection between her blog reviews and the academic review. As Davis remarks, however, that connection conceals more than it articulates. Unable to discern the *distinctions* between the book industry model of "the review-as-summary-and-recommendation" and the academic model of review as "summary, connection, and synthesis" (17), Natascha writes the academic review as though it were the blogging review. The perceived connection in this case, as Davis comments, is unhelpful: "the connection hasn't provided [her with] substantive ways of dealing with the challenges of a new context and new genres" (75).

In other cases, a kind of self-sponsored transfer can also be both appropriate and useful, as the next two examples illustrate. Sometimes the transfer is a quick carry-over from practice, as explained by Yun Moon, a student at the University of Nevada Las Vegas, who adapted her text-messaging practices for note-taking in school, a case of both transfer and deicity (the latter a situation where someone uses given technology for a purpose for which it wasn't designed: see Yancey 2004). Yun decides to use texting as a mechanism to take notes in class because it forces her to use English: "When I speak English, I use a mix of Korean," she says, "But when I text message, it makes me use English instead of Korean-English." Moon thus *repurposes* her newly developed personal texting practices for a school task, which she says also "helps me to write faster." We see in this example that students can and do intentionally self-initiate transfer as a kind of repurposing, as Wardle (2007) suggests.

Another student, Doppel, shows us a different kind of transfer, in his case based in work experiences that have provided him with writing *strategies* available for transfer. In Michelle Navarre Cleary's (2013) study of adult learners and the ways they attempt transfer between academic and non-academic settings, Doppel demonstrates what is possible. Doppel is something of a Renaissance employee and student, having worked in various jobs, among them as a researcher and a DJ. Having engaged in a variety of work situations, Doppel is adept at using what he has learned in them—in this case, from his architecture and project management training—to serve writing needs in other contexts, and he is quite articulate about how he understands his writing process:

> part of my secondary education was finishing my Architect's Associates for drafting. So I used to think of things on paper in blocks and chunks, and I would move them around like that. And eventually, when I was doing more projects and keeping schedules . . . what I do is I draw blocks out on a paper, and they'll go down the left-hand side, say from top to bottom, and then next to that block is the information of that project. And I think eventually I suppose in a way that's sort of a bullet point . . . I see it parsed out. : . when I'm thinking about writing five pages, I will visualize okay what's the first three quarters of the page supposed to look like? And the bottom quarter into the full second page, what is that going to look like? So again it visually parses out like that. And that actually helps me establish the rhythm of the paper and where the idea is going to be presented. How do they segue into one another . . . then I'm not so worried. It's like okay here are the ideas. They're not in your head in some grandiose amazing developing concept. (Navarre Cleary 2013, 677)

In this case, the highly personalized writing process Doppel uses is an adaptation, or repurposing, of what he learned in a specific field: as an older student, he has multiple experiences to draw upon and add to what he will learn in school.

However, the writing behaviors Doppel developed *in* school, in his case going back to middle school, haven't disappeared either. When a writer perceives learning to be relevant, wherever it occurs, it can serve as a resource to be tapped. Thus, when the writing demands of the workplace prompt Doppel to review his composing, he goes back to what he learned in middle school and carries that, first, to the workplace, and second, to college. As Cleary explains, Doppel

> initially learned about outlining, drafting and revising in middle school, but he did not apply these strategies until his experiences in the work world put him in situations where they became necessary. . . . In Doppel's case, it was not until the workplace that he found the need to apply the writing strategies he had learned in school. When he returned to school, he brought these strategies back with him. In describing his current writing process, he makes clear that "We'd be having a completely different conversation if this were ten years ago." (676)

More generally, what we see in these students' transfer is twofold. First, students develop both notions and processes—knowledge and practice—in many sites of writing, including the spaces of digital media and the workplace; students will draw on all of them, even when some of them are years, or even decades, old. Second, as in the case of writing experiences in school, some of these experiences will be helpful, others less so or not at all.

The Role of Students' Conceptions of Writing

In transfer, time matters. As we saw in Natascha's (Davis 2012) and Doppel's (Navarre Cleary 2013) experiences, past learning can be tapped in contemporary situations, but how it functions varies. As important are the conceptions of writing that students develop in the process of completing writing tasks—that is, how they understand writing—and the ways those conceptions motivate students, for good and for ill.

A comparison between two different journalism students illustrates how such conceptions can affect transfer, or put differently, how it can shape a writer's future. The first student, profiled in "'Big Picture People Rarely Become Historians': Genre Systems and the Contradictions of General Education," is Russell and Yañez's (2002) now well-known account of Beth, an aspiring journalist convinced of the integrity and objectivity of reportorial accounting. When asked to write in an Irish literature class that she needs for graduation, Beth is resistant, believing that "good" writing means her preferred writing, a clear, straightforward, and factually-based journalistic writing, not the historical writing required for the class, which to her feels inexact and duplicitous. What finally persuades her that it might be otherwise is learning about the relationships between two "kinds" of writing (i.e., history and journalism) and about how history—in its reliance on sources like newspapers—is created, in part, by the writing she values. In this case, once she has learned about how genres in these fields contribute to each other— that is, once she has a grasp of the bigger picture cited in the article's title—she is ready to write. And the bigger picture here, of course, is as much about a theory of genres, and their relationships, as it is about writing in a given genre.

A different case is outlined by Kevin Roozen (2009), who tracks the writing development of Angelica, a student who began writing in journals as a child, whose journal writing continues through her college years, and whose conception of writing is profoundly influenced if not determined by this activity. As Roozen explains, "over a span of twelve years, this literate activity developed from a brief fourth-grade handwriting exercise into a rich and complex set of literate practices and sustained engagement with multiple genres—from simple sentences into a blend of poetry, song lyrics, short stories, and daily observations" (550). As a college writer, Angelica continues her journaling practice and, much like Matt Davis's (2012) Natascha, she routinely attempts to transfer what she does in her outside-of-school writing to that inside school. For example, in completing a curricular literary assignment calling for a conventional kind of rhetorical development, Angelica employs a highly personalized style characterized by rich images, the kind of style typically found in a newspaper or magazine feature story, but with disappointing results. Although the instructor valued aspects of the completed text, he wanted a more genre-specific enactment. Here, a genuine disagreement between student and instructor occurred: whereas Angelica "viewed the opening sentence as a creative re-use of key practices developed through her journaling, and the paragraph as a whole as an inventive blending of multiple practices, her instructor read it as a failure to conform to the privileged conventions of literary analysis" (Roozen 2009, 558).

Having begun her academic career as an English major, Angelica switches to journalism: from "Angelica's perspective, further participation in English studies as a major and a career meant ignoring her penchant for vivid description and perhaps some of the cultural discourse practices she found so important." In her journalism classes, especially those focused on feature writing, Angelica finds her personal-journal style located in rich descriptions, accepted. Writing one story, for example,

> Angelica retooled a key literate practice from her private writing, redeploying it from her journals to journalism. Angelica's statements about the emphasis she placed on "the way the picture is painted" and "the forceful images" echo the penchant for rich description that marks her journal writing, and those practices resonated with the key aspects of feature stories: the use of creative and forceful language and the use of vivid imagery to capture the reader's attention. (Roozen 2009, 560)

Later, Angelica takes an internship with *Hispanic Magazine* in Miami, where she is also able to bring multiple writing experiences together into a writing process and text appropriate for a new venue:

> In addition to the colorful descriptions from her journaling so prominent in the story's opening paragraph, Angelica's reflection on her writing process points to the other practices that animate this story. Her reference to

the constant rewriting she engaged in, for example, echoes the drafting and redrafting emphasized by her Journalism 150 instructor, while her reference to "scene" and "mood" might index Angelica's experiences with literary analysis in her undergraduate English literature courses, or perhaps from earlier English courses in high school or before. (Roozen 2009, 564)

As was the case with Doppel, Angelica is able to transfer her writing practice and knowledge; drawing on various resources, she repurposes them for a new rhetorical situation. Moreover, in doing so Angelica draws on experiences from multiple spheres of activity to create a literate identity:

In repurposing what has commonly been dismissed as private writing to accomplish literary analysis and journalistic feature stories, literate practices from Angelica's journaling helped to splice together the dominant dichotomies (i.e., public/private, transactional/expressive, male/female, academic/personal, and intellectual/emotional,) and social spaces (i.e., home, community, school, work) traditionally used to divide the literate landscape that persons inhabit. And yet, this trajectory does not outline just the ontogenesis of literate practice but also the development of a literate identity. (Roozen 2009, 566)

In Angelica's case, her desire to include in her school writing tasks what she understood as successful practices motivated a shift to a new major, with a family of genres more hospitable to such transfer. More generally, students' conceptions of writing and of the value they assign to writing can motivate and inform choices small, as in writing assignments, and large, as in the choice of a college major.

The Role of Students' Perception of the Future in Motivating Transfer

The future—and in particular, the role curriculum can play in motivating students to prepare for future tasks—can also influence students, both negatively and positively. Three examples demonstrate how students' perception of the connection between current writing tasks and future writing tasks influence their behavior.

In the first example, Linda Bergmann and Janet Zepernick trace how students can discount FYC precisely because of its perceived *irrelevance* to their future writing lives:

Because [the students] saw the writing they are asked to do in English classes as personal, subjective, creative, and primarily intended "not to bore the reader," they failed to see any connection between what they have learned about writing in English classes and what they see as the objective, fact-based, information-telling writing demanded elsewhere in their academic and professional lives. (Bergmann and Zepernick 2007, 131).

Furthermore, without being able to make a connection between such contexts, the students weren't motivated. As Bergmann and Zepernick observe, "All of the many . . . concepts and skills that form the basis for composition pedagogy were perceived by our respondents as either inapplicable to their professional development (and therefore worthless) or as meddling with their self-expression or creative thinking (and therefore out of line)" (131). In sum, the students divided writing into two categories, one personal and thus not available for instruction, the second professional and not subject to the presumed expertise of faculty in English.

A second example turned out quite differently, in part because the students were further along in their academic careers, in part because in writing in the disciplines (WID) classes students could more easily make the connection between the writing in class and the writing they expected to be doing in the future. In other words, these students believed that the WID writing they were engaged in pointed them toward a future. In the aforementioned case of the Hilgers, Hussey, and Stitt-Bergh (1999) University of Hawaii study, "students on the brink of graduation were engaged in writing assignments that they believed prepared them for future employment or an advanced degree: more than 80% of the students reported preparedness for writing in their chosen fields" (345). In addition, a majority of the students, 68%, were sufficiently motivated to create their own goals for these assignments, much as did the "novice" students in the Harvard study of writing. As the researchers note, "the fact that the assignment was in their major, rather than in a general-education course, created a presumption of its relevance to personal interests and career goals" (330).

As important, however, is the fact that such relevance with an effect on motivation can be *designed* into a course. At Oregon State University, Tracy Ann Robinson and Vicki Tolar Burton (2009) found that students can be motivated to improve their writing when they understand that one course goal is for students to develop writing knowledge and practice that they can transfer into another context. In this model, students are explicitly told that transfer is an intent of the curriculum (Robinson and Burton 2009). Toward that end, the Oregon State project invited students to complete a Writer's Personal Profile (WPP), a start-of-term questionnaire to support writing and learning in upper-division writing intensive (WI) courses. Intended for use by students close to graduation, the WPP invites respondents to reflect on their college writing experiences, their strengths and weaknesses as writers, and the role of writing in their future careers. Then, based on these reflections, students set personal writing goals that will serve them in their post-graduation workplace and toward which they will work throughout the WI course. As well as laying the groundwork for their forthcoming course experience, the WPP also establishes a baseline reference for students' self-evaluation of their writing progress, both during and at the end of the term (Robinson and Burton 2009). In addition, instructors were invited to ask students to revisit their profile before the conclusion of the term. Students who used the profile tool

> collectively reported more growth as writers and saw more usefulness for the start-of-term tool than students who did not review their WPP responses before completing the end-of-term assessment. Perhaps the most striking difference in responses from these two groups pertained to personal writing goal achievement. Of those who did review their original WPPs, 42% reported having made significant progress toward their writing goals, while only 14% of non-reviewers reported significant progress. (Robinson and Burton 2009)

Belief that what a student is learning in a writing context will be useful in the future thus motivates students, and the reverse is true—that if no connection can be seen, students do not value the opportunity—as we see in the Bergmann and Zepernick study.

What does all this mean? When we consider this quick synopsis of what the research on transfer of knowledge and practice in writing shows, six patterns are clear.

1. As the graphic suggests, students write in many different sites: in high school before attending college; in personal venues before, during, and after college; in co-curricular sites like service learning and internships; in writing centers; in the workplace; and, of course, in college classes. Accordingly, there are abundant opportunities for concurrent, or cross-transfer, and students do engage in such transfer.

2. Students bring to college a sense of text and an ability to argue a claim, but as students begin college, they may fall into one of two groups, Reiff and Bawarshi's boundary guarders or boundary crossers, and it's also possible that such designations correspond to Wardle's problem-solvers and problem-explorers.

3. Time plays an often invisible but highly influential role in transfer: past experiences and future links contextualize it. Students draw on childhood experiences that can be formative; when they see a connection with the future, they are better motivated.

4. For several decades, we have been teaching process, and according to our students, they transfer process. In addition, there is some evidence that they also come to value composing process as a mechanism for learning.

5. Students have a sense of genre and write inside the conventions of genre, but they don't develop a conceptual understanding of or a language for genre, nor can they describe taking what they have learned about genre in one context and using it in another.

6. More generally, students don't create a mental map of writing that helps them move from one context to another and understand the relationships between writing in different contexts.

LAYER FOUR: McCARTHY'S DAVE, BEAUFORT'S TIM, AND THE TFT COURSE

We close this chapter by revisiting two students whose college writing experiences have, in some ways, framed the transfer question for composition, and we use the context presented here to outline the TFT course that we detail at the end of this book.

In 1987 Lucille McCarthy described Dave, a first-year college writer, as a stranger in a strange land—writing without a passport, a travel guide, or a portfolio to assist him in making some sense, some helpful meaning, out of diverse writing occasions and demands. In McCarthy's study, Dave wrote in three sites of writing, all of them early in Dave's career—FYC, literature, and biology—and perceived value in two of them, seeing value in each case for different reasons. Believing that first-year composition would set the stage for the rest of his academic career, Dave saw such writing as offering "four valuable functions":

1. Writing to prepare him for future writing in school and career;

2. Writing to explore topics of his choice;

3. Writing to participate with other students in the classroom; and

4. Writing to demonstrate academic competence. (McCarthy 1987, 253)

Dave thus saw first-year composition as providing him with generalized preparation for future writing tasks, both *in school and career*, as well as a site where he could *explore* and *participate*. The writing in biology, which

Dave also identified as valuable, served more specific writing functions for him:

1. Writing to learn the language of Cell Biology, which he saw as necessary to his career;

2. Writing to prepare him for his next semester's writing in Immunology;

3. Writing to make connections between his class work and actual work being done by professionals in the field; and

4. Writing to demonstrate academic competence. (253)

In the biology writing, Dave begins to make connections across classes and into a discourse community. He sees writing in the one biology course as a site that helps him *learn the language of Cell Biology* and prepares him to learn writing practices that he can transfer into another site, the class in Immunology; at the same time, he also sees writing in a specific academic discourse community as a preparatory link to *writing by professionals in the field*. As important, in identifying the values of both courses, Dave begins to create a set of links constituting a network, or mental map, of the writing cultures he values and the connections among them, both inside and outside the academy.

Ironically, however, Dave *does not* perceive relationships among them in terms of practices, nor does he understand or identify prior knowledge as a resource. McCarthy lists six resources Dave draws upon in writing for these two sites: (1) what teachers said in class about writing; (2) model texts; (3) talk with other students; (4) teachers' written response to writing; (5) Dave's prior experience; and (6) personal talk with teacher. But next to prior knowledge, McCarthy notes, "The extent to which Dave drew upon prior experience is difficult to say. In each class he believed he had no prior experience to draw from. However, we know he had had related prior experience" (259). In fact, it is that inability to call upon prior knowledge and, more generally, to frame the new in any way as relating to the old, that provides the grounding for McCarthy's depiction of Dave:

> As I followed Dave from one classroom writing situation to another, I came to see him, as he made his journey from one discipline to another, as a stranger in strange lands. In each new class Dave believed that the writing he was doing was totally unlike anything he had ever done before. This metaphor of a newcomer in a foreign country proved to be a powerful way of looking at Dave's behaviors as he worked to use the new languages in unfamiliar academic territories. (McCarthy 1987, 234)

A generation later, the field of rhetoric and composition followed the progress of another student, Tim, the subject of Anne Beaufort's

(2007) *College Writing and Beyond: A New Framework for University Writing Instruction*, and a college student whose writing experiences seem very like Dave's. In her study, Beaufort has two aims: on the one hand, she, like McCarthy, wants to document how students take up our assignments, and how in the process they do or do not develop as writers; and on the other hand, she also wants to know how we can foster student writing practices such that students can carry those writing practices and knowledge into other sites where they can be used, repurposed, and invented anew. To pursue these aims, Beaufort documents Tim's progress as he moves into very different writing situations across the curriculum and across six years, from general education courses to disciplinary writing situations and into professional life. Her conclusion is that academic writing, at least as it is often "delivered" in first-year composition, may enable students to learn to write in that context, but it does not prepare them to enter into other writing spaces.

Based on this study and on her 1999 work mapping four college graduates' transition into writing in professional spaces, Beaufort (2007) proposes a "conceptual model" of writing expertise located in five interacting domains: discourse community knowledge; rhetorical knowledge; genre knowledge; composing process knowledge; and subject matter knowledge. Useful for analysis, this model or a conceptual model like it, according to Beaufort, should be made explicitly available to students so they have a framework they can use to analyze writing tasks and then complete them:

> to aid positive transfer of learning, writers should be taught a conceptual model such as the five part schema I have laid out here for the "problem-space" of a writing task, i.e., the five knowledge domains they will need to draw from to complete the task. Then, they can work through each aspect of the writing task in a thorough manner, looking for what in the current situation is similar to past writing tasks, or analyzing new tasks with appropriate 'mental grippers' [or concepts] for understanding. (Beaufort 2007, 152)

In addition, Beaufort points to the role of reflection in assisting transfer, and in the process she highlights its role in helping writers discern relationships among writing tasks and situations:

> Literally thinking about thinking, meta-cognition implies vigilant attention to a series of high-level questions as one is in the process of writing: how is this writing task similar to others? Or different? What is the relationship of this writing problem to the larger goals and values of the discourse community in which the text will be received? These and other reflection-in-action kinds of questions, if part of a writer's process,

will increase the ability of the writer to learn new writing skills, applying existing skills and knowledge appropriately (i.e., accomplishing positive transfer or learning). (Beaufort 2007, 152)

Beaufort understands that helping our students make connections across writing tasks—the kinds of connections that Doppel makes but the very connections that Dave does *not* make—is a key to transfer, and to facilitate such connection-making she proposes a framework that can be used to articulate writing tasks one to the next. As important, this conceptual framework brings together two other virtues: as a model of writing expertise it articulates the domains writing experts engage with at the same time it invites students to develop such expertise by a similar kind of engagement. Not least, Beaufort's highlighting of reflection, while only briefly addressed (and principally in an appendix), aligns with the thinking on reflection mapped several years earlier by Kathleen Blake Yancey's (1998) *Reflection in the Writing Classroom,* where three kinds of reflection—reflection-in-action, constructive reflection, and reflection-in-presentation—constitute a theory of and framework for reflection on writing.

Given this context, and as we explain below, we are especially interested in two particular dimensions of Beaufort's model, dimensions at the heart of the transfer question but that haven't been well theorized or researched. First, what is the role of content knowledge in first-year composition as a mechanism for assisting with transfer? Second, what is the role of reflection in helping foster transfer?

Oddly, the role of content in first-year composition, in terms of how the content might impact transfer, has been infrequently considered and never reported in the literature. Although Beaufort's model identifies content knowledge as one of the domains needed for transfer, the assumption seems to be that content knowledge happens only in non-composition classes, and Beaufort herself suggests that she isn't at all certain what content in first-year composition might look like.[12] As a working assumption, and given practices across campuses, this uncertainty makes sense in that so many composition classes—from the curricular model at Duke (Harris 2006) to the composition program at FSU—are "themed," typically according to faculty interest; that is, faculty decide what interests them (topics are sometimes located inside their areas of expertise, sometimes not) and then this topic provides context and material for the course. Writing courses in the spring 2010 term at Harvard University, for example, included "The Art of Crime," "American Sports Culture," and "Family, Class and Nation in Nineteenth Century Britain" (Harvard College Writing Program 2010). Likewise, at Pennsylvania's Haverford College during the 2012–2013 school year writing courses were sufficiently "content-laden" that the word writing hardly appears, and then only in reference to the medical "story-tellers" whose texts provide reading material for the course:

> Courses: Medical Narratives (WRPRH110B01)
> Spring 2013
>   In "To Build A Case" Rita Charon asserts a polarity between the patient's oral tale and the doctor's written case history: "They are opposing entities. They are examples of language being used in fundamentally different ways. Their goals conflict." We'll test this pronouncement as we read across a spectrum of fiction and nonfiction texts. How does medical language illuminate, and how does it obfuscate, the patient's individual experience? Do the doctor's practices of "history-taking" and "case reporting" wrest narrative control from the patient—and, if so, what are the benefits and costs of a usurping authority? Can we detect the patient's subjective dilemmas finding expression in the doctor's own struggle for solutions? This course will attempt to place the two supposed narrative opponents into a larger context: a rich assortment of medical story-tellers. What types of medical narrative exist outside the consulting room and the "chart," and do they effectively reconcile the alleged conflict between patient- and physician-narrator? We'll look at illness through a variety of lenses, taking our readings not only from standard case reports but from patient memoirs, physician memoirs, medical journalism, essays in philosophy of mind, and (last but hardly least!) literary fiction. We will seek to understand the efficacy of each genre (even, one might say, its therapeutic implications) while training a clear eye on its inevitable evasions and oversights. (Haverford College Writing Program 2013)

In contrast, and as we detail in chapter 2, others in the field suspect that using writing *itself* as course content might contribute to transfer, an effort often referred to as "writing-about-writing" (WAW). At the same time, the role of content in first-year composition relative to transfer is still an open question: to date, there have been no studies inquiring into what difference, if any, the content of a composition course—be it Expressivist, cultural studies, or teaching for transfer—makes.

Another absence also made visible in Beaufort's model is a systematic study of reflection's relationship to transfer, especially as students take up reflective practices in a first-year composition classroom and use such practices to help them engage in new writing tasks in diverse classes the following term. We know from general theories of learning that metacognition is central to the development of expertise; we know from Beaufort's study, and theories of transfer like Beach's (2003), that metacognition focused on similarities and differences—across rhetorical situations, across genres—is a critical component of transfer; and we know from Yancey's theory of reflection something about the kinds of activities that would need to be interfaced for a robust set of reflective practices. But, to date, no one has inquired into how putting such activities together into a given class for the express purpose of facilitating transfer might contribute to students' ability to take up new writing tasks.

Our Study and the Role of Language

The study of transfer across contexts of writing that we share here is guided by these two questions: what difference does the content in composition make in the transfer of writing knowledge and practice? and how can reflection as a systematic activity keyed to transfer support students' continued writing development? In addition, our study makes several assumptions. We assume that on most, if not all, campuses, there are many writing contexts, opportunities, and tasks. We assume that no one course, nor one first-year writing program, can prepare students for all the writing occasions they are likely to encounter in such contexts. At the same time, we are taken by McCarthy's (1987) metaphor of a stranger in strange lands, and despite the controversy surrounding the metaphor of travel as a guiding concept for composition (see, for example, Clark 1998; Reynolds 2004), we understand the kinds of shifts students have to make—from course to course, from genre to genre, from writing task to writing task, generally across contexts—as a kind of travel, a kind of "boundary crossing" that might work much better, and be more satisfying as well as instructive, if students have the kinds of assistance expert travelers do: a passport, a travel guide, a portfolio of key terms. We also assume that we can help students, but we can't simply give students frameworks, and if we could, such giving would be futile given that transfer—as other scholars, our students, and ourselves conceive of it—is a dynamic rather than static process, a process of using, adapting, and repurposing the old for success in the new. The value of such frameworks, we believe, is more in the nature of a Bakhtinian exercise: students need to *participate* with us in creating their own frameworks for facilitating transfer, and at some level this study is also a study of the efficacy of such participation.

In the rest of this book, then, we pursue these lines of inquiry, and we do so with two overarching observations.

First, this project, writ large, is something of a hybrid. On the one hand, it's a detailed research study into the efficacy of a certain kind of curriculum intending to facilitate students' transfer of writing knowledge and practice, especially as compared to two other composition curricula. On a second hand, as indicated above and as chapter 2 details, it's also a synthetic account of scholarship, provided as context for the research, in several related areas—transfer generally, transfer in writing studies, composition curricula keyed to transfer and not, and prior knowledge, among others. And on a third hand, it's a text theorizing transfer of writing knowledge and practice while it considers, and at times speculates about, what we can, might, and should be teaching in first-year writing.

Second, and as important, this project is about the primary importance of language in conceptualizing writing, writing practices, and the transfer of writing knowledge and practice. As we saw in the Reiff and Bawarshi (2011) study, students coming into college don't have a language for writing, and as we saw in the Jarratt et al. (2005) and Hilgers, Hussey, and Stitt-Bergh (1999) studies, once in college, indeed even close to graduation, students haven't developed a language to describe key concepts in writing, such as genre. Likewise, as we saw in the discussion of general theories of transfer, several scholars are creating a new vocabulary to describe this phenomenon, whether that vocabulary be located in adjectives like high- and low-road (transfer), or in a new set of key terms like generalization and transition replacing the word transfer itself. And as is self-evident, we too are developing a vocabulary we hope will be helpful. Thus, rather than talking about students' declarative and procedural knowledge, which is admittedly a more conventional way of framing transfer, we talk instead

> ## A Set of Key Terms
>
> - Writing knowledge and writing practice
> - TFT: Teaching for Transfer, through key terms
> - Reflection as systematic theory and practice keyed to creating a theory of writing

about writing knowledge and writing practice. We do this in part because (1) it shows the distinction between the two spheres of knowledge and practice, while also showing their participation in the same construct with the word writing, (2) in part because of the specificity we thus gain, and (3) in part because this way of thinking about writing connects our work to other scholarship on transfer and curriculum. In other words, the language we propose here speaks both to writing specifically and to concepts like content knowledge and process knowledge that we find in Beaufort's model. As important, we see the role of language in conceptualizing transfer, and especially transfer in support of students *writing* their way into college and across the college years, as fundamental. In our project, we therefore introduce new vocabulary for three specific purposes: (1) to describe the TFT course that is the focus of our study; (2) to articulate the curriculum in reflection culminating in students' development of a theory of writing; and (3) to conceptualize students' uses of prior knowledge. Thus, although they are introduced separately, these three small vocabularies constitute a single set of key terms articulating our curriculum to support transfer and the ways that students enact that curriculum based on their use of prior knowledge.

Given this context, in chapter 2 we review the relationship between curriculum and curricular transfer. Given the relationship between expertise and transfer, we begin by succinctly summarizing what we know about expertise from the National Research Council (NRC) volume *How People Learn* (Bransford, Pellegrino, and Donovan 2000). We then turn our attention to a continuum of curricular approaches toward fostering transfer, with Smit's (2004) model of impossibility on one end of the continuum and Brent's (2012) model of a "naturalized" practice on the other end, noting the assumptions and affordances of each. Inside the continuum, we proceed similarly, reviewing four models of transfer-promoting curricular design: the Downs and Wardle (2007) Writing about Writing (WAW) curriculum; the Dew (2003) WAW curriculum with a focus on language; the Nowacek (2011) "agents of integration" model; and our Teaching for Transfer (TFT) model. In chapter 3, we detail our study examining the impact of composition content on students' transfer of writing knowledge and practice, in the process also considering the role that a systematic reflective practice likewise plays. Located in four distinctive features—key terms, theoretical readings, writing in multiple genres, and reflective practices—the TFT course is shown to provide more conceptual grounding to students, what we referred to above as a conceptual passport or travel guide, and therefore more help with transfer than two comparable FYC courses. In chapter 4, we provide findings related to prior knowledge and its role in students' ability to transfer writing knowledge and practice: (1) students' pre-college relationships with tests and other external benchmarks of success and efficacy in writing; (2) students' use of prior knowledge in one of two models, assemblage or remix; and (3) students' responses to and uses of a "critical writing incident" or setback. And last but not least, in the conclusion we take up several tasks, among them, identifying themes emerging from our research, making recommendations about how to teach for transfer and offer a TFT course, and identifying questions that have arisen in our work and that we hope others will take up with us.

In this volume, then, we assume that when it comes to assisting students' transfer of knowledge and practices in writing, we both should and can do better—and here, we explore how.

Notes

1   Not everyone agrees that we have moved beyond current traditional models of writing. See, for example, Matsuda (2003).

2   Interestingly, the relationship of the field's interest in academic writing, in genres, and in transfer is reciprocal: if all writing is (the same) academic writing, students don't need to transfer, at least inside school.

3   For a summary of the CCCC-sponsored discussion, see http://compfaqs.org /ContentofComposition/HomePage.

4   Given this set of course descriptions, how we distinguish first-year composition from writing intensive classes is a good question—or if we do at all, and why we might.

5   Reflection, of course, can take many forms, and at some level, asking students to argue that they have met outcomes they may in fact have not raises other questions.

6   For additional explorations of the utility of the consequential transitions perspective, see Jessie Moore's (2012) account in the *Composition Forum* issue focused on transfer.

7   Interestingly, "FCAT writing" appears here as a genre, and at the same time illustrates Wardle's point about the influence of institutional habitus.

8   See also Yancey's (1998) discussion of Kevin in *Reflection in the Writing Classroom*. He experiences a contradiction between his church-based conception of the history of the world's development and the version provided in a science class, which he documents but cannot resolve in reflective writing.

9   As we explain in chapters 4 and 5, there would seem to be a relationship between boundary guarding/crossing and dispositions toward problem solving and exploring. It may be that they both tap related tendencies; alternatively, they may be associated domains or constructs.

10   Dispositions point in at least four directions: one, a generalized sense as documented by Driscoll and Wells (2012); two, one sponsored by an environment, as theorized by Wardle (2012); three, a specific sense located in noviceship, as theorized by Sommers and Saltz (2004); and the sense we identify here as related to culture, defined and illustrated in chapter 4.

11   This model of a vertical curriculum seems to correlate nicely with William Perry's (1976) model of intellectual development, in which students generally move from dualistic to relativistic to reflective thinkers. Likewise, of course, students do transfer horizontally. The point of Nowacek's (2011) study is to trace such concurrent transfer given a set of linked courses, as we explain in chapter 2; we document our own findings in chapter 3; and we identify a set of options for concurrent transfer in chapter 5.

12   Beaufort (2012), in the August 2012 issue of *Composition Forum*, clarifies her position on subject-matter knowledge to advocate for two criteria for selecting a course theme that will promote transfer: (1) a focused theme rather than a multi-topic theme, and (2) a relevance to students. Furthermore, Beaufort suggests that there are many possible themes which might "encourage in-depth intellectual exploration into subjects from any number of discourse communities" and that teaching for transfer is a goal that can be achieved by using appropriate pedagogical strategies if content fits the two criteria she specifies.

2

THE ROLE OF CURRICULAR DESIGN IN FOSTERING TRANSFER OF KNOWLEDGE AND PRACTICE IN COMPOSITION
A Synthetic Review

*My theory of writing that has evolved in this class can help me in all
of my future classes, not just English. That will probably be the most
helpful thing that I take out of this class.*

— Rick

As we saw in chapter 1, we do know something about students' transfer of knowledge and practice in writing. We know, for instance, that when students come to college directly from high school, they bring with them some school-supported writing practices and understandings: an ability to create a text with beginnings, middles, and endings; and a nascent sense of genre, but one that is uninformed about the role of genre in shaping discourse. We also know that students bring with them writing experiences—and experiences they repurpose for writing—developed in other areas of their lives, as we saw in Davis's (2012) Natascha, Roozen's (2009) Angelica, and Navarre Cleary's (2013) Doppel. Moreover, some of this experience isn't in the immediate past, but rather in a past spanning several years and several sites of writing. Once in college, students transfer writing process and appreciation of process; their writing experiences seem more successful if they identify themselves as novices, particularly as they enter college and again as they enter their major. We know that college students develop a language for writing but that, even at the close of their college careers, this language isn't sufficient for the purpose of describing their own practice and theorizing their own knowledge.

Notably, most of what we know about transfer does not derive from curricula designed specifically to foster transfer. Recently, however, scholars

DOI: 10.7330/9780874219388.c002

have focused on how curricular design could support the transfer of writing knowledge and practice, and in this chapter we outline a range of such curricular models. On one end of what we might call a continuum of such models is the difficulty, if not the impossibility, of a model, as described by David Smit (2004); at the other end is a generalized, non-specific curricular model of general rhetorical education as put forth by Doug Brent (2012). And in the middle are four models, each with a distinctive contribution: (1) the Downs and Wardle (2007) Writing about Writing (WAW) model focusing on enhancing rhetorical awareness; (2) the Debra Dew (2003) WAW model focusing on language and rhetoric as content; (3) the Rebecca Nowacek (2011) "agents of integration" model focusing on genre as a portal to transfer; and (4) our Teaching For Transfer (TFT) model focusing on key terms, theoretical readings, writing in multiple genres, and reflective practices, including students' theories of writing.

Given our interest in fostering writing expertise and in the ways that transfer can support such development, however, we begin our chapter with an explanation of the National Research Council's *How People Learn* (Bransford, Pellegrino, and Donovan 2000) compilation of what we know about the differences between novice and expert.

WHAT WE KNOW ABOUT EXPERTISE

Published in 2000, the National Research Council-sponsored *How People Learn: Brain, Mind, Experience, and School* expands on the idea of how we might teach for transfer by focusing, as the title suggests, on how people learn, in this case evidencing the potential for the teaching of transfer by drawing from literature on learning across multiple sites and ages, from elementary school through graduate school. As the authors note, the promise of transfer is located, in part, in the difference between training and education:

> It is especially important to understand the kinds of learning experiences that lead to transfer, defined as the ability to extend what has been learned in one context to new contexts (e.g., Byrnes 1996, 74). Educators hope that students will transfer learning from one problem to another within a course, from one year in school to another, between school and home, and from school to workplace. Assumptions about transfer accompany the belief that it is better to broadly "educate" people than simply "train" them to perform particular tasks (e.g., Broudy 1977). (Bransford, Pellegrino, and Donovan 2000, 52)

In addition to pointing to the kinds of transfer (e.g., near and far) defined above, *HPL* identifies key concepts and explains why they are important, among them the relationship between novices and experts, which we understand as being particularly important for developing writers, not because there is a clear trajectory from novice to expert, and not because there aren't numerous forms of expertise, but rather because, as we saw in chapter 1, noviceship is a state all writers potentially inhabit and yet not one that students necessarily recognize they need to inhabit. For example, in the educational system it is commonplace that when students move from one context to another they begin as novices, especially novice writers, even in the case of students in graduate school, as documented by Paul Prior (1991). Likewise, whenever we take up a new task in a new genre—the faculty member writing her first grant application, the law student writing his first brief, the car driver completing the first accident report, and the insurance adjuster filing the first estimate—we are all novices. In sum, writing development is predicated on noviceship.

In this sense, expertise is always limited and contingent. At the same time, as Sommers and Saltz (2004) argue, developing expertise often requires that we behave as experts; we write our way *into* expertise. Given this claim, and given the intent of writing curricula to help students develop expertise, it's worth considering what expertise is.

HPL makes six claims about experts focused on the ways that experts behave:

1. Experts notice features and meaningful patterns of information that are not noticed by novices.

2. Experts have acquired a great deal of content knowledge, organized in ways that reflect a deep understanding of their subject matter.

3. Experts' knowledge cannot be reduced to sets of isolated facts or propositions, but instead reflects contexts of applicability—that is, the knowledge is "conditionalized" on a set of circumstances.

4. Experts are able to flexibly retrieve important aspects of their knowledge with little attentional effort.

5. Though experts know their disciplines thoroughly, this does not guarantee they are able to teach others.

6. Experts have varying levels of flexibility in their approach to new situations. (Bransford, Pellegrino, and Donovan 2000, 31)

Taken together, these statements help us understand the nature of expertise, both its behaviors and its limitations. For example, rather than collect information around discrete facts, experts organize knowledge around "core concepts or 'big ideas' that guide their thinking about their domains," allowing them to review data sets systematically, discern patterns, draw inferences, and raise questions (42). As important is what this means for teaching for transfer:

> The fact that experts' knowledge is organized around important ideas or concepts suggests that curricula should also be organized in ways that lead to conceptual understanding. Many approaches to curriculum design make it difficult for students to organize knowledge meaningfully. Often there is only superficial coverage of facts before moving on to the next topic; there is little time to develop important, organizing ideas. (42)

This claim is particularly important for a writing curriculum: the inference here is that students would understand writing differently and better were a course organized through key terms or concepts rather than through a set of assignments or processes. In addition, there are questions about the usefulness and appropriateness of the key terms common in first-year composition curricula. As we see in the WPA Outcomes Statement (Council of Writing Program Administrators 2000, 2008), we seem to focus on a limited number of fairly broad terms—composing process, drafting, revising, critical thinking, and so on—some of which, like the expression critical thinking, can belong to other disciplines as much as, or more than, to writing. Not least, some of the terms we use—draft is a perfect example—speak to the moment when writers relied exclusively on writing implements like pen and pencils put to paper, rather than on the kinds of digital technology, ubiquitous now, like word processors and blogging platforms that supply writers' sites of composition (Yancey 2004). Were we interested in supporting the development of student expertise through such big ideas—which we are—we might ask what the key terms for a composing curriculum might be, why those constitute the appropriate set, how they speak to each other, and how they might provide the starting point for a FYC syllabus.[1]

What it *means* to be an expert is also important, especially—as *HPL* explains—its very short shelf life and tentative quality. In this sense, expertise is a status always beyond reach; indeed, when one thinks that expertise has been achieved, deleterious effects can result. *HPL* explains this phenomenon by focusing on a common assumption about expertise among "veteran teachers and researchers":

> an expert is someone who knows all the answers (Cognition and Technology Group at Vanderbilt, 1997). This assumption had been implicit rather than explicit and had never been questioned and discussed. But when the researchers and teachers discussed this concept, they discovered that it placed severe constraints on new learning because

the tendency was to worry about looking competent rather than publicly acknowledging the need for help in certain areas. (Bransford, Pellegrino, and Donovan 2000, 48)

In response, the researchers gave up the idea of "answer-filled experts"—who sound suspiciously like the bankers in Paulo Freire's banking model of education—in favor of a model of "accomplished novices" (Freire 2000).

> Accomplished novices are skilled in many areas and proud of their accomplishments, but they realize that what they know is minuscule compared to all that is potentially knowable. This model helps free people to continue to learn even though they may have spent 10 to 20 years as an "expert" in their field. (Bransford, Pellegrino, and Donovan 2000, 29)

As important, one practice that supports the development and practice of expertise is meta-cognition, which allows experts to define a problem, based in part on the mental model of the problem or situation under consideration.

> The ability to monitor one's approach to problem solving—to be metacognitive—is an important aspect of the expert's competence. Experts step back from their first, oversimplistic interpretation of a problem or situation and question their own knowledge that is relevant. People's mental models of what it means to be an expert can affect the degree to which they learn throughout their lifetimes. A model that assumes that experts know all the answers is very different from a model of the accomplished novice, who is proud of his or her achievements and yet also realizes that there is much more to learn. (50)

What's interesting here, relative to writing, is how the mental model of writing students develop—or don't develop—can affect how they approach writing tasks. One way of thinking about this is to say that a mental map is very like a larger road map that allows one to see different locations, routes to those locations, and connections among those routes. With such a map, one has a fair amount of agency in deciding where to go and how, at least in terms of seeing possibilities and how they relate to each other—precisely because one can see relationships *across* locations. Instead of print maps, of course, many people now use a GPS device, which can be enormously helpful in getting from A to B, and, depending on the model, can offer various routes from A to B (the quickest, the most scenic), traffic alerts, and alternative routes. Still, what a GPS offers is the route from A to B: one doesn't have much sense of how the route is situated or its relationship to other routes or places. The analogy, though imperfect, is self-evident: without a large road map of writing, students are too often traveling from one writing task to another using a definition and map of writing that is the moral equivalent of a GPS device. It will help students move from one writing task to another, but it can't provide them with the sense of the whole, the relationships among the various genres and discourse communities that constitute writing in the university (and outside it), and the opportunity for an accompanying agency that a fuller map contributes to—nor will the GPS support the development of expertise.

In sum, distinctions between novices and experts are clear, but the value of seeing the differences is that we can put into pedagogical practice opportunities for students to practice expertise as they write themselves into expertise, as we shall see.

CURRICULAR APPROACHES TO TRANSFER: A CONTINUUM

As we detail here, the approaches to transfer developed in writing studies, in terms of the role that curriculum and pedagogy can play in supporting students' appropriate transfer of writing knowledge and practice, range widely. As previously introduced, on one end of the continuum of approaches is the argument that, given the complexity of writing situations students encounter, it's nearly impossible to devise a curriculum that could succeed. On the other end of the continuum is an argument that students transfer knowledge and practice in writing as a kind of "naturalized" activity, what some scholars describe as the function of "common sense" derived not from a specific curriculum, but rather from the experience of curriculum *in toto*. In the middle are four approaches that leverage different aspects of curriculum in an effort to help students transfer. One of these is the well-known Writing about Writing approach, which itself comes with different emphases; it takes writing as object and practice as its curricular focus. A second is a specific variation of the WAW approach, one with rhetoric and writing as content but focusing on language. A third is an "agents of integration" approach located in multidisciplinary contents and contexts providing real-time opportunities for transfer. And last is the curriculum we propose here, one that in some ways is aligned with all three in its attention to content and its positioning of students as "agents of their own learning" (Yancey 1998), but one that also *extends* this curricular program in two ways: (1) by incorporating a set of key terms as conceptual anchors for a composition content; and (2) by threading throughout the course a specific, reiterative, reflective practice linked to course goals, which themselves take transfer of knowledge and practice as a first priority.[2]

TRANSFER AS AN UNLIKELY AND TROUBLESOME
ENDEAVOR: CAN CURRICULUM MATTER?

Why transfer of knowledge and practice in writing can be such a troublesome endeavor was outlined cogently by David Smit (2004), author of *The End of Composition Studies*, in the chapter titled "Transfer." Smit begins his three-part argument by first, invoking David Russell's (1995) comparison of writing with "games that use balls"; second, distinguishing "between strong and weak strategies for learning"; and third, reanalyzing already-published case studies to argue that transfer is much more difficult than we assume. Smit concludes that in writing situations transfer functions differentially: transfer is likely for surface constructions like spelling, punctuation, and (to a lesser extent) syntax, but very unlikely for the composing behaviors or textual performance that compositionists think they teach, be it writing process, coherent text, or the claims and evidence of "academic" writing.

Smit's argument derives principally from what he considers the implausibility of what has come to be known as academic writing, a claim-and-evidence text typically familiar to those in the humanities. Precisely because writing is so different from one situation to another, however, and from one genre to another—a point Smit makes using a chart showing the differences in his sample of claim-and-evidence texts in the disciplines of business, history, psychology, and biology—there is no "global" academic writing, a claim that, as we saw in chapter 1, several compositionists (e.g., Russell 1995; Downs and Wardle 2007; Petraglia 1995) have likewise argued, and indeed expanded. It's not merely that situations are different; it's that the situations, even when they look similar, are located in very different activity systems and are contextualized by different goals, participants, and tools. Thus, the writing of a feasibility study in a business communication class, which is a system dominated by learning, power relationships, and grades, is typically a very different exercise than writing in what appears to be the same genre in an engineering company, a system where international collaboration may be the norm and enhancing the company's net profits a likely goal.

This difficulty in the possibility of transfer in writing is compounded by two other factors, according to Smit. One difficulty is that, given their preparation to teach writing, the faculty teaching composition are limited in their ability to help students. As a quick review of the Pytlik and Liggett (2002) *Preparing College Teachers of Writing* demonstrates, teachers of FYC may know writing theory and practice, typically from the perspective of the English Department or more generally from the humanities, but they are unlikely to know, or be asked to learn, the content and

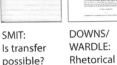

SMIT:	DOWNS/	DEW:	YANCEY/	NOWACEK:	BRENT:
Is transfer	WARDLE:	Language	ROBERTSON/	Concurrent/	Transfer
possible?	Rhetorical	as center.	TACZAK:	horizontal:	through
Not likely.	awareness	WAW.	key terms;	genre as	rhetorical
	for a vertical		reflection as	portal,	education:
	curriculum:		framework.	bricolage as	naturalized.
	WAW.		TFT.	practice.	

genres of the many disciplines inhabiting the academy in which their students need to write, a problem that, as we saw in chapter 1's discussion of the Bergmann and Zepernick (2007) study, students identify as a reason not to take FYC more seriously. Moreover, this unfamiliarity with the universe of differentiated texts extends to writing practices beyond the undergraduate years and outside the academy. As other scholars have demonstrated—Paul Prior (1991) focusing on the transition into graduate school, for example, and Anne Beaufort (1999, 2007) studying the adaptation to the workplace—the difficulties of teaching for writing beyond the baccalaureate are equally difficult. A second difficulty is the role that the individual writer plays in any situation available for transfer. Summarizing Lucille McCarthy's (1987) observations emerging from her study "A Stranger in Strange Lands: A College Student Writing across the Curriculum," Smit recounts the litany of potential obstacles:

> They include the function the writing serves personally to the writer, the role of the writer in relation to the subject matter, the task at hand, and the teacher. To her list I would add one more item: the individual ways that writers interpret the tasks that have been given to them in the first place. (Smit 2004, 131)

In sum, Smit's claim is that given what we know about writing and its social and cognitive character, about writing teachers' familiarity with the diversity of writing practices even inside the academy, and about the role of the individual composer in any writing situation, the likelihood of transfer is low, and the "degree to which any kind of knowledge or any given skill in writing is generalizable—that is, transferable from one context to another—will always be problematic" (133).

At the same time, Smit identifies four principles—ones that are often overlooked in the composition studies literature and that are very similar to those regarding the fostering of expertise recommended in *How People Learn*—that could point the way toward helping "novices develop the broad knowledge and skills it takes to write" (Smit 2004, 133). They include:

1. "First, writers may very well possess a kind of knowledge we might call 'general,' a kind of knowledge about many different things independent of particular contexts: knowledge of syntax, for example, or a general ability to adapt generic knowledge to particular rhetorical situations."

2. "Second, writers seem most obviously to apply general knowledge in situations in which they need to write outside the realm of their expertise. . . ."

3. "Third, expert writers learn to see analogies, to see similarities and differences between old and new genres and old and new contexts; novices don't. . . ."

4. "And last, writers seem to learn the general and the specific together, uncovering relevant generalizations, principles and strategies, and applying them and justifying that application in new contexts (Froertsch 378)." (133–134)

Finally, Smit sounds a note of cautious optimism: "We get what we teach for," he says. And: "if we want to help students to transfer what they have learned, we must teach them how to do so"—and do so in multiple contexts (134). In sum, Smit outlines how very difficult teaching for transfer is likely to be while endorsing the effort, and makes several general suggestions about how we might accomplish it, suggestions echoing those outlined in *HPL*.

"NATURALIZED" TRANSFER: THE EFFICACY OF A GENERALIZED CURRICULUM

At the other end of the continuum is a generalized, almost "naturalized" notion of transfer, this version of transfer researched by Doug Brent (2012). The claim is that students draw from the *entirety* of their academic writing experiences as they encounter new writing situations. More specifically, Brent seeks to learn about transfer of knowledge and practice across the two general contexts of school and work by observing six upper-level students engaged in various internships. Brent explains that his research intent is *not* to look for the resources a single writing course might provide to assist with transfer. Such a study—at Brent's host institution, the University of Calgary (as at most Canadian colleges and universities)—would be improbable given that first-year composition, while required in the US, is not available. Instead, most of Brent's students, as he explains, take only a single course in professional writing—if they take any writing course at all—and this dearth of writing-focused courses shapes both his study of transfer and the concept of rhetorical education whose effects he seeks to trace:

> Four out of the six students studied had taken or were taking this course [in professional writing]; the other two were not required to do so. As a result, my study does not primarily address transfer from any particular intentional source of rhetorical instruction. For the purposes of this study, the fact that some students had a single one-term writing course is interesting, and I paid close attention when students mentioned it. However, in the end, this one course is incidental to my larger purpose. (Brent 2012, 568)

The larger purpose here, as Brent puts it, is to trace how students who engage in an internship draw on their "rhetorical education," and the key to the study is Brent's definition of rhetorical education. According to Brent, rhetorical education could be defined dichotomously. On the one hand, it could refer to

> the sum of courses or programs designed explicitly to teach rhetorical knowledge and skill: first-year composition, first-year seminars with an emphasis on writing, courses in advanced composition and rhetorical theory, whether generalized or discipline-specific, Writing Across the Curriculum and Writing in the Disciplines programs, and the like. (559)

In other words, a rhetorical education might be the kind of curriculum we often see in US postsecondary education.[3] On the other hand, it might be defined very broadly, somewhat in the tradition of Roozen's (2009) Angelica or Navarre Cleary's (2013) Doppel, "as the sum of all experiences in a person's life, both inside and outside formal educational settings, that help him or her develop rhetorical knowledge and skills" (Brent 2012, 559). Brent's tactic here, however, is to stake out the middle ground between these two conceptual poles: he defines "a rhetorical education as the sum of institutionalized practices in the postsecondary education system that help a student develop rhetorical knowledge and skill, whether or not those practices are located in specific 'writing' courses" (559). Brent's sense is that as students move from course to course and task to task, "coping with the varying demands of the diffuse but pervasive rhetorical environment of the academy itself" (568), they develop a rhetorical education that includes both knowledge and skill.

The internships completed by the six students were diverse: students with various majors—including political science, marketing, sociology, and English—took positions as a Sunday school ministry assistant; a research assistant for a faculty member; an assistant in a financial services firm; an assistant in a human resources firm; an assistant in risk management for a telecommunications company; and an event planning assistant and media writer for a skin-care company. Several of them had already worked in that firm or office before becoming interns. Interestingly, when the four students who had enrolled in professional writing were asked about what they had learned in the course that was valuable in the internship—that is, what in effect they were able to transfer or use—they cited the values of clarity and concision (Brent 2012, 586). Brent also reports, however, that the students all experienced difficulty "explaining in detail on what prior experiences they might be drawing," in part it seems, because, like their US counterparts in the Hilgers, Hussey, and Stitt-Bergh (1999) and the Jarratt et al. (2005) studies, the Calgary students didn't have a language useful for describing the writing concepts or practices they called upon.

What students did describe, identified by Brent as themes, were three factors helpful in their internships, the latter two of which are writing-specific: (1) generalized workplace strategies; (2) models and genres that they could adapt; and (3) a sense of audience. In Brent's (2012, 588) conclusion, "the students seemed to be transferring not so much specific knowledge and skills as a general disposition to make rhetorical judgments."[4] Thus, students remarked on "highly general strategies for managing new task environments" that were helpful, and "almost all students referred to using models to determine what might be said and how information might be laid out, and even appropriate phraseology to use, in both their academic writing and in the workplace."[5] This "general sense of professional format" was particularly important for the students since it focused their attention on general rhetorical principles, such as ways "writers arrange information in hierarchies and how they use typographical conventions to signal those hierarchies." Such principles thus functioned as a kind of knowledge that could be adapted as students completed specific writing tasks. Moreover, such knowledge resulted not from explicit teaching or learning, but rather from what Brent calls "good rhetorical survival instincts that had been developed in order to survive varied academic writing tasks, but that appeared to carry over as a means of dealing with new workplace genres." While the students didn't always know "how they did so," they could "make complex rhetorical judgments about audience and genre, in some cases constructing for themselves ad hoc rhetorical genres such as the proposal, the mouseover text block, or the lesson plan, using models as starting points and then modifying by trial and error" (586–88).

Based on their interviews, Brent (2012) credits the students' successful internship experiences to three factors: "an understanding of how to extract genre features from models, how to analyze an audience, and how to use genre knowledge to interpret information." In terms of curriculum design to support even a generalized model of transfer, Brent recommends an emphasis on reflection and rhetorical awareness, so as to help "students become more conscious about what to observe and what questions to ask in new rhetorical environments" (588). Intentionality in this model, then, is enhanced through reflection.

There are three additional dimensions of this study that are worth noting, in part because they may have influenced the students' experience, and also in part because they may explain some of what Brent found. First, as Brent notes, since the University of Calgary doesn't offer a vertical writing curriculum, it's impossible to learn from his students how such a curriculum might support transfer. Instead, he studies a generalized rhetorical education and finds that students do indeed learn implicitly from their experiences: it's the curricular analogue to Roozen's (2009) and Navarre Cleary's (2013) findings, that students learn literate practices outside of school in a different kind of rhetorical education. Second, as suggested above and like their US counterparts, the students don't seem to have a language of writing, and without that it's difficult to know if what they tapped was generalized rhetorical knowledge, or whether there was something more specific they were drawing on but didn't have the language to name. Thus, when Celia says "I don't exactly know how I got better, but I guess it's just as you do more of it you just kind of get the grasp of it," it may be, as Brent suggests, that she is expressing knowledge that has become tacit and internalized (588). Alternatively, it could be that Celia attributes her success to practice because she doesn't have a vocabulary that would point her to other resources. Third, given that several of the students were already familiar with their internship workplaces, a good question is whether or how that prior socialization contributed to their ability to adapt. In other words, if students are already familiar with the workplace context, the task of transfer is different—and presumably easier—than it is for someone who is learning how to write at the same time he or she is also being socialized into a new workplace.

In sum, Brent's study, arguing for a kind of naturalized model of transfer based in a generalized rhetorical education, is provocative, raising numerous questions that speak to the complexity of studying transfer and the role of language in assisting students to describe their own writing activities.

WRITING ABOUT WRITING: A FOCUS ON WRITING AS AN AVENUE TO TRANSFER

The Writing about Writing approach to teaching composition, explained by Doug Downs and Elizabeth Wardle in their 2007 *College Composition and Communication* article, provides the parameters for a first middle-range curricular approach to supporting transfer of knowledge and practice in writing. In "Teaching about Writing, Righting Misconceptions: (Re)Envisioning 'First-Year Composition' as 'Introduction to Writing Studies,'" Downs and Wardle (2007) suggest that misconceptions about writing and composition pedagogy can be "righted" by using a Writing about Writing (WAW) curriculum designed to teach students about conceptions of writing that will help foster transfer (554). In part, their proposal is a response to the misconception assumed by those in the university broadly, or in FYC programs specifically, that academic discourse is universal. As a remedy, Downs and Wardle advocate a move from teaching writing to teaching *about* writing "in a course topically oriented to reading and writing as scholarly inquiry" (553). The curriculum they suggest intends to foster a level of rhetorical awareness in students by using writing studies theory as course content in which "students are taught that writing is conventional and context-specific rather than governed by universal rules," and that "within each new disciplinary course they will need to pay close attention to what counts as appropriate for that discourse community" (559). In addition, Downs and Wardle employ two case studies to illustrate that the WAW curriculum is appropriate for all levels of student proficiency and comfort with writing, noting that students in the study demonstrated improvement in three specific areas: (1) increased self-awareness about writing, (2) improved reading abilities and confidence, and (3) raised awareness of research writing as conversation (564–72). While they suggest that this course design includes content that will transfer, citing the proven means of transfer established by other researchers (Perkins and Salomon 1992; Smit 2004; Beaufort 2007)—such as "explicit abstraction of principles and alertness to one's context" (Downs and Wardle 2007)—their research focuses on the writing conducted within their own curriculum; it does not investigate whether or what students transferred to new contexts.

At about the same time the Downs and Wardle *CCC* article was published, Elizabeth Wardle (2007) also published preliminary results from a longitudinal study she was conducting with seven students at the University of Dayton, "a private, Catholic, liberal arts school of 10,000 students in Dayton, Ohio" (70). In "Understanding 'Transfer' from FYC: Preliminary Results of a Longitudinal Study," Wardle identifies the students as her former students from a FYC class who are majoring in a variety of disciplines—biology, chemistry, political science, and undeclared business—as she outlines the rationale and purpose of the study:

> Given the more complex understanding of transfer suggested by socio-cultural theories, what might a study of generalization—Beach's alternative to transfer—look like? Taking context, purpose, and student perception of writing both in and beyond FYC into account, I designed a qualitative, longitudinal pilot study following seven students from my Fall 2004 FYC course as they wrote across the university to answer four research questions:
>
> 1. What do students feel they learned and did in FYC?
>
> 2. What kinds of writing are students doing elsewhere?
>
> 3. How do students perceive that writing and what strategies do they use to complete it?
>
> 4. Do students perceive FYC as helping them with later writing assignments across the university? (70)

The students reported to Wardle that they learned both concepts and practices: "they learned about new textual features (including new ways of organizing material), how to manage large research writing projects (including use of peer review and planning), how to read and analyze academic research articles, and how to conduct serious, in-depth academic research" (72). The next term, however, students didn't draw on this knowledge; in Wardle's conclusion, they didn't see the need to draw on it, so there was what she calls a "failure to generalize." Although Wardle was disappointed in this result, the failure to generalize isn't absolute: through the FYC curriculum students had developed a meta-awareness that served them well as they wrote elsewhere in the academy, and fostering such an awareness, she argues, might be one of the most important goals for a transfer-supporting curriculum.

> The only ability students seemed to consistently generalize from one writing task to another within the various activities of schooling was meta-awareness about writing: the ability to analyze assignments, see similarities and differences across assignments, discern what was being required of them, and determine exactly what they needed to do in response to earn the grade they wanted. (76–77)[6]

A curricular approach oriented to WAW has been taken up by many, and with various alterations and change of foci, as Downs and Wardle (2012) explain. In their taxonomy provided in the Ritter and Matsuda (2012) *Exploring Composition Studies* volume, Downs and Wardle claim that those developing WAW curricula share a fundamental goal: "a desire to create a *transferable* and *empowering* focus on *understanding writing as a subject of study* (131). At the same time, Downs and Wardle identify variations in WAW curricula keyed to four factors:

1. The particular angle or perspective a course takes—what subjects it prioritizes and how student research is focused (if the course includes research);

2. The end of student learning that is emphasized—a primary focus on personal growth versus a primary focus on contribution to the field;

3. Types and numbers of readings; and

4. Types and numbers of writing assignments. (139)

In addition, Downs and Wardle report on three approaches to WAW currently in development.

> The first focuses on literacy and discourse, how writing and language demonstrate community membership. The second focuses on writing studies itself—the existence of the discipline qua discipline, with its knowledge and expertise on writing, emphasizing rhetorical strategies and its resultant strategies for writing. The third focuses on the nature of writing and writers' practices. . . . Other approaches, like the one at UCF, try to cover all of this ground by teaching "units" with particular declarative knowledge that must be covered. (139–40)

Schools offering these WAW curricula include Texas A&M, whose FYC curriculum addresses "how writing and language demonstrate community membership," and Marywood University, which highlights "the nature of writing and writers' practices" (Downs and Wardle 2012, 139–40).

In general, then, WAW curricula take a disciplinary focus as they respond to interest in transfer of knowledge and practice in writing, regardless of how explicitly this relationship is highlighted. It's also worth noting that rhetorical awareness, which is an important part of the Downs and Wardle (2007) model, *isn't* part of the Beaufort (2007) five-domain model. Nor has the relationship of rhetorical awareness to Beaufort's model been explored. At the same time, rhetorical awareness would seem to draw on some of the domains Beaufort identifies—on rhetorical knowledge or genre knowledge, perhaps—as well as on reflection; how it does so may provide a fruitful area for exploration.

A SPECIALIZED CASE OF WAW: FOCUSING ON
LANGUAGE AND RHETORIC AS CONTENT

A language-specific version of WAW, identified by Downs and Wardle (2012) as the version emphasizing "the existence of the discipline qua discipline, with its knowledge and expertise on writing, emphasizing rhetorical strategies and its resultant strategies for writing," is a second middle-range curricular approach to supporting transfer of knowledge and practice in writing. As explained by Debra Dew (2003), the writing curriculum at the University of Colorado–Colorado Springs (UCCS) was reimagined to achieve two purposes: (1) emphasize the disciplinarity of writing studies, and (2) focus students' attention on rhetoric and language.

In "Language Matters: Rhetoric and Writing I as Content Course," Dew (2003) cites David Kaufer and Richard Young's "conceptual parameters" as providing a beginning rationale for the new UC-CS curriculum (Kaufer and Young 1993):

> Our shift from a Writing-WNCP, "writing-with-no-content–in-particular," curriculum (77) to a Writing-WSC "writing-with-specific-content" curriculum, (82) follows David Kaufer and Richard Young's conceptual parameters as articulated in their theoretical inquiry into the relationship between writing and content. Kaufer and Young define the Writing-WNCP course as an instructional tradition that has long "dominated the thinking of most English departments," a tradition that encouraged "the splitting off of writing from the rest of what is taught and learned in the academy" via the establishment of the separate course in first-year composition (77). Such a course focuses on "mechanics, usage, style, and the paragraph" while other disciplines focus on "content, for which language is only a vehicle." (Dew 2003, 78)

Given this understanding of writing curricula, one dividing writing courses with "no particular content" from writing courses with "specific content," Dew and her colleagues engaged in a "curricular revision" aimed at writing instruction that "is now more fully a scholarly enterprise with disciplinary integrity." To accomplish this goal, the new course includes four specific features. First, it includes a subject matter: rhetoric and writing studies. Second, the combination of language and disciplinary content creates a renewed interest in rhetorical arrangement and an emphasis on "form as rhetorically contingent." Third, in this course the sentence itself has also received new attention. Fourth, the course is now conceptually at parity with other content courses (88).

Thus, much as the Downs and Wardle (2007) version of WAW focuses on rhetorical awareness, the Dew (2003) "Rhetoric and Writing Studies" has language awareness and use as its centerpiece. Using language as a lens, the faculty choose the topic or theme of the course:

> RWS content, locally understood as the study of language matters, encompasses the following subtopics: multicultural rhetoric and language practices; language and technology; language and literacy; pop culture and language practices; or writing in the disciplines (WID), as a survey of discourse conventions (skills and content) across the curriculum. Faculty choose their specific subtopic, but no matter the subtopic, students analyze diverse essays that address language issues. (95)

In addition to providing rich resources for invention, the course's focus on language provides material for students who "analyze diverse essays that address language issues," essays that resemble the kind of writing tasks students encounter in other disciplines (95). The intent, according to Dew, is that the subject matter of language will enhance transfer, since students learn in RWS that writing "principles and practices" are always situated in disciplinary contexts.

The centrality of language as content and the role of its disciplinarity—a role emphasized to students, of course, but also stressed to faculty across the campus—is the distinguishing feature of RWS. At the same time, the research showing the efficacy of this approach in fostering or enhancing transfer, according to the Downs and Wardle summary of WAW, has yet to be reported:

> Dew's curriculum is concerned that students recognize the study of rhetoric and writing as a discipline, which inherently carries some emphasis on changing students' conceptions of writing and showing disciplinary differences in writing (though these are not the main emphases). No explicit attention is devoted to transfer, conducting primary research, or writing to contribute to the field. (Downs and Wardle 2012, 142)

In this model of WAW, then, we see a very specific content, one focused on language, as the centerpiece of the course. Two good questions follow: what difference does this make for students in terms of transfer of knowledge and practice, and what difference does it make compared to other options?

AGENTS OF INTEGRATION

An approach different in kind rather than degree from the middle-range curricula reported thus far, the agents of integration approach is located in linked classes that students participate in concurrently: it exemplifies a third middle-range curriculum. This linked three-course seminar, an "Interdisciplinary Humanities Seminar offered to first-year honors students at a Catholic university on the East Coast," substitutes for FYC and provides, in Rebecca Nowacek's *Agents of Integration*, a study of what we might call concurrent transfer (Nowacek 2011, 4). Unlike the other models, agents of integration doesn't focus on the design of curriculum per se, but rather, given its linked-class design, on how students attempt to transfer writing knowledge across three different but concurrent classes of literature, history, and religious studies. Based on multiple sources of data—including classroom observations, student notebooks, more formal student work, and multiple interviews—agents of integration provides a window into how students transfer across concurrent contexts that aren't designed to support transfer specifically, but that make such opportunity available.

Influenced by the Beach (2003) notion of transfer as generalization outlined in chapter 1, Nowacek identifies five principles of transfer oriented to transfer-as-recontextualization: "multiple avenues of connection [exist] among contexts, including knowledge, ways of knowing, identities, and goals."

1. "transfer is not only mere application; it is also an act of reconstruction";

2. "transfer can be both positive and negative";

3. "there is a powerful affective dimension of transfer";

4. "written and spoken genres associated with these contexts provide an exigence for transfer"; and

5. "meta-awareness is an important, but not a necessary, element of transfer." (Nowacek 2011, 21–30)

According to Nowacek, "theories of transfer assume that an individual is moving among fundamentally *different* situations and seeking to identify some similarity," while "theories of genre assume that individuals find themselves in fundamentally similar situations and draw on socially constructed and constitutive genres in order to minimize the sense of difference in these different situations" (20). In Nowacek's model of transfer-as-recontextualization, both spoken and written genres can help students navigate writing tasks, and it is through genre, the study claims, that students use writing knowledge—defined here as "a constellation of knowledges and abilities linked together by genre"—across contexts (100). Moreover, in this model students and faculty play distinctive roles: much like Yancey's (1998) students-as-agents-of-their-own-learning, Nowacek's students are "agents of integration," with faculty, ideally, functioning as "handlers" helping students engage in recontextualization. In sum, agents of integration, as a concept, offers a means of joining transfer as an act of individual cognition with the institutional realities of a specialized academy that works against the recognition and valuing of transfer. Agents of integration are individuals actively working to *perceive* as well as to convey *effectively to others* connections between previously distinct contexts. (Nowacek 2011, 38, emphasis original)

And more specifically, the connections students draw on are genre and content.

What we see from this study is threefold. First, some students are adept at drawing on their prior knowledge of genre and/or information and using one or both in new writing tasks. For example, one student, Data, is able to draw on materials from his history class when making a successful argument in a literature assignment. Second, other students do not fare so well, transferring from one context to another, but, like Davis's (2012) Natascha, with disappointing results. In traditional terms, we would call such instances negative transfer, but Nowacek redefines them as cases of "frustrated integration." Assigned the task of writing one page of a medieval diary filled with material descriptions of life at the time, for example, Kelly instead composes a diary page oriented to the psychology of her subject, resulting in a lower grade than expected. Nowacek theorizes that Kelly does transfer, but it's more the transfer of what Kelly knows about the genre of a diary, which may sometimes be more oriented to thoughts and feelings rather than a report of material conditions. Kelly thus transfers, but it's a case of frustrated integration since the assignment specifies the genre of the writing task in a way at odds with Kelly's understanding. Third, while faculty in this model of transfer are identified as "handlers," their assignments—at least as they are presented in the study—not infrequently contribute to the difficulty students have in transferring, with the diary assignment as an interesting case in point.

As Nowacek observes, the diary assignment calls for a very specific kind of diary, one that fails to account for some students' prior experiences with diaries, but this difference is not mentioned or highlighted by the instructor:

> framing the assignment as a diary taps into associations with diaries prevalent in late twentieth century America: as personal and private, as focused on an individual's thoughts and feelings. A potential conflict, then, existed between the goals of the assignment (to focus on material detail) and the identities and goals often tacitly associated with the genre of diary (a self-absorbed author focused on feelings). (Nowacek 2011, 85)

Indeed, one of the points that Mary Soliday (2011) makes in *Everyday Genres* is related to this issue: what seems to help students, her research shows, is assigning them what she calls "wild genres," that is, genres that exist in the world. In this case, a diary is a wild genre, but in the history class it's been redefined to become something more "domesticated" to suit the needs of the class, and is thus doubly confusing to the students. In fact, Kelly is not the only student who encounters difficulty with the assignment. What's also interesting is that what Nowacek documents in Kelly's experience can be regarded as successful transfer if judged by the ability of the student to use prior knowledge successfully. What qualifies it as "frustrated integration" is the grade Kelly receives on the assignment; this in turn raises the issue of the relationship between what we consider success in transfer and the grade on an assignment, an important point we take up in later chapters.

More generally, here we see students recontextualizing, through genre knowledge and disciplinary context, what they have learned in one context in order to write in another, and again, good questions emerge from the study. One: as we have asked regarding other studies, if students had a working vocabulary, how might that support and inform their ability to transfer? Two, and as Nowacek (2011) observes, the role of meta-awareness is not clearly defined: "Finally, this study suggests the need—and a method—for future research into the role of meta-awareness in genre knowledge acquisition and transfer" (142). Third, Nowacek notes as well the need "for comparative studies. This study was not comparative, but an obvious question for future research is the relative merits of stand-alone FYC courses, linked courses, and the interdisciplinary L.C. model of FYC described in this book" (142), a research task we begin to take up in chapter 3.

TEACHING FOR TRANSFER: INTERLOCKING CONCEPTS AND A THEORY OF WRITING

The last middle-range curricular model is designed for transfer, the TFT course that is the focus of the study we share in chapters 3 and 4. Developed as the first step in the study, this course includes particular content for first-year composition, content that seeks to teach for transfer explicitly. It also provides material for students to write to, write with, and think with as they develop as writers and approach other writing tasks, both as they are enrolled in the class and as they participate in other courses. Different than that of the other approaches documented here, the course content is distinguished by two features. First, the TFT readings and assignments focus on writing-rich and writing-specific terms, concepts, and practices. Second, we include specific concepts and practices of reflection pointing students toward developing their own "theory of writing," a theory intended to help students frame and reframe writing situations. Students' development of their own "theory of writing" is a signature of the course, which engages students in a semester-long reflective process with the purpose of exploring the ways they develop, understand, use, and repurpose their knowledge and practice of writing. Thus, through a set of interlocking rhetorical concepts and practices, students in the TFT course learn content they are then able to transfer: (1) key rhetorical terms that aid in the understanding of writing as theory and practice; (2) the use of reflection as a tool for learning, thinking, and writing in the course and beyond; and (3) the development of a theory of writing that helps students create a framework of writing knowledge and practice they'll take with them when the course is over.

The first component, key terms and writing concepts, helps students describe and theorize writing; eleven such terms anchor the course. These terms, representing the core concepts about writing that students learn and practice in the course, are introduced in four sequential sets—(1) audience, genre, rhetorical situation, and

> **Sequence of Key Terms**
>
> 1. audience, genre, rhetorical situation, and reflection
> 2. exigence, critical analysis, discourse community, and knowledge
> 3. context, composing and circulation
> 4. knowledge and reflection (reiterated specifically in this unit)

reflection; (2) exigence, critical analysis, discourse community, and knowledge; (3) context, composing, and circulation; and (4) knowledge and reflection again—each set intended to support a specific writing assignment or course unit. In addition, earlier concepts are recursively integrated into the learning of subsequent concepts, as the general trajectory of the course, below, indicates.

> Unit 1: Students are introduced to key concepts/terms about writing while they learn to analyze and incorporate sources as evidence in their writing.
>
> Unit 2: Students work with key concepts/terms about writing while they learn the importance of research and to conduct research, identify appropriate sources, and integrate sources into their writing.
>
> Unit 3: Using the key concepts/terms about writing, students draw upon what they discovered and wrote about in the research phase (unit 2)

for the development of strategically planned composition in multiple genres, or "Composition–in–three–genres."

Unit 4: Writing a reflection-in-presentation, students work from substantial reflections and other writing activities completed throughout the course to articulate a *theory of writing* that integrates the key concepts and terms learned in the course with the practical experience gained in applying those concepts to their own writing.

The second component of the course, reflection, is introduced as a theory and a reiterative practice that students engage in before, during, and after their writing process. Reflection is integrated into the course in three ways: (1) students learn reflective theory by reading about it; (2) students complete successive reflective assignments, including one accompanying every major assignment in which students theorize about key terms, writing processes and practices, and their identity as a writer; and (3) students engage in other reflective activities connecting readings, key terms, and assignments.

And last but not least, the final component of the course is the theory of writing that students develop; its intent is to ensure students can theorize about and practice writing using key terms and concepts learned in the course, and to support their development as reflective writing practitioners who are able to abstract their theories and employ them in new contexts. As part of the reiterative course design, students reflect on their theory of writing at ten different points—six different journal assignments ask them to think through one or two specific key terms they are learning at that point, and the short writing assignments that work toward one of the four major assignments also require students to define their theory at that moment. The final reflection, then, which is the fourth and final major writing assignment in the course, represents for students the culmination of writing knowledge they have been developing all semester. Given the aim of the course to foster transfer, the last assignment is critical in that it calls for reflection on transfer specifically—students are prompted to reflect and write about how they might apply writing knowledge learned in the course to other writing situations—and it functions to help students continue developing as they exit the course. As a reiterative process, the development of a theory of writing asks students to bridge the learning acquired in first-year composition to the writing required in other college situations. How it does so in the TFT course, especially in comparison to more conventional FYC courses, is the topic of our next chapter.

Notes

1   Thus far in transfer literature there have been two efforts to use key terms as a major curricular element, ours in the TFT course, and Linda Adler-Kassner's (2012) use of "threshold concepts," a very different approach located in the Meyer and Land (2003; 2006) theory of threshold concepts as a gateway to a discipline. See her article discussing these in the Fall 2012 issue of *Composition Forum.*

2   There are many different models of WAW; see the Downs and Wardle (2012) chapter for a fuller account.

3   Rhetorical education seems to be something of a floating signifier. Suzanne Bordelon (2010), for instance, uses it as a term to describe the kinds of experiences women at the turn of the twentieth century encountered in colleges and as a function of their commencement speeches for the public. In its attention to the civic sphere, this notion of rhetorical education seems to be very different than the usage employed by Brent (2012).

4   Here we see another use of the word disposition.

5   The role of models, while often emphasized in pedagogy, seems undervalued in their influence on writers more generally. See, for example, our findings regarding the role of models—and their absence—in chapter 4, as well as Michael Bunn's (2013) research on their role in shaping student response to writing assignments.

6   The value of meta-awareness has been emphasized by other programs as well. The Stanford Study of Writing (2008), for instance, notes that "Participants who scored high in rhetorical awareness of audience in their freshman year showed their greatest amount of growth in subsequent years, indicating this variable as statistically significant ($p > .0001$)."

3

TEACHING FOR TRANSFER (TFT) AND THE ROLE OF CONTENT IN COMPOSITION

Initially, the amateur writer doesn't consider everything that goes into composing a paper. They do not concisely acknowledge that you need to first figure out what audience you are conveying your message to and what genre you are going to put your composition under. As time goes on, the author begins to acquire more experience, and their skills progress so that they can formally seek out the audience and genre.

— Renee

As explained in the last chapter, while several teacher-scholars have created new curricula designed to support students' transfer of knowledge and practice in writing, we have yet to fully explore if or how the content in a first-year composition class influences the writing knowledge and practice students develop in such a setting, and thus the knowledge and practice they can use in other sites of writing. Intuitively, it makes sense that the content of a writing class—as indicated by readings and assignments, for example—would at least influence students' experience. Alternatively, the content might be viewed as *more* than minimally influential; it might be seen as required, as the window or fulcrum through which students learn about writing and how to write. In this case, selecting content would be less peripheral and more fundamental to the design of a first-year composition class. Anne Beaufort's model suggests that content or subject matter knowledge is one of the five critical domains of writing; if this is so for writing in other disciplines, it must be so for writing in first-year composition, since the salient issue isn't disciplinarity per se, but rather the content that is inherent in any given writing task. Indeed, given that first-year composition functions as a gateway to writing in college, selecting the content—and it's fair to note that in very few disciplines can the content be "selected" in the sense in which we are using the term here[1]— would be a first-order concern.

DOI: 10.7330/9780874219388.c003

Given this context, we begin this chapter by detailing the particulars of our research into the "content" question, including the local institutional context hosting our study, after which we detail our research investigating the role that content in FYC plays in transfer. As suggested in chapters 1 and 2, we pursue this question by comparing the content taught in three different sections of first-year composition and exploring the efficacy of each in supporting students' transfer of writing knowledge and practice. More specifically, we report on students' experiences in three FYC courses differentiated by content: first, an Expressivist course; second, a course with content from cultural studies and media; and third, the Teaching for Transfer (TFT) course. We also pay close attention to the role of the teacher in these courses, finding that the differences across the courses are not a function of differentiated proficiency in teaching, but rather a function of *curriculum*. And as we suggested in chapter 1, one of the major findings we report is the role of language in helping students transfer writing knowledge and practice; as is conventional practice, each course included a language locating both writing and theme, but it was the language of the TFT course that provided students with the passport to writing across multiple sites.

To forecast our findings, then, the content in first-year composition does matter, contributing in very specific ways to students' intentional transfer of knowledge and practice in writing.

INSTITUTIONAL CONTEXT

Our research took place at Florida State University (FSU), a large, flagship, Research–1 institution in the Southeast US, had IRB approval and spanned two semesters totaling thirty-five weeks, over the fall of 2009 and the spring of 2010. We began in the fall with the second course of the two-course composition curricular sequence; then in the spring we followed students as they continued to write in their general education classes—what we call liberal studies classes—which included a wide range of offerings, from chemistry and biology to religious studies, history, and humanities. FSU's first-year composition program—constituted by two sequenced courses entitled ENC 1101 and ENC 1102, the first emphasizing elaborated writing processes, and the second writing with sources—is guided by a mission statement that views the teaching of writing as "a recursive and frequently collaborative process of invention, drafting, and revising" (English Department 2011/2012).

The program presents writing as both personal and social, teaching students to perceive writing in those ways and to learn to write for a variety of purposes and audiences. First-year composition courses are capped either at twenty-five students in a "regular" classroom—supplied with a whiteboard and multimedia instructor station allowing the display of digital and print resources—or at twenty students in computer-equipped classrooms. Both courses in the FSU first-year composition sequence emphasize a workshop format incorporating peer collaboration and multiple drafts of writing. In addition, first-year composition courses are almost exclusively taught by graduate teaching assistants in the three departmental programs: rhetoric and composition, literature, and creative writing. The content of first-year composition varies, as graduate students have the choice of teaching according to one of several program-approved "strands." Such strands may focus on personal writing, literature-based writing, a mix of personal and creative writing, or writing about media, culture, and cultural issues.[2] Besides the approved strands, graduate teaching assistants with experience in the program can apply to teach writing content according to specific themes, which are approved on an individual basis by the program director. Each themed course, like those in the strands, is designed to reflect the institution's commitment to process writing and incorporate attention to the outcomes articulated in the WPA Outcomes Statement.

Graduate teaching assistants in the writing program, including both first-time teachers and experienced teachers who are new to the program, are provided with considerable preparation and support for their teaching. New TAs enroll in a pedagogy "boot camp" provided through two credit-bearing, graded graduate courses completed the summer before they teach; experienced instructors attend a two-day orientation to the writing program. Once teaching begins, all graduate assistants new to the institution are supported by a year-long program of support for teaching, including weekly meetings to discuss pedagogical issues, regular small-group gatherings with experienced mentors, regular workshops, and an online resource of teaching materials and classroom activities supplied by the program. However, as with most programs of its size—nearly 100 sections of FYC are offered each fall and each spring, and nearly that many during the summer—and with such a variety of instructors, daily course content is up to the individual instructor to develop and share with students, as long as it fits within program guidelines.

Given several factors—the nature of the FSU program; our observations of FSU first-year students, especially in the context of our experiences teaching FYC at eight other very different institutions of higher education; and our own questions—we were interested in ways that students moving from FYC into other writing sites *use* what they have learned in the FYC class to help them complete other writing tasks. Put another way, we were interested in students' ability to take writing knowledge and practices from the first-year composition classroom and employ or repurpose them in other writing sites. Moreover, based on our own experiences and on the kind of empirical research on writers' development reported in chapter 1, we were persuaded that students do transfer writing practices; we thus wanted to design a curriculum that continued to support students' development of elaborated practices. However, we were also persuaded that there is a kind of writing knowledge—articulated in the types of language students did not use, and more particularly in the kinds of key terms characterizing expertise, as *HPL* (Bransford, Pellegrino, and Donovan 2000) explains—that students didn't seem to develop. As important, we were persuaded that such key terms, if put in dialogue and used to frame students' own writing experiences, could position students as agents of their own learning who would create their own theory of writing to use as they encountered new writing tasks, some of which are completed in the FYC class, some of which are tackled in other classes concurrent with FYC and after, and some of which may be outside of school. And last but not least, based on our prior work in reflection and the emphasis on metacognition expressed in all theories of transfer (see, for example, Bransford, Pellegrino, and Donovan 2000; Beaufort 2007), we believed it important to build into our curricular model a very specific kind of reflection, one that was interwoven into the course as a regular, systematic, and knowledge-producing practice—indeed, as a kind of curriculum consistent with, current with, and integrated with the writing curriculum. Put simply, we believed that students can make knowledge from their own writing practices if asked to do so and if supported in their efforts. Specifically, then, our interest in transfer centered on two main areas—content and transfer, and reflection and transfer—providing the foundation for the course we call Teaching for Transfer (TFT).

In our curricular design for the TFT course, and in the research for our project exploring the role of content in transfer, we chose to focus on the second of the two FYC sequenced courses, and for three reasons all related to local context but also, we believe, of interest to the field at large. First, over 55% of FSU's first-year students—using AP, SAT, CLEP, or other standardized measures—exempt the first writing course, so our decision to focus on the second course allowed us to draw from a much larger population. Second, because of the high number of students at FSU with test scores exempting them from the first of the two FYC courses, more than half of the students in the second-semester course are actually participating in their *first* college writing class, at least as delivered on a college campus. So in that sense, it is the second-term course that provides students with a gateway to writing in college at FSU. Second, since students come to this course with a wide variety of possible prerequisites or experiences in different writing sites, the starting point for students in this course varies greatly, which again we thought would contribute to the diversity and richness of student experiences.[3] And third, although our second course maintains an emphasis on elaborated writing process, its primary outcome is introducing students to research-based writing; since FSU had no WAC program (at the time; one is currently in the proposal stage), this is the course that will be for most students the last opportunity they have to receive explicit instruction in writing, and it is this instruction that they are likely to call on as they continue in their academic careers. Given our interest in transfer, then, the efficacy of this course was of special interest.

RESEARCH PARTICIPANTS AND DATA SOURCES

Study participants were recruited from a wide range of sections: classroom visits were made to a total of eighteen different sections of the same first-year composition course, all taught by different instructors. Each visit consisted of a brief verbal explanation of the research and what would be required of participants, supplemented by a letter providing the same information in written format and further detail. The "content" for the FYC classes varied widely, as the program description above suggests. Initially forty-one potential subjects from eleven possible sections responded, and a number of these were the only volunteers from their section. There were five sections that yielded four participants each, but several of these subjects dropped out of the study in its initial phase. Ultimately, seven total subjects in three sections of first-year composition—one of those sections being the TFT course—continued to the end of the study.

The goal of the study was to provide the widest range of comparison, based on three factors that would ensure the study could continue to its conclusion: (1) that the highest number of participants were available from each section to ensure a good rate of response; (2) that one section consisted of the TFT content so it could provide part of the content comparison; and (3) that the three sections were different enough from each other in terms of content so that a more varied comparison would be possible while at the same time ensuring that the content to be studied was not atypical of FYC content available at this institution and elsewhere across the country. In other words, we sought to compare the TFT content to typical first-year composition course content, using as many subjects from each type of course as possible. While acknowledging that there is no ubiquitous content featured in FYC anywhere, this inquiry aimed for relevance to a wide range of first-year composition programs in its design.

To that end, a number of methods were used to gather data: student interviews, instructor interviews, analysis of student writing samples, and analysis of course materials. The research was designed in two phases: (1) a comparison of the content taught in three different sections of FYC over the fall semester, and (2) an exploration of the transfer of content from each of those three sections to other academic writing contexts encountered by study participants in the spring semester of 2010, including courses in the sciences, social sciences, and humanities. More specifically, we explored two connections between content and transfer: first, whether students transfer *between assignments within each section of first-year composition*, and if so, whether and how that transfer is connected to the specific content of each course; and second, whether students transfer knowledge and practice *between the first-year composition course and other curricular writing contexts in college*, and in what way the transfer that does occur relates to the content a student engaged with in the FYC classroom.

Each of the three FYC sections took a specific approach to content, and, according to Richard Fulkerson's (2005) analysis of patterns in FYC curricula, the first two are fairly common approaches. One section took an Expressivist approach, guiding students to explore their own and others' interpretations of what is written about and in our culture, and to write personally inflected process-based essays reflecting those interpretations. A second section focused on media and culture, exploring the influence of media on our society and on ways our cultural awareness is mediated; students were required to write and research content related to this theme. The third section featured the TFT course; its content, as explained in chapter 2, was located in key terms representing writing content and in reflection as a means of theorizing writing.

INTERVIEWS AND TIMELINE

Interviews with each of the three instructors were conducted at the beginning of the "composition" semester, the first phase of the study, to learn about the instructional design of the course and each instructor's approach to teaching. Interviews with each of the seven study participants—Expressivist course participants Emma and Glen; media and culture students Darren and Carolina; and TFT students Marta, Clay, and Rick—were conducted at various intervals in the composition semester, with the first interview occurring just a few weeks into the semester. Its purpose was to provide context about students in terms of their history with writing instruction, their writing behaviors or preferences, and their expectations about the writing they would do in the course. Two additional sets of interviews with participants took place during this phase, one midway through the fall semester and one at the end of the fall semester, both intended to further explore participants' interpretations of the writing assignments in which they were engaged. This phase also included analysis of instructional materials from each of the sections—including the course syllabus, assignment descriptions, and writing prompts—and a mid-term check with the three instructors regarding any adjustments they might have made to course content.

In its second phase in the spring semester, following the three-week holiday break, the research continued with document-based interviews with the seven study participants as they now tackled writing assignments in new courses. The intent of these interviews was to analyze how the content did or did not facilitate students' transfer of writing knowledge and practice, especially relative to the writing content provided to that participant in first-year composition. In the interviews participants were asked to analyze their approach to writing and to identify connections made between the writing they did in FYC and their current writing. Students were also asked to reflect on completed assignments, writing approaches and behaviors, resources consulted, and, ultimately, what they believed they had transferred from their first-year composition course to use in new writing contexts (or, conversely, what they had not transferred), and whether the writing knowledge transferred contributed to or detracted from their writing success.

As Table 3.1 illustrates, each participant was enrolled in one of three sections of first-year composition, each section varying by content. In the second phase of the study, participants wrote in a range of new disciplinary contexts for writing, including the sciences, social sciences, and humanities, as well as one extra-curricular writing context.

COMPARATIVE CONTEXTS: THREE COURSE DESIGNS WITH VARYING CONTENT

As we explain below, the three courses varied significantly in approach, goals, and assignments. The Expressivist course, so named because of

Table 3.1 Study participants, content of FYC course, and post-composition writing analyzed

Study Participant*	FYC Course Content Design	Writing Contexts Analyzed in Post-composition Semester
Emma	Expressivist approach: personal writing, interpretation of print and visual texts	Essays in three courses: Religion, Family and Child Sciences, Humanities
Glen	Expressivist approach: personal writing, interpretation of print and visual texts	Humanities essay; film essay; personal statement; physics lab report
Darren	Media and culture theme: analysis of media and its influence on the shaping of our culture	Biology lab reports; chemistry lab reports; theater essay
Carolina	Media and culture theme: analysis of media and its influence on the shaping of our culture	Biology lab reports; chemistry lab reports; sorority fundraising letter
Marta	Teaching for Transfer design: comprehensive writing concepts approach using key terms, theory of writing, and structured reflection	Reading responses in Philosophy of Literature course; essay in Fantasy Literature course
Clay	Teaching for Transfer design: comprehensive writing concepts approach using key terms, theory of writing, and structured reflection	Meteorology essay; biology lab reports
Rick	Teaching for Transfer design: comprehensive writing concepts approach using key terms, theory of writing, and structured reflection	Biology lab reports; chemistry lab reports and poster; physics lab reports

*Names have been changed

its focus on the writer and the writer's perspective, featured content that dealt with current social topics and reflected instructor interest in creative writing as it encouraged students to develop as writers through an evolving perspective on the world. The media and culture course, so named because of its focus on the many aspects and influences of culture and media on our society, included content that addressed the impact of iconic images, many forms of media, and our interpretation of culture based on media influences. The Teaching for Transfer course, so named because of its curricular intention to support transfer, involved content that featured key terms, reflection, and a theory of writing designed as interlocking components aimed at helping students develop a conceptual framework of writing knowledge that would transfer across contexts.

The Expressivist Course Approach

The course we refer to as Expressivist reflected the values of its instructor in terms of writing: voice narrative, character development, identity as a writer, perspective, and dialogue. The instructor was a third-year MFA student in creative writing and had five years experience teaching a variety of courses in composition and creative writing. The instructor's goal was to ease students away from the five-paragraph essay structure so common in high school writing (especially for tests) and help them learn to use a narrative rhetorical strategy, as well as narrative tactics like dialogue, imagery, and character complexity, all of which were keyed to creating voice in writing.

> "What I'm trying to do in this class," the instructor explained, "is get them [students] to develop a voice, and to be able to create the imagery and dialogue that makes for a great character story. I'm also attempting to push their thinking beyond the personal essay to more sophisticated narrative using points of view other than their own. And in the research essay, they should learn the obvious citations and how to research, but I'm looking for a great story, well told, too."

This course featured four major writing assignments, each one heavily process-driven, with three drafts and extensive review before the final version of each assignment was submitted. The course also included a multitude of free-writing assignments and reflection assignments, the latter referred to interchangeably by the instructor as "cover letters" or "process memos," which are accounts of the writing process leading to the text in question.[4] Each of the four assignments, although different in scope, focused on the loose theme that guided this course: cultural identity and its impact on the writer. The writing values inherent in each assignment reflected the instructor's goals for helping students grow as writers: to be accomplished through the creation of an increasingly sophisticated narrative, the incorporation of their own perspective on their work and the work of others, and a consideration of various cultural identities that shape a writer's perspective and the written work that results from that perspective.

Expressivist course assignments

In the Expressivist course, the first assignment consisted of a "snapshots" essay in which students created five, short written pieces describing an aspect of their lives from different perspectives. This was an assignment that focused on the development of a narrative and the use of imagery, while also using the social and cultural contexts that affect us as its axis. More specifically, the assignment asked students to "consider how the stories of our lives have been shaped," to "create a picture with words," and to "think about the social and cultural contexts that have affected your opinions of yourself as well as others' perceptions of you," in the words of the instructor. Students were also encouraged to consider their audience, identified as members of the classroom who "will be interested in and want to read" the piece. To assist students in identifying content for this essay, the instructor used selections from a textbook themed around identity within American culture—including short stories, essays, and memoirs capturing the experiences of marginalized groups, or groups with different cultural identities found within our society—readings that provided students with a means of thinking about their lives and cultures in ways they might differ from their own. In addition to the readings, students interviewed classmates to gather additional perspective. Using these perspectives, their own cultural experiences, and visual images they gathered, students created the five "snapshots" describing their lives from different points of view. In addition, students wrote a "cover letter" process memo about how they approached this assignment and how it differed from other writing assignments they had completed.

The values associated with a narrative genre or rhetorical strategy, as outlined in the first assignment, were echoed in the second assignment, a research project written first as an essay and then repurposed in the form of a magazine feature article that might call on a specific emotional appeal to reach an intended audience. Students also had to identify a magazine for their article, and include all of the information from their research essay in that article. Research topics students wrote about varied, but were from a list suggested by the instructor and themed around the course focus of cultural identity. In this assignment, students learned to conduct research, incorporate research sources into an essay, and cite sources according to MLA style. In repurposing the research essay as a magazine feature, students were first required to develop a written strategy for moving the essay information into the format of a magazine article by considering various popular magazines available to consumers, as well as their audiences. While students were tasked with composing in a new genre, they did not explicitly discuss the concept of genre, but rather relied on models, exploring various samples of the genre in the form of popular magazines—*Newsweek, Rolling Stone, Men's Health, Vanity Fair, Southern Living*, and others—brought to class by the instructor. Likewise, although students were also asked to consider the audience for their magazine and write using the idea of an emotional appeal to that audience, a broader concept of audience was not explicitly discussed.

The third assignment asked students to write a "converging analysis," described by the instructor as "an essay that analyzes the chosen text, your experiences with or reactions to the text, as well as an in-depth analysis of the intended audience and the ways in which that audience may relate." Students were to find a text of personal significance from any source of their choosing and from any medium, particularly focusing on how the writer/creator used "images, character construction, dialogue, and/or text to capture and sustain the audience's interest and imagination." Students were given a variety of texts they might consider for this assignment, including excerpts from the course textbook; a television program such as *Project Runway, Weeds,* or *Deadliest Catch;* a video game such as *World of Warcraft;* a blog; a home video; a photo; a billboard or other advertisement; a poem; or a movie. The instructor used the example of a home video of a family gathering as something students could analyze for "how the creator of the video constructs via narrative movement and particular scenes and images a sense of family identity and the roles of individuals within that collective identity." Although audience is again listed as a key consideration in the description of this assignment, the instructor described it as "a chance for students to compare their own writing, which will hopefully be improving with each assignment, to the writing of others outside the class, to get a sense of how other writers use the same techniques I'm teaching them to use."

The final project, a "radical revision," asked students to revise one previous major assignment, making it a visual piece to present to the class. While the instructor did not suggest particular concepts or goals for this assignment, students were asked to identify their own goals and writing process in an accompanying reflection that "explains why you chose your particular project, how you went about completing the project, changes you would make if you had more time, and what you learned as a result of completing your project." All four of the major assignments developed by the instructor were designed to follow program guidelines and were aimed at helping students find their identities as writers and enrich their writing by exploring different perspectives.

Media and Culture Course Approach

The media and culture section of FYC also reflected the interests and values of the instructor, specifically four such interests: the use of digital technology in writing; the influence of social media; the impact of visual design; and the ways that all of these aspects work together to shape our culture and the writers who write in it. Students were expected to compose digital texts as well as more traditional written essays, the intent to build students' confidence as writers and to include their varying experiences, backgrounds, interests, and accomplishments as important values in the course. The course also intended to teach students to use social media and tools of technology to foster collaboration and develop a stronger understanding of their role in multiple communities within and outside college. The instructor for this section believed that the more opportunities students were given to experience writing in different modes and media, including the digital and visual, the better they would perform in different writing situations. The instructor explains:

> I think my students will respond well to the relevance of these assignments to the writing they do in their lives, and the various media they encounter on a daily basis. They need to be able to make sense of the barrage of messages we all receive from various media on a daily basis, and to understand how those influence us.

The instructor, a first-year MA student in rhetoric and composition, had completed the program's summer pedagogy boot camp, during which she also interned with an experienced instructor just prior to teaching this section of first-year composition.

This course featured three major writing assignments and a final portfolio assignment, each process-driven and generated through invention exercises such as free-writing and brainstorming. The assignments were developed to align with the overall goals of the composition program, while mirroring the values about writing in the digital age that the instructor sought to use as a focus. The instructor, despite teaching for the first time, was recognized as enthusiastic and innovative, and won one of four coveted teaching awards at FSU during the academic year in recognition of exemplary performance as a first-year instructor.

Media and culture course assignments

The first major assignment in this class required that students research the biographical, historical, and social context of an iconic image—such as Warhol's Campbell Soup can or Rosie the Riveter—and write an analysis of their response to the image using the design principles of contrast, repetition, alignment, and proximity (CRAP) that the instructor had previously introduced in class. Images for the assignment were provided by the instructor and initially discussed in class so students could explore their impact on our culture and discuss intriguing themes they represented; students were asked to research one of those iconic images using the Internet or the FSU library to gather information from sources. Using one of the sample iconic images and their own research, students were required to produce a seven to eight page essay reporting on the image they researched and ways the information they found changed their initial response to that image.

In the second assignment, students generated a research question from any theme they identified in Hemingway's "Hills Like White Elephants" and developed an essay around the issue or topic their question addressed. The in-class work for this assignment featured a variety of writing strategies, including outlining, brainstorming, and free-writing; students also completed a free-write at the beginning of each class, posted regularly to the class blog, and participated in brainstorms and other writings online and in the classroom. Building on the research learned during the first assignment, this segment of the course also featured instruction on using MLA style and finding sources of good quality and relevance to the goals of each student's essay. Throughout the assignment students engaged in a multi-draft process, peer collaboration, and reflection writing oriented, as in the case of the Expressivist course, to the processes the students were engaging in as they researched.

The third of the major assignments, functioning in a cumulative way, asked students to create a visual argument and analysis, which required that they develop a visual piece conveying a specific message and then analyze that piece for its effectiveness. It was designed to help students "transition" what students learned in the first two assignments into an analysis of something they themselves had created, and the assignment required that students specifically analyze three dimensions or aspects of text: audience, message, and medium. Students were also asked to analyze it using the CRAP design principles introduced during the first assignment in creating their visual piece.

All three of these assignments included multiple drafts and a final reflection on the process for each assignment that mirrored the reflection assignments in the Expressivist course. Revision and reflection were the main components of the final digital portfolio for the course, which involved a revision of the three major assignments and a collection of the visual and digital components of assignments the students had created over the entire semester. Students presented their revised work, commented on their improvement as writers, and tied their work together through a written introduction to each section of the portfolio.

The Teaching for Transfer Course Approach

The content for the TFT course featured four specific components: (1) the introduction of key terms or concepts; (2) readings supporting the writing assignments, including reading in writing theory and readings in reflection; (3) structured reflection writing through activities and assignments; and (4) a reiterative assignment in which students develop a theory of writing throughout the entire semester and which culminates in a final "theory of writing" assignment. All four components are designed to work together; none of them works toward transfer without the benefit of the others, and all are taught using a reiterative approach communicating clearly to students that transfer of writing knowledge and practice is a goal of the course. To that end, students both practice their development as writers and theorize a framework for approaching concurrent and future writing tasks.

The course features eleven key terms, identified in chapter 2, that represent core writing concepts students can use and apply in other situations. These are introduced throughout the course in four sequential sets—(1) audience, genre, rhetorical situation, and reflection; (2) exigence, critical analysis, discourse community, and knowledge; (3) context, composing, and circulation; and (4) knowledge and reflection again—each set of concepts employed within specific writing assignments and integrated into the learning of the remaining concepts. Reflection, as both theory and practice, is also a key feature of the course that students engage in before, during, and after their writing assignments. By focusing on key terms and reflection, students engage in both theory and practice about writing, which allows for the development of a theory of writing—or a framework of writing knowledge they can apply to new writing contexts—both within the course and beyond it.

The instructor for the TFT course was a third-year doctoral student in rhetoric and composition, with five years prior experience as an adjunct professor and teaching assistant at four different institutions. This instructor, as one of the designers of the TFT course, had the same goals for this course as detailed above: (1) to help students develop a theory of writing that includes some (if not all) of the key terms and rhetorical strategies they practiced inside the classroom; and (2) to aid them in developing as writers. This instructor had also extensively studied reflection and was both knowledgeable about and invested in teaching the structured reflection described as necessary to the success of this course. The course had been piloted on three previous occasions, and by the time the instructor taught it during the research term, she was practiced and familiar with its nuanced approach.

Teaching for transfer course assignments

Featuring four major assignments, the TFT course opened with the four key terms that make up the subject of the first major assignment: develop a source-based article analyzing genre, audience, and rhetorical situation, and in the process use reflection to understand them. The first four terms provide a foundation from which students begin to develop their own theory of writing, which over time helps them create a framework providing for the transfer of knowledge about writing and writing practices. In addition, the two-part format of the assignment forecasts the design of the succeeding assignments, with each one having a writing task *and* a reflection task (written concurrently with the writing task) that is keyed specifically to the writing task and the terms locating it, as we see in the first assignment:

> For this assignment, **you will write a 6–8 page source-based article**, in which you will go beyond summarizing to **analyze and make connections between the concepts of genre, audience, and rhetorical situation**, and begin to **develop a theory of writing**. You will choose from the assigned reading sources (which represent a variety of genres) to incorporate evidence as support for your ideas about these key concepts and to reflect on a possible theory of writing. You must first define the key terms *audience, genre*, and *rhetorical situation* and investigate their relationships within the context of your sources in order to determine the connections between them. You will closely analyze the sources you choose to write about in your article, looking at how each writer uses genre, handles the rhetorical situation, and reaches an audience. As you develop your article you will incorporate both the rhetorical strategies we will explore in class and your understanding of *audience, genre*, and *rhetorical situation*. At the same time as you are developing your article, **you will also create a 2–3 page reflection piece in which you begin to develop your theory of writing**, considering the concepts of genre, audience, and rhetorical situation and how they connect.

In the second assignment, a research essay, students incorporate the second set of terms into their writing—exigence, critical analysis, discourse community, and knowledge. They analyze information from researched sources and intentionally explore the genres their research fall into—both the role of those genres and their audiences—working recursively to integrate the first set of key terms into the next set for this assignment. The writing practice is also recursive: students incorporate evidence from sources and analyze concepts, much as they did in the first assignment, but this time without sources provided and with the addition of four new key terms.

The third major assignment incorporates the next three key terms— context, composing, and circulation—as it moves students from researching and analyzing information to composing in three different genres, each of which communicates to a targeted audience on the initial research topic, but in new genres.

> For this assignment you will move from researching and analyzing your topic, as you did in the Research Essay assignment, to creating a composition which uses different genres to communicate to a targeted audience about that same topic. You will use your previous research, along with new sources, to inform your strategy and help you make the rhetorical choices necessary to create an effective composition. Your genres are your choice, based on your analysis of the rhetorical situation learned in the research process. In this assignment, you will relate your topic to an audience more strategically and specifically than you did in your research essay, incorporating additional evidence and new arguments designed for audience expectations. You will target your audience(s), consider the rhetorical situation, and develop genres to communicate to that audience based on the knowledge you gained in developing the research essay. You will also develop a *rationale* to communicate the strategy behind your genre choices, and a *reflection* to discuss the development of your project. This assignment requires critical thinking, rhetorical awareness, and reflection capabilities to most effectively communicate to your audience.

Students are encouraged to choose from a wide range of genres, from memoirs/personal essays, obituaries, and advertisements to short-feature videos, academic journal articles, case studies, and brochures. In addition, students compose a reflection that, again, is focused on what they have learned about composition by way of the key terms:

> In this reflection, you will analyze the approach to and process of creating your composition project as well as thinking through questions that involve the key terms. Think about what rhetorical choices you have made and consider the following questions: What barriers in communicating to your audiences did you encounter? How did you overcome these barriers? Why did you choose the three genres that you used? How did genre affect audience choice and how did thinking about audience reflect genre choice? Reflection—what rhetorical practices did you find yourself using? Were they effective in the way you presented them? How was your original discourse community affected in new genres? How was the composing process different than with your research essay?

The final major assignment, a reflection-in-presentation, reintroduces two earlier key terms: reflection and knowledge. This reflection-in-presentation assignment—similar to Yancey's reflection-in-presentation model but designed as a single text commenting on students' composition over the duration of the course, rather than on a portfolio of work—asks the students to develop a theory of writing using key terms and their own writing from the semester as evidence for their theory.

Reflection allows you the **opportunity to process knowledge and then apply that knowledge**. In doing this, you can **come to an understanding** and **interpret** what it is you have learned. This semester we have used reflection in this way. In the final assignment you will use reflection to analyze and interpret your learning process. Over the semester, you have had the opportunity to create a knowledge base of writing and its practices. You have been developing a theory of writing as we've moved along, and in this final reflection you will finalize that theory, exploring the following:

1. What is your theory of writing?

2. What was your theory of writing coming into ENC 1102? How has your theory of writing evolved with each piece of composing?

3. What has contributed to your theory of writing the most?

4. What is the relationship between your theory of writing and how you create(d) knowledge?

5. How might your theory of writing be applied to other writing situations both inside the classroom and outside the classroom?

Through this final reflection students combine their experiences of writing with the key terms to create a writing theory for themselves. To prepare them for this culminating task, students reflected on their theory of writing at ten different points during the term: six different journal assignments asked them to think through a specific key term they were learning at the time, and four short writing assignments—that worked toward one of the major assignments—also required students to define their theory at that moment. Given that the aim of the course is to foster transfer, the last question students address in the reflection-in-presentation is critical: it functions to underscore the idea and practice of transfer of writing knowledge and practice as it helps students continue developing after exiting the course.

More generally, as we shall see, students in all three classes offered different perceptions of course content, as well as different ideas about which type of content from their first-year composition course was applicable to future contexts. They also used their knowledge about writing in different ways, both successfully and unsuccessfully, in the writing situations they faced in the semester following the completion of each of the three courses. But compared to the other students, the ones enrolled in the TFT course had the advantage of a language and framework they had made their own. By working with key concepts reflectively, the TFT students created a composing passport to help them cross new writing boundaries.

EXPRESSIVISM, WRITING, AND TRANSFER:
THE EXPERIENCES OF EMMA AND GLEN

The first of the FYC courses in the study, the Expressivist course, provided the participants in this section, Emma and Glen, a set of tasks they found familiar. Emma and Glen were eighteen-year-old, first-year students during this study, and both graduated from public high schools in Florida—Emma in Daytona Beach and Glen in the Tampa area—with both of them testing well enough on their AP English Literature and Language exams to be exempt from the first course in the two-term sequence. Emma and Glen also reported being successful at writing in their high school courses, where they felt they had learned much from their English courses about writing, a learning that they drew upon in FYC. Since the high school and college writing assignments contained a common literary-informed thread—interesting narrative, imagery, dialogue, and character—the college writing assignments seemed "natural" to Emma and Glen. In other words, though the setting was new, the assignments were familiar, given their extensions of what was familiar from their high school literature-based English classes. In one case, as we will see, the familiarity was seemingly an asset, while in another one it was not. More specifically, Emma and Glen's experiences of collegiate writing were very different: Emma pursued a two-part strategy imported from high school—avoiding error and meeting teachers' expectations—that resulted in a kind of school-success, while Glen—in the process of navigating some *unsuccessful* writing experiences—began discovering the content of composition through experience rather than curricular design.[5]

Emma's approach to writing throughout the two terms was framed doubly: (1) correctness, in particular through the "rules for correctness" she had learned in high school, and (2) the meeting of teacher expectations for each assignment. In her mind the two were linked, as she explains: "I do like choosing what I write about as long as I have specific guidelines to write on. I like to know what I'm being graded on and what the criteria is. That way I can't do anything wrong." Emma's definition of writing didn't change during the two terms, especially since her approach to writing was consistently rewarded all the way up the food chain by good grades in all three contexts: high school; FYC; and the courses she took in the post-composition semester. She transfered what she had learned about writing in high school—that is, her writing knowledge, captured in her perception of the role of error in writing and the need to avoid it—to her college composition course. Moreover, in responding to her post-composition writing requirements, rather than calling on her FYC experience, Emma "leapfrogs" her writing knowledge from high school over the FYC context as she takes up post-composition writing assignments. In one humanities course, for example, Emma was required to write about gender representation in film by looking at the work of a specific director. Emma approached this assignment by drawing on other writing knowledge, what she knew about writing high school literary analyses, as she explains: "I've done analysis since high school, so it was no big deal. I did it like an analysis of a piece of literature, only it was film, and just followed the specific format. And the research we did was like we learned in high school and in 1102 [the second term of the two-term sequence], so I knew where to go to look at the databases, or to just Google the director." Drawing on her knowledge of literary analysis to write in the context of film, Emma engages in *near transfer* as defined by Perkins and Salomon (1992), moving from one context to another without consciously realizing that she is considering the differences in situation and material. She doesn't identify writing knowledge from her college writing course as helpful—even though both the college and the high school class shared some of the same practices and thus some of the same content—because she cannot identify any content from FYC that might apply, other than Googling for information. In a very common sense way, what Emma can identify as applicable—her high school knowledge of the genre of literary analysis and how to compose one—is what she transfers.

As important, the sense of expertise communicated by her successful grades in high school and college writing gave Emma the impression that two factors—(1) knowing the instructor's expectations and meeting them and (2) knowing how to write without error—*are* the keys to success in any writing situation; and given her success in terms of grades, it's in some ways difficult to counter her perceptions. At the same time, it's fair to note that Emma was largely able to maintain this view because the contexts in which she wrote during both semesters were all very similar; she was basically repeating the same writing task in each assignment. Put another way, Emma doesn't see herself as a novice, in the Sommers and Saltz (2004) sense, because her college writing assignments don't ask her to be one. Perhaps, then, it was not surprising that her theory about writing that she shared in her penultimate interview echoed what she had said as she entered FYC: avoid error, please the teacher—in her words, "appease the teacher"—and, if possible, connect empathetically with the teacher for feedback: "Talking to my teacher and going over my paper with her was always a plus also. It gave me some extra direction into what she wanted and I also got a chance to show her how much I cared."

In contrast, Glen's post-composition writing experience—which was not completely successful—created a kind of dissonance, prompting him to begin thinking about writing differentially and thus rhetorically. As he began the post-composition term, Glen brought two minds to his writing assignments. On the one hand, he was able to read across situations, as *HPL* suggests (Bransford, Pellegrino, and Donovan 2000), in this case observing how various writing sites and assignments were alike and different. For example, in describing the genre of his physics lab reports, he noted similarities to and differences from his writing in a humanities context. The physics lab report, he explained, "required a step-by-step description of the lab process and plenty of math, plus drawings, if necessary," and he commented that the purpose of writing was "to understand the properties of light and sound." This purpose, he noted, was similar to the writing in his humanities course, where the goal "was also to show understanding of the subject matter, but also to analyze the works of important figures and see how they relate." Thus, Glen saw *both* similarities and differences in the writing of the two situations. On the other hand, Glen sometimes projected more similarity between two writing sites than was actually the case, especially when, to him, they seemed to be "naturally" similar. In fact, he expected connections between the writing in first-year composition and his post-FYC humanities course, and here his expectation, at least in part, set him up for an unsuccessful experience, or failure.[6]

In the humanities class, Glen was required to write an essay in which he first explored and analyzed the connections between the moral philosophies of two authors, philosophers, or political leaders of an earlier time, and then connected those to the course discussion on morality in the present day. As Glen reported in an interview, he intentionally transferred knowledge from his Expressivist FYC class when working on this assignment, employing writing knowledge and practice from the composition course for the purpose of writing the humanities essay: "I used the outlining process that helped me during ENC 1102. I also used the knowledge of resources available to me, such as the books and space available at the library." However, the documentation we collected doesn't support this observation. In other words, Glen reported transfer from FYC that wasn't evidenced in the FYC course materials or teacher interviews: the outlining process Glen used in his composition course, and the knowledge of resources he developed, were *not* addressed in his FYC class. Apparently, he, like Emma, either leapfrogged, drawing on high school instructional experiences, or intuited them from writing situations more generally, much as Doug Brent's (2012) students report.[7]

Glen *had* learned how to compile research from his Expressivist FYC course, however, and for the humanities essay he did a thorough job of compiling information. He was also adept at comparing the moral philosophies of two authors, as required, but he did not connect those to the moral ideologies being discussed in his class. Basically, his approach to the assignment relied on replicating prior experiences—compiling information and presenting it in a FYC-type research essay (as he had experienced it)—rather than on repurposing or developing a new or adaptive strategy to write in what was in fact a new genre, the fully researched and synthetic humanities analysis connecting ideas from multiple contexts. Nor did Glen consider the rhetorical situation of the humanities assignment, especially the broader social perspective of the context in which his humanities course's discussions on morality were based. Instead, perhaps misled by the similarities between this assignment and the FYC assignments, he reverted to the writer-centered approach informed by the values of imagery and interesting narrative from the content of the FYC course. In other words, Glen employed the specific writing techniques he learned in FYC, which focused more on expressing oneself as a writer, rather than on writing an effective and rhetorically objective analysis. Thus, although Glen did transfer writing knowledge he learned in FYC, it was not writing knowledge that was appropriate to the new context.[8]

Glen's grade on the humanities essay was an unpleasant surprise to him, but it also prompted him to approach writing differently. After his humanities essay was returned, Glen reported that his professor talked to him about expectations for analysis in writing, and it was in that conversation that Glen realized that the context was different than it had been in the FYC course. Here, then, as Glen widened his reading across writing situations in order to discern differences at least as much as similarities, he began to understand the differences in context, and thus the relationship of writing to situation:

> In ENC 1102 we covered a multitude of topics related to media and how it affects the past, present, and future. The class also allowed more introspective thought as we wrote about our own lives in addition to the lives of others. In humanities, the assignment was very direct, and while we were required to analyze, it was using only evidence and not feelings.

Later that semester, Glen demonstrated that he had taken the learning from this experience and used it in a new situation, a short assignment for a class studying film, where he was required to write another analysis, this one addressing certain aspects of *Raiders of the Lost Ark*. Glen's analysis was successful in this context, as reflected in two ways, by his A grade and, more importantly, by his understanding. In discussing his approach to the assignment, he indicated his new understanding that writing an analysis requires analytic distance, rather than the writer-centric focus on voice and imagery that he experienced in his first-year composition course:

> It was just facts, kind of dry, but supported by evidence, and the key was making sure the significance to the final film is explained. It was more like what I expected college writing would be like than 1102. More restricted, less personal. In 1102 the writing was vivid, emotional. That wouldn't work for this.

Glen here begins to differentiate between genres, although he—like the students in both the Jarratt et al. (2005) and the Hilgers, Hussey, and Stitt-Bergh (1999) studies—doesn't have the language of genre. More generally, Glen was beginning to transfer differentially and appropriately: he does transfer the compiling of information from FYC, but he does not transfer the "vivid, emotional" approach that was rewarded there. Likewise, Glen was able to transfer writing knowledge acquired through a set-back, his failure in the humanities course writing assignment, to his film class. As he does so, he is inventing a theory of writing.[9] Part of that theory, not surprisingly, is located in the differences among different writing tasks, even though, or perhaps especially because, they looked alike: in the non-composition humanities courses "the key was making sure the significance to the [text or issue] is explained." In this adaptation and summary of learning, Glen demonstrated that he was beginning to develop both general knowledge about writing and local knowledge about writing tasks. As we've seen, however, Glen's development was fostered within the context of writing for other college courses rather than within his first-year composition course: he begins to learn this content of composition through experience. Relative to our interest in how we can support student transfer of knowledge and practice, what's lost in Glen's case is the travel guide or passport that the FYC class can make available to help students explicitly understand how writing works and to develop a frame for approaching new writing tasks.

In sum, the two students from the Expressivist course either did not draw upon, or *learned* not to draw upon, the content of that course as they moved forward, with one of the two discovering that the de facto writing theory inherent in the course itself—valuing a personal approach, for example—was at odds with the expectations of their post-composition writing assignments. Emma simply continued to exercise the generalized student behaviors of avoiding error and satisfying teacher expectations she'd successfully practiced in high school, and unfortunately her post-college composition classes didn't demand anything more. Without such demands, there is no prompt for development, and transfer is unlikely to occur: there is no exigence. Glen does progress, largely as a result of *reverse transfer*. Through an unsuccessful experience, a setback, he learns that transfer may not be appropriate even when contexts look similar. Based on this experience, he begins to develop the writing knowledge that helps him understand why the limited analysis and personally oriented Expressivist content of his first-year composition course will not assist him in meeting the genre expectations for the writing tasks in his humanities course. Furthermore, both students are without a robust language for writing: thus writing in a genre in FYC doesn't link to a *conception* of genre, to ways that genres are related, or to their role as responses to recurring situations (in Carolyn Miller's (1984) famous formation).

The content of this first-year composition course, then, did not support transfer for Emma and Glen, and in two ways. First, since it did not provide the opportunity for students to develop a broader set of terms for writing, or a conceptual writing framework, they had no passport with which to transition from FYC to other contexts. Second, while the Expressivist course included the *practice* of reflection, it did not engage students in using reflection to theorize, as recommended by *HPL* (Bransford, Pellegrino, and Donovan 2000): put simply, reflection functioned in practice as a process addendum to writing assignments rather than as a source of invention for understanding writing. In sum, without an explicit theoretical construct of writing organizing and anchoring the course, course content was not supporting these students as they took on new writing assignments.

THE MEDIA AND CULTURE EXPERIENCE: DARREN AND CAROLINA

The media and culture themed course presented a situation very different from the Expressivist course, in large part because, for Darren and Carolina, the content was both new *and* unfamiliar. Darren and Carolina were eighteen-year-old students in their first semester at Florida State University, the former from the Jacksonville area and the latter from a small town on the western edge of Fort Lauderdale. Both had completed ENC 1101 before coming to FSU, Darren through dual enrollment at a community college and Carolina through dual enrollment at her high school. At FSU, Darren's major was bio-mathematics and Carolina's was bio-chemistry, with both aspiring to attend medical school and eventually practice medicine in their areas of specialty. In the media and culture course, they were provided with different spaces, online and in print, where students were required to write. The course also required students to analyze and produce many different types of writing. Darren and Carolina indicated in later interviews some uncertainty about the purpose of assignments, though independently they identified three areas of focus overall: writing strategies, research techniques, and the content of their individual research projects. Consequently, for both Darren and Carolina this course content was, in large part, focused on the *how* of writing as filtered through their own research, and their report of what they learned in the course echoes observations McCarthy's (1987) Dave made about writing: writing is simply different from one situation to the next.

In Darren's case, research provided the link between assignments—especially the first assignment, the visual analysis, and the second, the research essay—because both required that students find sources to support claims. He did not connect the visual analysis to the written analysis later in the semester, however, possibly because he did not have the knowledge of genre as a category that could link the two. He focused instead on the *process* he used to complete the writing, rather than on a conceptual definition of writing, genre, or the strategy of *rhetorical analysis*. Darren researched Andy Warhol for the assignments, and understood the topic of his text to be Andy Warhol, but he didn't understand the learning goal of the assignment to be the *analysis* of, or *writing* about, Warhol. He thus "fills in the blank" of the course content with the content of his research, which was Andy Warhol; in other words, Darren identifies Andy Warhol, not the rhetorical analysis of the Warhol material, as the subject matter of the course. Later in the course, in one of his interviews, Darren identified the course content as "research" for the same reason; he knew the course involved research and there was no other explicit content he was able to name, so he perceived it as a research course. Without being able to identify a conceptual framework around which to organize both the assignments in the course and the information he was finding through research, Darren perceived the course, as demonstrated in his written assignments, as one centered on *research* and on *process*—an understandable conclusion given that the content wasn't in fact directly related to writing and that he wasn't presented with any writing-specific knowledge.

Carolina also defined the course according to *how* writing was done, not *what* writing was or is: for her, the FYC was a class "about writing" as acts of writing rather than a subject. Carolina saw the purpose of writing the research essay as "to fulfill the requirement," adding that, while she found her topic interesting, she doubted she would use it in the future. Carolina also reported that in composing this text, she did not write with a specific audience in mind: "I assumed it would be college students and/or professors but that didn't exactly influence the way I wrote it." She did, however, report that she learned some writing techniques she would find helpful again: "I did find that [reverse outline exercise] extremely useful because it allowed me to see the paper as a whole and fix the order of it. I've never made a reverse outline before but I will probably use it again." Later in the interview, Carolina mentioned the reverse outline again when she commented on the challenge of revising her draft for this essay:

> I had to rewrite my paper after draft two, which was a challenge. I don't like when I have to choose my own topic because I end up picking a very vague one. That happened with this paper, but making a reverse outline really helped to see the structure of the paper and which ideas were strong.

The process of multiple drafting was new to Carolina—as it is to many first-year college students (Jarratt et al. (2005); Scherff and Piazza 2005; Denecker 2013)—and she reported several times that this practice was helpful, just as she lauded the reverse outline. However, she also believed that the amount of process writing was too extensive, especially since she did not see its relevance to writing in other courses. Darren expressed the same view: the process requirements, involving multiple drafts, peer reviews, and a process memo, were tedious. In particular, because they perceived the amount of writing in the course as randomly decided and designed to make students work hard rather than help them, Carolina and Darren questioned the need for more than two drafts.

As Darren continued classes in the post-composition semester, he noted that he could see no similarities between the FYC course and the writing he did in other courses, but he, like Glen, saw connections between post-composition courses and his high school English classes. When explaining the writing in his theater class, for example, he pointed to the similarities between high school literary analyses and college theater writing tasks, at least in terms of the "freedom" (or lack of same) he associated with those kinds of assignments:

> Analyzing a play is like what we did in the literature class, where it's a literary text, and honestly it sounds like my theatre instructor wants the exact same thing. In 1102 the analysis was about visual text so it was more up to the writer what to say; I mean no one can argue with however you see it.

For each of his postcomposition courses, Darren developed a strategy: for example, in "Chem Lab I know that nothing but the data was important and I would be successful if I showed that I knew what I was talking about." His strategy for the theater class was keyed to topic sentences and grammar; he was careful to include "introduction sentences for each paragraph. Plus I knew that the content was only worth forty percent of the points so it was important to use good grammar." Much like Emma keying her writing to faculty expectations, Darren keyed his to formulaic textual strategies and an analysis of the points any assignment could earn.

Given this context, it's not surprising that Darren believed there was nothing he learned in the composition course that was applicable to writing in any other context: "Everything I learned about writing, I learned in high school." In the sense that it was in high school that he learned about types of analysis, basic research protocols, and grammar, Darren's account is, of course, accurate. Darren also explained that the techniques he learned in the composition course did not fit with his writing style because he doesn't plan or outline, and much as the students in the Bergmann and Zepernick (2007) study, he described a view of FYC process as one at odds with the values of writing in his other courses, where process is either not expected or extra-curricular, in the sense that students are assumed to be completing whatever processes they choose to employ outside of class. Darren thus perceived the extensive, multi-draft process of the FYC course as content, or partial content, that was not as important as the content he learned in other classes. Since he could not articulate the FYC content, he struggled to understand what it was, filling in the writing process as the content he could not otherwise discern. Further, because the writing process was so explicitly elaborate in the FYC course, he perceived it as irrelevant to writing in other courses, as the writing there was dominated by clearly communicated subject matter and nonexistent or implied process. He explains:

> It's entirely different. In 1102, your grade is dependent on being able to do things the way other people want you to do them. Content really doesn't matter too much in that class, although it is somewhat important. In other classes, the grade is almost completely dependent on content. In other classes you can write any way that you want as long as the final result is good. 1102 is about the process; other classes are about the product.

Carolina's perception of the differences in writing in FYC and in other classes matched Darren's: "The writing in other classes is really simple, or factual, or explanatory. As long as you understand the information you are writing about and explain it clearly through your writing you will do well." She viewed FYC as focused on unnecessary process rather than on the end result; in particular, she didn't understand the logic of the amount of process.

> Writing multiple drafts of an essay can be annoying, but it is definitely helpful to check your work. It did help me correct my work and understand information I wrote about. But I wasn't sure why we focused on the work that goes toward an end result instead of actually trying to get there. Isn't that the point of writing, to have something finished and good?

Carolina anticipated no trouble completing any of her writing that semester. She was already familiar with writing lab reports: "since I love science and doing experiments, it is easy to write those. Plus it's just simple writing, you just report what happened." She characterized lab reports as "summaries with enough details to make the experiment clear." Her approach to writing lab reports was to take notes during the experiment and the lecture or discussion, and then to replicate that experiment in words. She also noted that correctness in the writing is necessary, but not limited to just one author's perusal: "your whole lab group can read it over so you'll see if there are any mistakes."

When discussing this process of writing up lab results, Carolina drew connections across sites of writing, much as an expert would, remarking that "having a lab group is kind of like a peer review workshop in 1102." However, Carolina also understood that the lab was different than FYC. She viewed the lab environment as a place of collaborative work, including the writing of the report and the feedback, in large part because the lab writing was focused on correctness and collective authorship: "The group in the lab is so you can do the experiment properly and check your work in writing up the report. There is no opinion or suggestions for writing involved, it's just about being correct in your report." Given her perceptions of the differences in values and practices—evidenced personal opinions as opposed to correctness, for example, and single authorship gaining response from peers as opposed to collaborative authorship with review for correctness—it's not surprising that Carolina was unable to see a connection between what she had learned in FYC and any future writing tasks, which she assumed would be like lab writing.

> The type of writing I'm going to be doing isn't that type, like writing and analyzing about someone. I'll be writing lab reports and things. I'm going to be a doctor, so I don't expect much writing other than lab reports and that kind of thing, unless I go into research.

Carolina was doing writing in other sites, however, one of which was for her sorority, in this case the writing of a fundraising letter. While the letter genre was not new to her since she had been a summer employee at a financial advising office where writing business letters was a regular task for her, the purpose of this letter was different and, again reading across sites, she recognized that.

> This letter is harder than I thought because it's not just reporting on an account or updating, like the letters I wrote for the summer job; it is asking people for money or something they can give us. It's for charity so that's good, but it's still hard to ask for money and make it sound good. You really have to sell the event and make sure they understand why it's important and what could be in it for them.

Once Carolina was attempting to write in a real-world situation with a very specific persuasive purpose and audience that were meaningful to her, writing became challenging. She also understood how, in terms of strategy, the appeal in this letter would be different than the approach she took in FYC: "The art pieces were really vague, and so my analysis was too. I can't do that here or we won't get sponsors." Still, while Carolina reported that she saw audience and purpose as ideas she had learned in the composition course, she did not believe these ideas were helping her write better fundraising letters; they weren't central enough as key terms of writing to provide a lens into or frame around this writing task. What did help her, much as they helped Doug Brent's (2012) internship students, was a set of models that she could draw from or imitate:

> Well, I had to learn how to write these letters, with help from the rest of the committee, but basically on my own. We had some from two years ago that I looked at and those helped. But it's different writing than in 1102. I see that there are similar things when you ask me to think back, but the writing is not the same.

Without discernible content, students fill in their own content; without a theory on which to build and apply knowledge, Carolina turned to models and Darren turned to process. In cases like this—when content or theory is absent or indiscernible, and especially when it is perceived to be at odds with writing in other university sites—models of writing become the teacher and the curriculum.[10]

The confusion of both Carolina and Darren about the content of the composition course—that, from the instructor's perspective, it (among other aims) was intended to help prepare students to write in other situations—was exacerbated by the design of the course, especially its key terms. The media and culture course employed two sets of key terms, one set using imagery, research, analysis, audience, message, and medium, and a second set communicated through class activities and assignments—process, peer collaboration, visual text, design of text, digital media, and writer identity—all woven into the course through free-writes, discussions, and exercises. Content was lost in translation, or was too ambiguous to discern, as Darren and Carolina tried to decipher the code to achieving a good grade for each assignment—and for all the students in the study, good grades mattered (a point that we take up more thoroughly in the next chapter). Too much "floating" content—content unmoored to specific writing theory or practice—resulted in a lack of cohesion, a common thread absent throughout the course design that students could discern or use as a guide or passport. Without the coherence of an explicit course design integrating relevant assignments, large and small, students were confused about course content, goals, and concepts that might transfer. Accordingly, when Darren and Carolina take up new post-composition tasks, like McCarthy's (1987) Dave, all they see is difference.

TEACHING FOR TRANSFER (TFT): MARTA, CLAY, AND RICK

In Florida, students with an Advanced Placement score of three on either of the "English" AP exams are exempt from the first term of the two-term composition sequence, an exemption earned by all three of the students in the TFT course. Majoring in philosophy and interested in a career in politics, journalism, or public relations, nineteen-year-old, white, middle-class Marta was from Tampa. Clay—eighteen years old, middle-class, and white—was a first-year student from Boca Raton majoring in actuarial science. And Rick, another eighteen-year-old, middle-class, white student, came to FSU from Orlando to major in physics and astrophysics, in his case aspiring toward a career in physics research. Still, from the beginning of the TFT course, there were differences among these three students. For example, of the three participants from this section of composition, Marta was the only one who self-identified as a strong writer based on previous experience. She reported writing success in both her high school classrooms and the school newspaper, whereas Rick and Clay, both science majors, did not consider themselves to be strong writers. Her multiple writing experiences, however, did not advantage Marta. As we shall see, both Clay and Rick were better at adopting the novice stance that many researchers (e.g., Carroll 2002; Hansen et al. 2004; Sommers and Saltz 2004) claim is so important for writer development, and that development was in large part facilitated through a new language they used to frame writing across contexts.

Enactments of the Prior: Marta

When the TFT course began, Marta demonstrated that she was already familiar with some of the writing concepts presented in the course and that her future professional plans included writing. Put simply, she identified as a writer. During the TFT course, then, she largely continued the practices she had brought with her. For example, she expanded the writing strategies she had developed in high school, using multiple outlines and revising several drafts, but she did not adopt any *new* strategies other than the highlighting of research notes to enhance her research essay writing, a strategy she did not categorize as one learned in the composition course. Likewise, she continued to consider audience in her writing and knew that the purpose for writing was different depending on the situation. Thus, in her second interview, when discussing the research essay in the composition course, she described her audience as broad and imagined beyond the classroom, without mentioning the teacher as part of the audience—an unusual absence in this population of students. She also discussed the purpose of her essay as "creating awareness" and, unlike the other students, did not mention anything about grades or writing to fulfill an assignment. Still, despite her comparatively sophisticated understanding of audience and purpose, and despite the course design, Marta did not employ or think in terms of the key terms linking assignments in the TFT course. While she was able to define the concepts required in the first assignment—genre, audience, and rhetorical situation—she did not *recognize* those concepts as operating in the second or third assignments. When prompted, she acknowledged that rhetorical situation was a consideration for the third assignment, but she did not understand it as a requirement for it. In other words, she *understood* the concepts in the course, including that of rhetorical situation— and at the end of the semester she listed rhetorical situation as one of the key terms in the course—but she did not *incorporate the idea* of rhetorical situation as a way to think about or frame a writing task. Instead, like her colleagues in the two other versions of FYC, Marta's focus remained on the process of writing rather than on a theoretically informed practice of writing. She discussed the techniques that enhanced her process, specifically in the areas of outlining and revising, but her fundamental writing process did not change, and she did not allow a theory about writing to inform her writing and thinking practices, at least during the scope of this study.

Because Marta had enjoyed writing success in the past, and because that success had been validated by others, she either did not recognize or chose to ignore the writing concepts in the TFT course that could have contributed to her theoretical understanding of writing. But a good student, Marta was canny about her inclusion of terms in the various reflective assignments. For example, in her final in-class reflection about her theory of writing, Marta cites three key terms from the course: audience, genre, and rhetorical situation. She defines these concepts as "working together in the process of writing. Rhetorical situation is important because it adds different layers to the writing; it makes the writing intriguing when in consideration with the other two elements of good writing." Marta's theory of writing identifies the three key terms of genre, audience, and rhetorical situation, but she lists these terms not because she uses them—and she defines rhetorical situation incorrectly—but because she believes they make the writing *intriguing*, and they provide content the teacher will expect to see in the assignment.

In the same reflective assignment, Marta also contributes her own list of terms she believes to be important to writing: integrity, persistence, revision, thought, emotion, borrowing, and character. She explained, "My key terms list at the beginning of the class consisted of consistency, integrity, persistence, revision, and thought. I would keep all of these key terms today as they are all very valid in the writing process." But, as Marta's explanation demonstrates, these are not the content-specific terms recommended by *HPL* (Bransford, Pellegrino, and Donovan 2000), but rather terms that describe life itself:

> If you were to take the word "writing" out of my theory, you could almost say it was a theory to anything we do in life. My writing theory involves ideas of emotion, borrowing, and character. Emotion can be applied to everything we do. We use emotion when talking to our friends, watching TV, or even while interacting in a class discussion. Emotion makes our lives worthwhile; life would be boring without it, just as writing would be nothing without it. When we write, we borrow the ideas of other authors we have read. Just as when forming our own identities, we borrow what we see in the places we go and the people we meet. No one can be considered original. We all come from something. We're all made up of the different elements we meet in life. Our personalities are fractions of our parents, family, and friends. They are influenced by what we read, the music we listen to, and the hobbies we participate in. The main idea of my theory of writing involves the relationships built and built upon, through what we write and the different elements in them. We build relationships with people through writing and verbal communication. Every step in our life is a building block on each other. Each piece we write builds upon each other, whether we are aware of this or not.

The terms Marta includes here—for instance, integrity and persistence—are valuable traits, of course. But they serve as a kind of "general-intention response," as discussed by Faigley et al. (1985, 192), one that "suggest[s] only a student's abstract motivation to succeed in the writing task" rather than as the components of a writing situation or as a theory of writing.

During both semesters of the two-semester study, Marta, like Emma from the Expressivist class, encountered no exigence for change: given affirmation in terms of good grades and favorable feedback, she—all too understandably—did not see the need to change her approach to writing. Not that she didn't see connections across sites of writing: like the students in the Hilgers, Hussey, and Stitt-Bergh (1999) and Jarratt et al. (2005) studies, Marta made connections between the writing in the TFT course and that in other courses, but those connections involved writing process or writing strategies exclusively. While she may have applied these strategies in new contexts, and was therefore practicing what Perkins and Salomon (1992) refer to as *low-road transfer* to new writing situations, Marta did not appear to engage in *mindful transfer* of any of the larger concepts of writing from the FYC course to post-composition writing.

The Role of Context: Clay

Clay articulated as much confidence as Marta in his writing, but less interest. Clay's challenges with the research essay in the TFT course, however, provided him with an exigence prompting him to adopt a novice mindset, which in turn allowed him to embrace new concepts offered in the course. More specifically, by realizing he had not learned all he needed to know about writing, especially about the citation information that confounded him until the end of the research essay segment of the composition course, Clay was able to take up a novice stance, in large part by letting go of expertise based on earlier success in writing. However, assuming a novice stance may have been easier for Clay than it was for Marta because Clay was not as invested in writing as an indication of his current or future worth, whereas Marta identified as a lifetime writer and thus had her future leveraged on writing. In contrast, Clay, as an actuarial science major, did not have the same outside or internal pressures to excel in writing, so for him adapting a novice mindset may well have been a non-threatening step toward improving his writing.

Clay had the same broad conception of audience for his writing as Marta: indeed, he took up the role of audience in his research essay as he explored the negative influence of Facebook, with the purpose of creating awareness of what can happen to users when they post inappropriate content. His sense of audience bled into his awareness of a broader purpose for writing: he identified his audience according to Facebook user demographics, and he was reasonable and realistic in his rhetorical intent. He didn't expect his readers to cease their Facebook participation, but he wanted them to participate more knowledgeably. Clay thus demonstrated an awareness of writing as a meaningful rhetorical engagement, going beyond writing for the teacher to fulfill a course requirement, instead writing to fulfill a genuine purpose for a specific and salient audience of peers. As important, his conceptual understanding allowed Clay to approach aspects of the research essay that were creating a challenge. Although the assignment called for inquiry, for example, Clay was prone to argument; he thus adapted a writing strategy on his own—outlining—to try to overcome his propensity for argument, a writing mindset he found difficult to shed given the deeply embedded prior knowledge of his high school writing experience and—probably more important—his successful debate team experience that privileged argument above everything else. [11]

Engaging in peer review was also a helpful strategy to Clay because he got feedback on the organization of his writing, not on the surface errors, which had been his previous experience with peer review. Although he did not change his writing process significantly during the course, he did give new strategies a chance. He also discovered a benefit to reflection writing for the first time, practicing metacognition through reflection and discovering what he thought about genre and audience. When asked if he learned any particular writing strategies in FYC that might have changed what he did in response to an assignment, Clay reported:

> I didn't get that [strategies] from the class, I got a greater understanding of what I was doing. I realized things that could help me. Like now, before I sit down to write a paper, I think about the topic for a bit and think about what the genre or audience or rhetorical situation might be. I became more aware of trying to write a good paper instead of just writing, which is what I did before.

By the time the third major assignment arrived, Clay was beginning to look beyond the writing strategies toward the theoretical concepts behind writing. In creating the three genres for the composition-in-three-genres assignment, and by engaging in the critical thinking that the project demanded in order to develop an audience strategy, genre proposal, and research on genres of writing, Clay was able to understand how the theoretical writing concepts worked in context. Clay realized that writing requires both theoretical knowledge and practice; by working through how to present the "same" material in different genres and for different audiences, he came to understand how genres were both different and similar, a reading across contexts that is congruent with the advice given in *HPL* (Bransford, Pellegrino, and Donovan 2000). This was a turning point for Clay; he suddenly understood how contextual writing is, which helped him to clarify the concepts, such as rhetorical situation, that he'd worked with earlier in the term. Likewise, Clay marked this shift himself when, in the interview at the end of the first semester of the study, he observed that what he learned in FYC were not strategies, but *ways of thinking* about how to write in any situation.

In this process, as Clay began to think about the connections between his writing in various situations, he applied the concepts of genre, audience, and rhetorical situation to an assignment he had in a literature class that same semester, with much success. As he then worked on his final assignment for FYC, the reflection-in-presentation, he began to see reflection as a tool for making these connections. He also saw connections to his other courses and the potential writing situations he would face in the future. As he pointed out in his final interview that first semester, he realized how reflection had been the means of connection—writing to thinking and thinking to knowledge—and that's, he said, how his writing had developed. Through reflection, Clay was able to develop knowledge about writing and use it appropriately both inside and outside FYC.

When asked how he defined the course, Clay responded that it "compare[ed] genre, audience, and rhetorical situation to everything we did with writing. Not comparing, analyzing." He described the first assignment as "developing a theory of writing" that "became something we built on the rest of the course—it kept coming up as we learned new things like context or how the research we did made us think more about our theory of writing." By the end of the term, Clay's theory of writing captured this new understanding of *writing in context*; he particularly focused on the idea that because context is constantly evolving, a fluid rather than static theory of writing was appropriate. He also spoke of the idea that context was important because each situation influenced the writing. He described this in the familiar terms of his major, actuarial science: "the context of a statistic is what matters, not the statistic itself." He also applied this thinking to the composition-in-three-genres project: "I knew that each genre would have its own specific audience because each genre had its own goals." In Clay's final assignment, the reflection-in-presentation, he emphasized both his "remodeled" theory and the way it helped him write:

> This remodeled theory will be continuously changing, but what is important to remember is that my definition is not what is important; it is the application and usage of my theory to the classroom and real world situations. Part of my theory of writing is both my methodology and composing process. My theory of writing allows me to approach certain situations with a certain manner. I will continue to use an appropriate composing process in the classroom for assignments. What my theory of writing allows me to do outside the classroom, however, is approach many tasks in manners that require a lot of thinking, carefulness, and application of knowledge and skill. My theory will help me think clearly in "gray areas of my future." Theory of writing will be different for everyone. My definition is still not clearly defined, nor do I believe it ever will be. I can only hope that my knowledge base continues to grow as my writing becomes exceptionally better.

Clay applied this theory and his notion of writing context to his research project in meteorology the following semester. After being given this assignment, Clay's instinct was to return to the writing theory he knew, as he might in any situation return to what he knew; here he drew on the key terms he had learned and expanded on in the TFT course. He developed the research essay for his meteorology course by using his favored process of planning out the writing in his head, doing extensive research, and writing a single draft in one sitting, and in constructing this essay he drew specifically on the concepts of genre and audience he learned in FYC.

Thinking ahead to his future courses and his career, Clay continued to see many opportunities for transfer. He began to read across contexts, as Glen from the Expressivist course learned to do: he moved from seeing the writing strategies in the TFT course as something he needed to learn to succeed in the course to using and repurposing them to benefit other sites of writing. For example, he did not at first see the value in writing a reflection, but after participating in the set of structured reflection activities, he began to understand its role in helping him (1) think through the key terms and concepts and (2) learn to use them in new situations. In sum, he progressed beyond just adopting writing strategies to developing conceptual knowledge he could use to respond to writing tasks in other contexts. For instance, in applying what he had learned in the TFT course to the meteorology essay he wrote the following semester, he realized that he had knowledge he was able to transfer and that his work with the concepts learned in FYC were responsible for that transfer, particularly genre, context, and audience.

Once you understand that writing is all about context you understand how to shape it to whatever the need is. And once you understand that different genres are meant to do different things for different audiences you know more about writing that works for whatever context you're writing in.

For Clay, the connections across writing sites and the role of the key terms in approaching new writing tasks didn't occur until later in the TFT course, and again the next semester when he was completing his meteorology essay. "I believe it was at the end of the assignment when it hit me that what I picked up on in that class are indeed skills that I will use for the rest of my life." Moreover, in the *practice* of writing using *knowledge* he successfully transferred, he sees more potential transfer ahead. In the same way that he transferred *knowledge* about the concept of genre while engaged in the *practice* of writing the composition-in-three-genres assignment, Clay deliberately transferred his knowledge of writing from FYC to the meteorology essay. In sum, Clay's experience illustrates one of the major premises of the TFT course: both theory and practice, working together, can help students facilitate transfer of writing knowledge and practice.

The Importance of Science in Developing as a Writer: Rick

The idea of transfer was not as clear to Rick as it was to Clay, but Rick eventually demonstrated that he too had transferred writing knowledge to new contexts. Rick had confidence in his writing, just as Clay and Marta had when they began the composition course, but as a physics and astrophysics major, Rick, like Clay, did not generally identify as a writer, though he did identify as a *science* writer. In his first interview Rick revealed that he liked to watch YouTube video lectures of famous physicists in order to learn more about physics and see how writing works in science. He credited both these videos and lab report samples he had collected as helpful in developing the lab reports for his various science classes, using the samples to help him understand writing in an unfamiliar genre.[12] He noted: "I think I write well in my science lab reports because I have read so many lectures and reports that I can just kind of copy their style into my writing."

Early on in the TFT course it was clear that Rick, like his classmates, was drawing on prior knowledge, although in a different way than the others. For his research essay, he chose subject matter he knew well and that was so interesting to him that he neglected the second of two features of a successful response to the assignment: (1) conveying subject matter and (2) helping an audience understand why the information is significant. Put differently, Rick's knowledge and enthusiasm for quantum mechanics got in the way of effectively sharing its significance to a "layperson" audience—with a lower grade as a result. In response, he reported that he had learned a valuable lesson about audience: he " . . . ended up focusing more on the topic than on the research, which is what mattered. I explained too much instead of making it matter to them." This experience proved to be similar to Clay's in that it provided Rick with the opportunity to see himself as a novice, as a student with something to learn. And as a science major, Rick worked in theories rather than absolutes, so the novice mindset was relatively easy for him to adopt.

Like Clay, Rick was not invested in writing as much as he was invested in his major. An emerging physicist, Rick thus used the frame of science as a way to understand writing and look for patterns that would cross both fields of activity: Rick looked for patterns in the writing expectations for each of his three science courses, just as he looked for concepts that would cross contexts. He acted, in this sense, as a "novice expert" by looking for patterns. He also connected all his science courses to composition through the practice of reflection, which he had previously mentioned as something that all scientists do when they're drawing conclusions.

> Reflecting is something all scientists must be very familiar with, because that is what they do. They design and run experiments and do the calculations and then reflect on the data to draw conclusions. The process of writing is sometimes very similar to Bacon's scientific method, with reflection in writing being the equivalent of observing and drawing conclusions in science. When I reflected in [ENC 1102] class I focused on looking back on assignments and thinking about what I have learned from them. In my physics class for our conclusions we use this thing called "RERUN."

> **R**ecall what you did during this lab.

> **E**xplain why you did this lab and what you were trying to find out.

> **R**eflect on the lab's meaning (a.k.a.: did it match your hypothesis or was your hypothesis wrong?)

> **U**ncertainty (errors that were in the lab that you could not control [a.k.a.: weather problems, measurement mistakes] or just any errors that you came across during running this lab that you could fix for the next time you perform the lab).

> **N**ew questions or new discoveries (normally you put in at least two).

> I tried to do the same thing in [ENC 1102] class, saying what we learned from the assignment, why we did the assignment, what the assignment

> meant; we didn't talk about the measurements of uncertainty but instead
> we talked about our problems in the assignment, and we talked about
> what we learned or are still wondering about after the assignment. My
> theory of writing that has evolved in this class can help me in all of my
> future classes, not just English. That will probably be the most helpful
> thing that I take out of this class.

By making these connections, Rick transferred the practice of reflection
in FYC to reflection in his science courses, but he also transferred what
he knew about reflection in the science lab to the composition course,
a "360-degree transfer," as he put it.

One of the major hurdles Rick encountered had to do with audience: he struggled with the idea that audience plays an important role
in writing, which in turn meant he did not fully understand the concept
of rhetorical situation and exigence, two of the key terms in the course.
To him, the most important key term was discourse community, most
likely because it gave him greater entry into the world he loved, science,
and the community he was anxious to join. He discussed the concept of
discourse community as helping him understand the communication
among members of the academic sciences community and allowing him
to better communicate with his professors. Perhaps because of his interest in discourse community knowledge, he also better understood context and the fact that context is always a factor influencing writing. Not
least, Rick used the concept of discourse community to help him transfer understanding and practice from the TFT course to writing conclusions. He reported, for example, that his process for writing lab reports
in chemistry had not changed, but that he was thinking intentionally
about the conclusions he was writing: "I did better on the conclusions
when I started to think about the discourse community and what is
expected in it. I remembered that from ENC 1102, that discourse community dictates how you write, so I thought about it." Rick perceived that
there was a connection across many of the writings he had done in the
sciences, and he saw "a little more of a connection to 1102 and the writing I'm doing now, because making it good means considering some of
the same things like discourse community and purpose."

As Rick began to better understand his conceptual knowledge about
writing, he was able to draw upon additional concepts. For example,
genre became another key term applicable to new situations: this
occurred as Rick began to compose in a new genre, that of the scientific poster. By drawing on his experience in FYC with how research
is presented in different genres, he began to explore—much as *HPL*
(Bransford, Pellegrino, and Donovan 2000) predicts—the similarities

and differences across the two genres of academic research essay and academic poster.

> I have this poster I had to create for my chemistry class, which tells me what genre I have to use, and so I know how to write it, because a poster should be organized a certain way and look a certain way and it is written to a specific audience in a scientific way. I wouldn't write it the same way I would write a research essay—I'm presenting the key points about this chemistry project not writing a lot of paragraphs that include what other people say about it or whatever. The poster is just the highlights with illustrations, but it is right for its audience. It wasn't until I was making the poster that I realized I was thinking about the context I would present it in, which is like rhetorical situation, and that it was a genre. So I thought about those things and I think it helped. My poster was awesome.

What's interesting here—as we will see from another vantage point in chapter 4—is how the composing and textual features in one genre can illuminate those in another: in this comparison, Rick continued to develop his theory of writing intentionally, as a function of linking knowledge *about* writing with practice *in* writing. Like several of the students we talked to, before he took the TFT course Rick had an understanding that *different genres exist*, but in the TFT course he developed *conceptual knowledge about genre* that facilitated the writing in his science classes. He then reversed that transfer by connecting knowledge about genre in his science courses back to the writing he was working on in the TFT class at the same time.[13] And because he was able to develop conceptual knowledge about genre, he was able to apply that knowledge to the concepts of audience and purpose, and consider how they too might transfer to new contexts in scientific writing. At the same time, it's fair to note that Rick understood that genre was only one of a larger constellation of terms; he was quick to qualify that his success on the poster assignment was also a case of understanding expectations: "I learned what the Chemistry TAs wanted in the lab reports and the poster presentation and that influenced what I did. It was part of the context of the course, knowing the expectation."

Most importantly, Rick understood the fact that he didn't yet fully grasp the concept of rhetorical situation, so he continued seeking connections between it and other writing concepts. In his final reflection-in-presentation, for example, he indicated he understood that audience shapes writing, and that this concept, or the idea that "you should write differently to different people," was the most important lesson he learned. Nevertheless, at the same time he remained tied to the notion of the writer's agency, particularly in the context of his science courses, where he may have developed a weaker novice stance than he did in

FYC. By the end of the study, however, Rick indicated that his understanding of the writing concepts and the connections between writing contexts was much stronger. He connected genre in the TFT course to the sciences more concretely, observing that the science genres were different than those in English, but that they share analysis as a rhetorical strategy. With this understanding, he demonstrated that he had a framework within which to apply writing knowledge to new contexts.

In some ways, the students in the TFT section were very like their colleagues in the Expressivist and media and culture sections. Some—like Emma and Marta—entered as strong writers and didn't change very much, in part because the strategies they drew upon were successful, and in part because of absences—of a vertical curriculum, of sufficient challenge built into writing tasks, and of sufficient diversity in the types of assignments they encountered. Other students—like Glen, Clay, and Rick—evolved, in part because they encountered less success, or even outright failure, a point we take up in some detail in the next chapter. But what differentiated Glen from Clay and Rick is that the latter two had a language that facilitated their application and reworking of knowledge and practice from one site to another. Additionally, language isn't merely a set of terms for a class, but the material for a theory of writing and a heuristic for approaching new writing tasks, developed over the course of a term and useful as a tool of analysis and invention, as we saw in Rick's analysis and composition of the poster. As Clay and Rick kept building their theory of writing, then, connecting key terms and concepts to one another and layering in new concepts as they learned them, they became increasingly sophisticated at articulating and practicing their theory of writing.

These aspects of composition content do not work in isolation, but instead are interdependent pedagogical and metacognitive tools for helping students adapt and repurpose what they learn in composition courses to other sites of inquiry.

GOOD TEACHING, IMPACT OF THE CURRICULUM, AND DISTINGUISHING BETWEEN THE TWO

Perhaps what we have documented here is simply the function of good teaching; better teachers, one might say, help students develop as writers in ways others do not. Were this the case, then this study would be more properly focused on pedagogy. But while the teaching of these three classes doesn't distinguish them one from the next, the attention to curriculum and kinds of curriculum do.

Each of these FYC courses—the Expressivist approach, the media and culture themed, and the TFT design—had by definition "good" teachers, and all were graduate students. Two of the three teachers had won teaching awards at FSU; one, as mentioned earlier, was recognized during the study for excellence as a first-time instructor. Each teacher was dedicated to teaching writing, and all three desired that students would learn useful writing knowledge in their courses that would help them develop as writers for diverse contexts.

One major difference in the three courses, however, is the extensive effort in curriculum design that went into the making of the TFT course. As we might expect from a large FYC program, the writing courses that are a routine part of the program, like the Expressivist and media/culture courses, are based on established principles and practices from the field. In contrast, the Teaching for Transfer course is unique because it was more carefully considered by its developers, was the first of its kind, and because it would be used in a research study. Nonetheless, while the TFT course was labored over and piloted prior to the research study, the other two courses were developed and adjusted by the FYC program in much the same way, adapted and honed by the input of the many instructors who had previously taught these courses.

Even with a design such as that featured in the TFT section, of course, students' needs are continually assessed and attended to as the course progresses. Sometimes that means modifying a reading or slowing down an assignment in response to what we understand the class to be learning and doing. This kind of adjustment was exercised by all three instructors as the semester proceeded. Given the extensive program support and mentoring provided by this institution, and given the level of commitment and excellence of the three instructors, our sense is that the students in all the FYC sections involved in this study were provided with "good teaching" as defined by the institution hosting the study.

Good teaching, though, does not necessarily guarantee that students learn what they need to learn in a course. As noted by Bergmann and Zepernick (2007), even with the best of intentions and years of experience, instructors are not always able to provide students with knowledge *about* writing they can then use to frame new writing tasks. It is fair to note, however, that some factors might make a difference, among them the amount of teaching experience of instructors and their educational background, especially if the background, as is the case for rhetoric and composition and writing courses, is directly relevant to the course in question. What we observed in this study was consistent: students looking for identifiable content regardless of course design; and students using the content they could identify—in the case of Emma and Glen, content from high school, and in the case of Clay and Rick, content from the TFT course—to assist them as they approached new writing tasks. In this analysis, then, where the quality of the teaching seems similar, the distinguishing factor isn't the teaching, but rather the curriculum. Moreover, even in a course designed to assist transfer, and in which some students demonstrated successful transfer, others may not transfer due to various factors not related to the quality of teaching, as was the case for Marta.

In this regard, what this study suggests—and as was suggested earlier by Hilgers, Hussey, and Stitt-Bergh (1999), Jarratt et al. (2005), and Reiff and Bawarshi (2011)—is that students need a vocabulary for writing in order to articulate knowledge and ensure more successful transfer. Without a curriculum explicitly based on a writing vocabulary or set of key terms, students often leave the classroom unsure of what they did learn; they then leapfrog to earlier knowledge and practice that may be more or less helpful, rather than employing a writing-rich language model of curriculum as an approach to understanding and responding to new writing situations. Key terms, fully conceptualized and reiteratively learned and used in the classroom, offer students a vocabulary with which they can articulate learned writing knowledge and which is available for use in other rhetorical situations. In sum, such a vocabulary contributes to the passport students need to transition to new contexts. Without such a language, students cannot easily describe individual writing tasks or similarities and differences across them; without such a language, borders to these new worlds represented by new ways of writing and thinking too often remain closed to them.

In the next chapter we examine two factors influencing students' willingness and ability to make use of the kind of content featured in the TFT course: what we call a point of departure and prior knowledge.

Notes

1   In most disciplines, of course, one doesn't *select* content: content and method are at the heart of disciplinarity.

2   The strands, which are continually changing, are available on the web.

3   The point of departure—that is, what students perceive as their starting point in any class, but particularly in their first college class in writing—exerts considerable influence on how students engage with composition and what they expect from it, as we will see in chapter 4

4   Reflective memos at this institution are invariably process memos of the kind described by Jeff Sommers (1988). More recently, Sommers has developed a

sophisticated, individual, and collective set of reflective activities focusing students' attention on their beliefs about writing and the ways they change, or not, as they progress in FYC. See "Reflection Revisited: The Class Collage" (Sommers 2011).

5   Students can learn at least some of the content of composition through experience, as we saw in the case of Doppel (Cleary 2013); such learning can happen in school as well, as we saw in the case of Glen.

6   What's interesting here is the ability to see both similarity and difference across sites, and to see similarities only where they exist and differences where they exist. Those distinctions, we believe, are at the heart of transfer.

7   The value of using multiple methods is obvious here—and in other of the case studies—since it allows us to trace the source of students' perceptions. As Jarratt et al. (2008) note, students' pedagogical memories are, like ours, hardly perfect.

8   In Nowacek's (2011) schema, we might call this an example of frustrated integration.

9   See chapter 4 for a fuller explanation and examples of setbacks.

10 The influence of models is another outcome of the study we had not anticipated, and their role in curriculum is an issue we take up in chapter 4.

11 It's interesting how debate influences the view of argument, and how an awareness of this also shapes the writing experience. It reminds us that prior knowledge and experience come from many sources.

12 It's also clear here that models for writing are available in many places.

13 As Nowacek (2011) observes, and as we have seen in portfolios (a point made in chapter 1), when students write concurrently in multiple contexts, there may be exceptional opportunities for transfer. These contexts, however, can also occur "naturally," as a function of students' schedules, and when they do they can be remarkably serendipitous, especially since they inherently position students as agents of their own learning, as in the case of Rick. It's also the case, as Baird and Dilger (2013) explain, that by design, the curriculum, especially for students in their majors, can include such concurrent opportunities through service learning and internships. As we explain more fully in chapter 5, the composition-in-three-genres assignment works toward this end, we think, precisely because it invites students to engage in the kind of current activity that makes opportunity for transfer available.

4

HOW STUDENTS MAKE USE OF PRIOR KNOWLEDGE IN THE TRANSFER OF KNOWLEDGE AND PRACTICE IN WRITING

In high school, I received a six out of six on the writing portion of my FCAT. . . . I figured I knew all there was to know [about writing]; I was surely mistaken.

— Kevin

As the previous chapter suggests, one significant factor influencing students is their prior experience. Marta and Emma, for instance, who brought to college very positive writing experiences from high school, continue to draw on that prior knowledge almost mechanically, while Rick and Clay develop new knowledge as a function of their TFT class. Put more generally, a significant factor in all the case studies that we didn't appreciate until we began examining the data was the influence of prior knowledge on several dimensions of students' writing experiences: their attitudes toward writing; the strategies they drew upon; the knowledge about writing contextualizing their practices and, consequently, their development as writers. Prior knowledge, we learned, became one of the more important factors in how writers developed—or *didn't* develop. Moreover, students tended to use prior knowledge in different ways, that is, how they would draw upon and employ what they knew in new situations, whether such knowledge and practice was efficacious in the new situation or not.

In this chapter, drawing on and reviewing some of the research presented earlier as well as incorporating new research,[1] we trace how students make use of prior knowledge and practice in the context of our understanding of transfer: as a dynamic activity through which students, like all composers, actively make use of prior knowledge as they respond to new writing tasks. More specifically, we theorize three dimensions of prior knowledge, and again we have a set of terms that describe key concepts. First, we articulate what we call *a point of departure*: we theorize that

DOI: 10.7330/9780874219388.c004

students progress, or not, relative to their past performances as writers—not so much relative to their experiences as writers, but rather as they have found themselves *represented* as writers by others, through external benchmarks like grades and test scores. Second, we learned that students often find themselves entering college courses with an *absence of prior knowledge*, that is, a dearth of information or experience that would be helpful as they begin writing in college. Our students bring with them, for example, very little knowledge or practice in reading the non-fiction texts that are a staple of college writing contexts. And third, despite these impediments, we found that students actively make use of the prior knowledge and practice they do have, and in three ways:

1) by drawing on both knowledge and practice and adding a limited number of new key concepts to this critical knowledge base, an unsuccessful use of prior knowledge we call *assemblage*;

2) by reworking and integrating prior knowledge and practice with new knowledge as they address new tasks, a more successful use of prior knowledge we call *remix*; and

3) by creating new knowledge and practices for themselves when they encounter what we call a *setback* or *critical incident*, which is a failed effort to address a new task that prompts critical ways of thinking about what writing is and how to do it.

We begin this chapter, then, with a quick review of the ways prior knowledge shapes learning, as explained in *How People Learn* (Bransford, Pellegrino, and Donovan 2000), before considering what we call the point of departure, defining it and explaining how it influenced writers' sense of writerly self and their general conceptions of writing. We then define absent prior knowledge and its effect on transfer, linking it to research on high school language arts curricula, before turning to our typology of uses of prior knowledge—assemblage, remix, and critical incident/setback.

HOW PEOPLE LEARN

As we saw in earlier chapters, a little-referenced but rich source of research on transfer is the National Research Council volume *How People Learn: Mind, Brain, Experience, and School* (Bransford, Pellegrino, and Donovan 2000). In addition to plotting the differences between novices and experts, it also reports on prior knowledge and the ways we all use prior knowledge in new situations. *HPL* clarifies that transfer "is best viewed as an active, dynamic process rather than a passive end-product of a particular set of learning experiences." According to this generalized theory of transfer, all "new learning involves transfer based on previous learning" (53). All such prior learning is not efficacious, however, as we saw in chapter 1 and in our case studies. According to this theory, prior knowledge can function in one of three ways. First, an individual's prior knowledge can match the demands of a new task, in which case a composer can draw from and build on that prior knowledge. We might see this when a first-year composition student—much like Clay in the TFT course—thinks in terms of audience, purpose, and genre when entering a writing situation in another discipline. Second, an individual's prior knowledge might not fit with a new writing situation. We saw this when Glen attempted to use his Expressivist FYC approach for the humanities assignment requiring synthesis. And third, an individual's prior knowledge—located in a community context—might be at odds with the requirements of a given writing situation. There are hints of this in Roozen's (2009) study of Angelica, whose use of vivid imagery and personal voice seemed to be valued by her family but not by faculty in English. As this brief review suggests, and as we saw in our case study students, we know that college students call on prior knowledge as they encounter new writing demands: the significant points here are that students actively use their prior knowledge and that some prior knowledge provides help for new writing situations, while other prior knowledge does not.

POINT OF DEPARTURE

One form of prior knowledge is the knowledge we have about our own writing practices—how we typically begin a text; what genres we prefer to compose in; what editing struggles dog our best efforts—and students bring that knowledge with them to college. But in all the case studies, students saw themselves as writers through the lens of what we call a point of departure, which functioned as a primary point of reference as they began college composition. In our formation, the point of departure assists students, for good or ill, much like it influences a traveler. Ideally, the point of departure can and should include all things a student might need to continue on his or her writing journey—a passport identifying key rhetorical concepts, a travel guide of the writing process, and a portfolio of key terms.[2] Not all students are so equipped for travel, however, and without this preparation or guide students look elsewhere for help or signs of progress, to tests and grades especially. These progress markers are ubiquitous, and for many they *become* the passport, the identity marker for them as writers that frames their new learning. Put simply, the point of departure is constituted by external benchmarks like grades and tests that in effect tell a writer what kind of, and how good, a writer he or she is.

Although national policy rewards students for completing AP courses and earning a high score on the culminating AP test, research suggests that students who identify as AP writers are less likely to see themselves as novice writers when they enter college (Hansen et al. 2004). Likewise, as Tinberg and Nadeau (2011, 2013) explain in both "Contesting the Space between High School and College in the Era of Dual- Enrollment" and "What Happens When High School Students Write in a College Course? A Study of Dual Credit," students coming into college with an experience that pretends to substitute for the college experience are often not as prepared as they believe, and thus are not ready to "benefit in the college classroom" (Tinberg and Nadeau 2011, 704). As one student told us:

> It's funny how your high school advisors tell you the advantages of taking fourteen A.P. and I.B. courses, but they don't tell you how severely constricting coming into college with 39 credits is . . . I, the first year sophomore, was positive that I could walk into college and take easy courses because I was just so damn prepared.

The students profiled here had a bimodal reaction to the high school experiences constituting their point of departure. On the one hand, for some students the experience was positive and contributed to a strong writer identity, which in some cases—ironically—translated into an unwillingness to learn or explore. These students exhibited (as we saw in chapter 1) what Reiff and Bawarshi (2011) call boundary guarding and what Wardle (2012) conceptualizes as problem solving behavior. On the other hand, for some students the high school experience was a negative one, but it motivated students to try new approaches. These students exhibited a willingness—in Reiff and Bawarshi terminology—to boundary-cross, and in Wardle's—to problem-explore. Marta, one of the TFT students we met in chapter 3, exemplifies the first type. A successful writer in high school, Marta cited "what I learned in my AP Literature class in high school" as sufficient for *all* new writing situations. Marta's point of departure was thus constituted, at least in part, by her preparation for the AP exam and her successful performance on it. Additionally, her sense of herself as a writer-per-AP was complemented by her co-curricular work as a features writer and weekly columnist for her high school newspaper, both activities which also evoked praise. Together, these experiences suggested to Marta that she was already more than an experienced writer: she was an expert.

The point of departure can also motivate students to attempt a new approach. Andy, a first-year student majoring in political science, entered the TFT course believing he had been "brainwashed" with the five paragraph assignments teachers use to prepare students for the Florida standardized writing exam, the Florida Comprehensive Assessment Test, or FCAT. He felt "uneasy" about writing generally, and it's probably not surprising since he had no composing process to call on. Because the totality of Andy's writing instruction had been test-specific, he had developed no composing method other than an abbreviated process attuned to the test environment. Upon entering FYC, he attempted to use the single approach he had relied on in high school, writing up an assignment in an hour. This approach to writing, as Scherff and Piazza (2005) discovered, is common for 90% of high school students in Florida. Not surprisingly, as Andy entered college he felt unprepared and ill-equipped for the process approach that was expected and didn't understand what it was, but by the conclusion of the TFT course Andy observed that he had not experienced a "real" writing course until coming to Florida State. For Andy, the FCAT writing test was a point of departure: his "unease" combined with the instruction he received at FSU helped him understand and practice writing very differently than before.

Without their own standards for assessing their work, students participating in this study were also especially sensitive to grades. Grades, or the approval of the instructor, led the students to see writing dichotomously, as either good or bad, and to see themselves similarly, as writers whose identities as either "good writers" or "bad writers" were fixed and unchangeable. Darren and Emma, whom we met in chapter 3, believed they were involved in a kind of game of playing up to teachers, not only to meet teacher expectations, but also to project that they cared, that they were concerned about expectations. Both Darren and Emma follow what they perceive to be one of the rules of school: find out what the instructor wants and then write in a way that meets those expectations. For both students, this idea—discover expectations, deliver expectations—had emerged through the success of their method in each local writing context: delivering what they perceive as the marks of good writers, which is rewarded with good grades, and which then confirms their sense that, indeed, they are good writers across contexts. With such powerful experiences of successful writing, it's not surprising that a student wouldn't want to change. What this means, however, is that satisfying teacher expectations as the goal contributes to a fixed sense of writer identity: students see themselves dichotomously, as the good writers or bad writers they are now and will be forever. Moreover, the expectations themselves substitute for a more theoretical understanding of writing located in a concept like the rhetorical situation. In such cases, the concept of the rhetorical situation has been distilled into a student-teacher interaction dominated by Britton et al.'s (1979) teacher-as-examiner.

Although not always visible, the point of departure for students—created by test scores and grades—often influences the approach students will take as they experience college composition—and sometimes shapes it entirely.

ABSENT PRIOR KNOWLEDGE

As documented above, it's a truism that students draw on prior knowledge when facing new tasks, and when that acquired knowledge doesn't fit the new situation, successful transfer is less likely to occur. This is so in writing generally, but it's especially so as students enter first-year composition classrooms in college. Whether students are border "guarding" or "crossing," they draw on similar high school experiences (Applebee and Langer 2009, 2011). What this seems to mean for virtually all FYC students is that as students enter college writing classes, there's not only prior knowledge providing context, but also an *absence* of prior knowledge, and in two important areas: (1) key writing concepts and (2) nonfiction texts that serve as models.[3] In part, such a situation exists because the curricula at the two sites—high school and college—don't align well, a point underscored by proponents of the Common Core State Standards. In addition, as Applebee and Langer's (2011) continuing research on the high school English/language arts curriculum shows, the high school classroom is a literature classroom, whereas the first-year writing classroom, which—despite the diverse forms it takes, from first-year seminars to WAC-based approaches to cultural studies and critical pedagogy approaches (see Fulkerson 2005; Harris 2006)—is typically a writing classroom. The result for our students—and, we think, others like them—is that they enter college inexperienced in the kinds of writing and reading the first year of postsecondary education demands.[4]

In terms of how such an absence might occur, the Applebee and Langer (2011) research highlights two dimensions of writing in high school that are particularly relevant in terms of absent prior knowledge. First is the emphasis that writing receives, or doesn't receive, in high school classrooms. Their studies demonstrate an emphasis placed on literature with deleterious effects for writing instruction:

In the English classes observed, 6.3% of time was focused on the teaching of explicit writing strategies, 5.5% on the study of models, and 4.2% on evaluating writing, including discussion of rubrics or standards. (Since multiple things were often going on at once, summing these percentages would overestimate the time devoted to writing instruction.) To put the numbers in perspective, in a 50-minute period, students would have on average just over three minutes of instruction related to explicit writing strategies, or a total of 2 hours and 22 minutes in a nine-week grading period. (21)

Second is the way that writing is positioned in the high school classes Applebee and Langer (2011) studied: chiefly as preparation for test-taking, with the single purpose of passing a test, and the single audience of Britton et al.'s (1979) "teacher-as-examiner." Moreover, this conclusion echoes the results of the University of Washington Study of Undergraduate Learning (SOUL) on incoming college writers (Beyer, Fisher, and Gilmore 2007), which was designed to identify the gaps between high school and college that presented obstacles to students. Their findings suggest that the major gaps are in math and writing, and that writing tests themselves limit students' understanding of and practice in writing. As a result, writing's purposes are truncated and its potential to serve learning is undeveloped. As Applebee and Langer (2011) remark, "Given the constraints imposed by high-stakes tests, writing as a way to study, learn, and go beyond—as a way to construct knowledge or generate new networks of understandings . . . is rare" (26). The scholarship on the transition from high school to college thus focuses on a fundamental key concept: a definition and practice of writing for authentic purposes and genuine audiences.

Writers are readers as well, of course. In high school the reading is largely (if not exclusively) of imaginative literature, whereas in college composition it's largely (though not exclusively) non-fiction. For evidence of the impact of such a curriculum, and a second source of absent prior knowledge, we turn to students enrolled in a second section of the TFT course. We learned from this particular group of six students—through questionnaires and interviews—that their prior knowledge about texts, at least in terms of what they *chose* to read and how such texts represent good writing, is located in the context of imaginative literature, which makes sense given the school curriculum. When asked "What type of authors represent your definition of good writing?" these students replied with a list of imaginative writers. Some cited writers known for publishing popular page-turners—Michael Crichton, James Patterson, and Dan Brown, for instance; others pointed to writers of the moment—Jodi Picoult and Stephenie

Meyer; and still others called on books that are likely to be children's classics for some time to come, such as Harry Potter. Two other authors were mentioned: Frey, whose *Million Little Pieces*, famously, was either fiction or non-fiction given its claim to truth (or not); and textbook author Ann Raimes. In sum, we have a set of novels, one "memoir," and one writing textbook, none of which resemble the non-fiction reading characteristic of first-year composition and college more generally. Given the students' reading selections, what we seem to be mapping here, based on their interviews, is a second absence of prior knowledge.

However, the number of students is small and their selections are limited; these interviews don't prove that these students, much less others, have no prior knowledge about non-fiction. But the facts that (1) the curricula of high schools are focused on imaginative literature and (2) none of the students pointed to a non-fiction book—other than the single textbook, which identification may itself be part of the problem—suggest that these students may not have models of non-fiction they can draw upon when writing their own non-fiction. Put another way, when these students write the non-fiction texts characteristic of the FYC classroom, they have neither pre-college curricular experience with the reading of non-fiction texts nor mental models of non-fiction texts, which together constitute this second absence of prior knowledge. Given the consistent tendency of students—the students we saw in chapter 3 and the students in Doug Brent's (2012) study—to turn to models for assistance when taking up new tasks, this absence seems particularly important.

Perhaps not surprisingly, what some students do in the absence of prior knowledge is draw upon and generalize their experience with imaginative texts in ways that are at odds with what college composition instructors expect, particularly when it comes to concepts of writing. When we asked these students how they wrote and how they defined writing, we saw a set of contradictions. On the one hand, students reported writing in various genres, especially outside of school. Unlike the teenagers in the well-known Pew study (Lenhart et al. 2008) investigating teenagers' writing habits and understandings—for whom writing inside school is writing, and writing outside school is not writing but communication—the students we interviewed did understand writing both inside and outside school as *writing*. More specifically, all but one of the students identified writing outside school as a place where they "use writing most," citing three specific practices—taking notes, texting, and emailing—as frequent (i.e., daily) writing practices. In addition, two writers spoke of particularly robust writing lives: one of them noted, for instance, writing

> Inside school. Taking notes. Inside the classroom doing notes. If not its writing assignments. Had blog for a while; blog about everyday life [she and three friends]; high school sophomore through senior year; fizzled out b/c of life; emails; hand written letters to family members.

A second writer described a similar kind of writing life, his located particularly in the arts: "Probably [it would] be texting . . . the most that I write. I also write a little poetry; I'm in a band so I like to write it so that it fits to music; a pop alternative; I play the piano, synth and sing."

On the other hand, given that many of these genres—emails and texts, for example—are composed to specific audiences and in that sense seem to be highly rhetorical, it was likewise surprising that every one of the students, when asked to define writing, used a single word: *expression*. One student, for example, defined writing as a "way to express ideas and feelings and to organize my thoughts," while another summarized the common student response: "I believe writing is, um, a way of expressing your thoughts, uh, through, uh, text . . ." Thus, in spite of their own experience as writers *to others*, these students see writing principally as a vehicle for authorial expression, not as a vehicle for dialogue or an opportunity to make knowledge, both of which are common conceptions in college writing environments. We speculate that this way of seeing writing—universally as a means of authorial expression in different historical and intellectual contexts— may be influenced by the emphasis on imaginative authorship in the high school literature curriculum, in which students read the writing of poets, novelists, and dramatists as forms of (canonical) expression. Likewise, the emphasis on reading in high school, at the expense of writing, means that it's likely that reading exerts a disproportionate influence on how these students understand writing itself, especially since the writing tasks, often involving a form of literary analysis, are also oriented to literature and literary authorship. In additon, what we see here—through these students' high school curricula, their own reading practices, and their writing practices both in but mostly out of school—is reading culture as a prior experience, an experience located in pre-college reading and some writing practices, but one missing the conceptions, models, and practices of writing, as well as practices of non-fiction reading, which could be helpful in a new post-secondary environment emphasizing a rhetorical view of both reading and writing. Or: absent prior knowledge.

A TYPOLOGY OF PRIOR KNOWLEDGE

Type One: Assemblage

While we speculate that incoming college students, like our students, enter with an absence of prior knowledge relevant to the new situation, how students *respond to* and *use* the new knowledge relative to the old can vary. Here, based on interview data, writing assignments, and responses to the assignments, we describe three models of prior knowledge activity. Some students, like Eugene, use new knowledge in a way we call *assemblage*: by grafting isolated bits of new knowledge onto a continuing schema of prior knowledge. Some, like Alice, take up new knowledge in a way we call *remix*: by integrating the new knowledge into the schema of the old. And some, like Rick—whom we met in chapter 3—encounter what we call a *critical incident*—a failure to meet a new task successfully—and use that occasion as a prompt to rethink writing altogether.

Eugene was a nineteen-year-old middle-class Hispanic male majoring in business and international affairs, who, like so many of his colleagues, did not take the first writing course in the FYC sequence at FSU because he received AP credit for the literature and language exams. As important for our purposes, Eugene exemplified Reiff and Bawarshi's (2011) border guarders. Given a successful writing experience in high school, and with his AP scores as a positive point of departure, Eugene believed that what he was learning in FYC was very similar to what he learned in high school; he thus had no need to cross the high school-college border because he didn't really see one. In terms of his use of prior knowledge, he engages in what we call *assemblage*. Such students maintain the concept of writing they brought into college and use it as a foundation. Taking the new learning and breaking it into bits, they graft those isolated "bits" of learning onto the foundation without either recognition of differences between prior and current writing tasks and concepts, or synthesis of them.

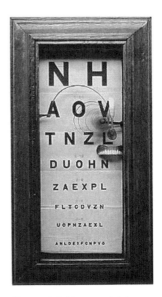

Figure 4.1. Vorwarts! Johann Dieter Wassman

Such bits may take one or both of two forms: key terms and strategies. Taken together, the conception of writing that students develop through assemblage is very like the assemblage "Vorwarts!" Here, we see an eye chart functioning as a foundation. Although new bits—a set of teeth and a spring—are added to it, they are not integrated, but instead are pasted on top. Consequently, the basic chart isn't significantly changed at all. The chart, much like Eugene's conception of writing, stands relatively unaltered by the additions.

When Eugene entered the TFT course, he articulated a dualistic view of writing oriented to a rhetorical conception of right or wrong. For writing to be successful, Eugene observed, "you have the right rhetoric and the right person in the right manner." Conceptualizing writing as transmission, Eugene noted that it enabled him "to get his message across." Interestingly, he also believed he was "really prepared for college": "[in high school] we were doing a lot of papers that talked about literary devices so I basically knew a lot of literacy devices so there wasn't a lot more to learn necessarily, I guess more fine-tuning of what I had already learned." (And in this observation, we see a confusion that plagued several students: between litera*ry* and litera*cy*, the former connected to devices, the latter not.) Furthermore, when he began to understand what learning opportunities were available in the TFT class, Eugene wasn't very interested, oddly, precisely because it fell outside what he *did* know: "I don't like research papers because I don't know how they work very well and collecting sources and analyzing." He noted that he was better at "evaluating an article and finding a deeper meaning," which is the purpose, of course, of the literary analysis texts he wrote in high school.

As he began his college writing career, Eugene exhibited a three-part pattern that he continued throughout the TFT course and into the next term: (1) he confused and conflated the literary terms of high school and the literacy and rhetorical terms and practices of college; (2) he continued to believe that "there wasn't a lot more to learn"; and (3) he relied on his prior knowledge of writing, one located chiefly in the role of the unconscious in writing process. In analyzing his progress in terms of writing, for example, he noted the central role of the unconscious:

> my main point is that writing is unconsciously understanding that certain genres that have certain formalities where I have progressed and so where I have progressed is I can put names and places to genres; writing is pretty much unconscious how you are adjusting the person you are talking to and how you are writing.

In this case, the unconscious element of writing provided the defining feature of Eugene's concept of writing—the eye chart of his writing theory—and as the TFT course continued and in the semester that followed, Eugene struggled to find terms he could comfortably graft onto that central understanding.

During his four interviews, when Eugene was asked to nominate key terms for composing, Eugene struggled to make his prior conception of writing align with the new conception of writing to which he was being introduced. In all, he nominated sixteen terms: audience and genre were both mentioned three times (once each in three of the four interviews), with the other terms each suggested once: reflection, tone, purpose, theme, exigence, diction, theory of writing, imagination, creativity, and rhetorical situation. Given this range of terms, there is no center to Eugene's conception of writing. Moreover, some of the terms—rhetorical situation and exigence, for instance—came from his first-year composition class, while others—diction and imagination—were terms located in his high school curriculum; that might be no surprise, but the sets of terms are neither semantically parallel or congruent. As he moved into the semester following the FYC class, Eugene continued to cite genre, saying in one interview immediately following the composition class that "I still have to go with genre [as] important and everything else is subcategories," and in the next interview he said genre was still important, but not something he needed to think about as he worked "unconsciously":

> A lot of my writing is like unconsciously done because it's been ingrained in me to how writing is done. Even though I probably think of genre I don't really think of it. Writing just kind of happens for me.

In the final interview, Eugene retrospectively observed that what he gained was a "greater appreciation" of genre, "for the role genre plays in writing. [I]t went from being another aspect of writing to the most important part of writing as a result of ENC1102." For Eugene, genre is mapped assemblage-like onto a fundamental and unchanging concept and practice of writing located in expression and the unconsciousness he calls *ingrained.*

In the midst of trying to respond to new tasks like the research project, but unable to frame them anew, Eugene defaulted to two strategies he found particularly helpful. One of these was multiple drafting, not to create a stronger draft, but to have the work scaffolded and organized according to goals: "Most useful was the multiple drafts, being able to have smaller goals to work up to the bigger goal made it easier to manage." The second strategy Eugene adopted for both the TFT class and for writing tasks the next semester was a practice students often mentioned: "reverse outlining," a strategy in which (as its name suggests) students outline a text once it's in draft form to see if and how the focus is carried through the text. Eugene found this particularly helpful:

"something new I hadn't experienced before was the reverse outline because it helped me to realize that my paragraphs do have main points and it helps me realize where I need main points." Interestingly, the parts-is-parts approach to writing Eugene values in the multiple drafting process—because of the smaller goals leading to larger ones—is echoed in his appreciation of reverse outlining, where he can track the intent of *each* paragraph rather than how the paragraphs relate to *each other*, a point he makes explicitly in his end-of-FYC interview:

> Um, my theory of writing when I first started the class was very immature. I remember describing it as just putting your emotions and thoughts on the paper I think was my first theory of writing and I think from the beginning of fall it's gotten to where I understand the little parts of writing make up the important part of writing, so I think in that way it's changed.

As the study concluded and Eugene was asked to comment retro-spectively on what he learned in the TFT class, he restated not what he learned, but rather the prior knowledge of writing he brought with him to college: "For me, there wasn't much of a difference between high school and college writing." And he explains that, given his point of departure, he was ready for college:

> Like I came from a really intensive writing program in high school, so coming into [FYC] class wasn't that different, so, um, I mean obviously any writing that I do will help me become better and hopefully I will progress and become better with each piece that I write, so in that regard I think it was helpful.

What seemed to help, according to Eugene, was simply the opportunity to write, which enables him to progress naturally through "any writing that I do." In describing his writing process, Eugene also repeats the definition he provided as the TFT class commenced:

> I mean writing is like when you break it down it's a lot more complex than what you describe it to me. I mean you can sit all day and talk about liter-ary devices but it comes down to writing. Writing is, um, its more complex so it like anything if you are going to break down its going to be more complex than it seems. Writing is emotionally based. Good writing is good and bad writing is bad.

Writing here is complex; it is something to be analyzed, much like literature "when you break it down." But it's also a practice: "you can sit all day and talk about literary devices but it comes down to writ-ing." Likewise, the strategies Eugene appreciated—revising toward larger goals and reverse outlining to verify the points of individual paragraphs—fit with the assemblage model. Rather than calling into question an "unconscious" approach, these strategies can be used to *support* this approach and *verify* that it allows him to produce texts whose component parts are satisfactory. Of course, this wasn't the intent of the teacher introducing the multiple drafting process or the reverse outlining strategy. But, as Eugene makes use of prior knowledge in an assemblage fashion, the conceptual model of unconscious writing he brought to college shapes new learning and his response to the curriculum more broadly, from key terms to process strategies.

Type Two: Remix

Students who believed that what they were learning differed from their prior knowledge in some substantive way(s), and who valued that difference, behaved differently: they began to create a revised model of writing we characterize as a *remix*, or prior knowledge revised synthetically to *incorporate* new concepts and practices into the prior model of writing. Remix, in this definition, isn't purely a characteristic of hip-hop or modernism more generally, but a feature of invention with a long history:

> Seen through a wider lens . . . remix—the combining of ideas, narratives, sources—is a *classical means of invention*, even (or perhaps especially) for canonical writers. For example, . . . as noted in *Wikipedia*, Shakespeare arguably "remixed" classical sources and Italian contemporary works to produce his plays, which were often modified for different audiences. Nineteenth century poets also utilized the technique. Examples include Samuel Taylor Coleridge's "Rime of the Ancient Mariner," which was produced in multiple, highly divergent versions, and John Keats's "La Belle Dame sans Merci," which underwent significant revision between its original composition in 1819 and its republication in 1820. ("Remix"). In sum, remixing, both a practice and a set of material practices, is connected to the creation of new texts. (Yancey 2009a, 6)

Here, we use remix with specific application to writing: a process that links past writing knowledge and practice to new writing knowledge and practice, as we see in the experience of Alice.

Alice, an eighteen-year-old, middle-class, white freshman majoring in music, entered the TFT class with a conception of writing influenced by three sets of experience: preparing for and taking the FCAT; completing her senior AP English class; and taking her English 1101 class (the first course of the two-course sequence), which she had completed at her local community college in the summer before attending Florida State. In Alice's formation, she had literally grown up as an "FCAT writer," but in her senior year of high school Alice enrolled in an AP English class where she learned a different model of text that both built on and contrasted with her experience as an FCAT writer: "[my senior English teacher] explained his concept as instead of writing an intro, listing your three points, then the conclusion, to write like layers of a cake. Instead of spreading out each separate point . . . layer them." The shift here, then, is one of remix: the arrangement of texts was to remain the same, while what happened *inside* the texts was to be changed, moving from a listing of points to an analysis of them. During the third experience, in the summer before her first year in college, Alice learned a new method of composing: she was introduced to "process writing," including drafts, workshops, and peer reviews.

When Alice entered the TFT class, she defined writing as a Murray-esque exercise: "Writing," Alice said, "is a form of expression that needs to have feeling and be articulate in order to get the writer's ideas across. The writing also needs to have the author's own unique voice," an idea that acted as a passport for her as she encountered new conceptions of writing located in key terms like rhetorical situation, context, and audience. In Alice's retrospective account of the TFT class, in fact, she focused particularly on the concept of rhetorical situation as one both new to her and difficult to understand, in part because it functioned as something of a meta-concept: "Rhetorical situation had a lot of things involved in that. It was a hard concept for me to get at first but it was good."[5] By the end of the course, however, Alice was working hard to create an integrated theory of writing that included three components: her own values, what she had learned during the summer prior to the TFT class, and what she had learned in the TFT class.

> I still find writing to be a form of expression, it should have the author's own voice and there should be multiple drafts and peer reviews in order to have the end result of a good and original paper. Along with that this year I learned about concepts such as rhetorical situation. . . . This opened me up to consider audience, purpose, and context for my writing. I need to know why I am writing and who I am writing to before I start. The context I am writing in also brings me to what genre I'm writing in.

Alice's conception of writing here seems to rely on the layering strategy recommended by her AP teacher: voice, mixed with process and framed rhetorically, defined here layer by layer.

As Alice continued into the post-composition term, two writing-related themes emerged for her. One: a key part of the process Alice began to embrace was reflecting on her writing, both *as* she drafted and *after* she completed a text. Two: she found that the study itself helped her develop as a writer, but Alice felt she needed more time and more writing activity to make sense of all she'd been offered in the TFT course.

As explained earlier, Alice was asked to reflect frequently in the TFT class: in the midst of drafting; at the end of assignments; and at the end of the course in a reflection-in-presentation. She found these reflective practices particularly helpful, and when she wrote for her humanities and meteorology classes in the next term, she continued to practice a self-sponsored reflection: it had become part of her composing process. As she explained, she felt that through reflection she was able to bring together the multiple factors that contribute to writing:

> I do know that I really liked reflection, like having that because I haven't done that before. And whatever term was writing with a purpose, and I like that, so I guess writing with some purpose. Like when you are done writing you do reflection, because before I would be done with a writing and go to the next one, and so then in between we go over each step or throughout.

As the study concluded, Alice pointed to reflection and rhetorical situation as the two most important concepts for writing she learned in the TFT class, but as she did earlier, she also included a value of her own—in this case "being direct"—in her remixed model of writing.[6]

> Two of the words I would use to describe my theory of writing would be the key terms, rhetorical situation, reflection, and the last that isn't would just be being direct. Rhetorical situation encompasses a lot about anybody's theory of writing. It deals with knowing the purpose of my writing, understanding the context of my writing, and thinking about my audience. I chose being direct for lack of a better term. I don't think my writing should beat around the bush. It should just say what needs to be said and have a purpose. As for reflection, that's something we do in life and not just writing. In the context of writing it really helps not just as a review of a grammar or spelling errors but as a thought back on what I was thinking about when I wrote what I wrote, and that could change as I look back on my writing.

Being direct, of course, was Alice's contribution to a curricular-based model of writing informed by reflective practice and rhetorical situation. She defined reflection as a "thought back," a variation of the "talk backs" (Yancey 1998) that students were assigned in the TFT class, here a generalized articulation of a metacognitive practice helping her "change as I look back on my writing." In addition, Alice worked toward making reflection her own as she theorized about it—"that's something we do in life and not just writing"—in the process seeing it as a life-practice as well as a writing practice, and even distinguishing between the two. More generally, we see that Alice is developing her own "remixed" model of composing, one that combines her values with new curricular concepts and practices. Thus, reflection was more than an after-the-fact activity for Alice; rather, it provided a mechanism for her to understand herself as a learner and prepare for the future, be it in writing or any other aspect of her life.

Alice was also aware of the impact of the study and of the need for more time to integrate her TFT education into her model and practice of writing. On the one hand, she seemed to appreciate the study since it functioned, in her view, as a follow-up activity extending the class itself, which was particularly valuable as she took up new writing tasks the next semester.

> I feel as though I forget a lot about a class after I take it. I definitely don't remember everything about my English class, but I feel I remember what will help me the most in my writing and I think that information will stay with me. This study has helped me get more from the class than just taking it and after not thinking about it anymore. The study helped me in a way to remind me to think about what we went over in English as I wrote for my other classes.

On the other hand, Alice admitted she had been unable to use all that was offered in this class:

> I feel like I haven't used everything; there were a lot of terms that [we] went over I don't use and there are some that I do and those are the ones that [the teacher] used the most anyways. I feel like this has helped me remember those that I will use and I feel like this has helped me retain a lot of information, and now I have had to write a lot more besides our class and the stuff I gave to you. I was still thinking about what we did in that comp class, so it has really helped me. But I still think I could use a lot more experiences with writing papers and getting more from a college class, I mean like getting away from the FCAT sound I wrote like that until 10th grade.

Alice hoped she had identified the best terms from the class, and she thought that she had, given that "those are the ones that the teacher used the most," a repetition that was, as she observed, one reason she remembered them. Because of the interviews, she "was still thinking about what we did in the comp class"; she was continuing to think about the terms more intentionally than she might have if no interviews had taken place. Additionally, Alice believed that she "could use a lot more experiences with writing papers and getting more from a college class," here pointing to the need to get "away from the FCAT." Given that Alice "wrote like that until 10th grade," "getting away from the FCAT sound" is more difficult than it might first appear.[7]

In sum, there is much to learn from Alice's experience. Through her integration of prior knowledge, her own values, and new knowledge and practice, we see how students remix prior and new knowledge, and how they create new understandings of composing that may change over time in a continuing process of remix. We also see how a composing practice like reflection can be generalized into a larger philosophy of reflection, one more characteristic of expertise. And not least, we see, through a student's observations, how a term viewed as a single concept functions more largely as a meta-concept and how hard it can be to remix prior knowledge, especially when that prior knowledge is nearly deterministic in its application and impact.

Critical Incidents: Motivating New Conceptions and Practices of Composing

In various writing situations, students often encounter a version of what's called a "critical incident," a phrase common in fields ranging from air traffic control to surgery to teaching. A critical incident is a situation where efforts either do not succeed at all or succeed only minimally. We have found that writing students who encounter critical incidents—like Clay and Rick in the TFT course—can become willing to let go of or relax prior knowledge as they rethink what they have learned, revise their model and/or conception of writing, and write anew. In other words, the setbacks motivated by critical incidents can provide the opportunity for conceptual breakthroughs, as we detail in the case of Rick.

The surgeon Atul Gawande (2002) describes critical incidents as they occur in surgery, and how they are later understood, in his account of medical practice titled *Complications*. Surgical practice, like air traffic control, routinely and intentionally engages practitioners in a collective reviewing of what goes wrong—in surgery, operations where the patient died or whose outcome was negative in other ways; in air traffic control, missteps large (e.g., a crash) and small (e.g., a near miss)—in the belief that such a review can reduce error and thus enhance practice. Accordingly, hospital-based surgeons meet weekly for a Morbidity and Mortality Conference, the M&M for short, its purpose both to reduce the incidence of mistakes and to make knowledge. As Gawande explains,

> There is one place, however, where doctors can talk candidly about their mistakes, if not with the patients, then at least with one another. It is called the Morbidity and Mortality Conference—or, more simply, M & M—and it takes place, usually once a week, at nearly every academic hospital in the country . . . Surgeons, in particular, take the M & M seriously. Here they can gather behind closed doors to review the mistakes, untoward events, and deaths that occurred on their watch, determine responsibility, and figure out what to do differently next time. (57–58)

The protocol for the M&M never varies. The physician in charge speaks for the entire team, even if she or he wasn't present at the event under inquiry. In other words, a resident might have handled the case, but the person responsible—called, often ironically, the attending physician—speaks. First, information is presented about the case: age of patient, reason for surgery, progress of surgery. Next, the surgeon outlines what happened, focusing on the error in question; that there was an error is not in question, so the point is to see if that error might have been discerned more readily and thus have produced a positive outcome. The surgeon provides an analysis and responds to questions, continuing to act as spokesperson for the entire medical team. The doctor members of the team, regardless of rank, are all included but do not speak; the other members of the medical team, including nurses and technicians, are excluded, as are patients. The presentation concludes with a directive about how such prototypic cases should be handled in the future, and it's worth noting that, collectively, the results of the M&Ms have reduced error.

Several assumptions undergird this community of practice, in particular assumptions which are at odds with those of compositionists. For example, we gave up a focus on error long ago in favor of the construction of a social text. Likewise, we might find it surprising that the M&M is so focused on what went wrong when just as much might be learned by what went right, especially in spite of the odds—for instance, the young child with a heart defect who surprises everyone by making it through surgery. Still, the practice of review in light of a critical incident suggests that even experts can revise their models when prompted to do so, a point also observed in *How People Learn* (Bransford, Pellegrino, and Donovan 2000). Moreover, these experts are not confined to the medical arena, although there is a good deal of interest in using critical incident theory as a centerpiece of medical

```
         CASE RECORD FORMAT

1. THE PROBLEM
   Who was involved?
   What was the pertinent background information?
   What was your role in the problem?

2. OUTCOME and/or OBJECTIVES DESIRED
   What did you hope to accomplish?

3. ALTERNATIVES CONSIDERED
   What alternatives did you consider to
   solve the problem?

4. STRATEGIES IMPLEMENTED
   What action did you take in an attempt to
   achieve your objectives?

5. RESULTS
   Were your objectives achieved?
   What happened as a result of your actions?

6. ASSESSMENT
   Did your plan work as intended?
   What critical events, decisions, situations
   influenced the outcome?
   What would you do differently, if anything?
```

Figure 4.2. From Reflective Practice for Educators, 2nd ed. (Osterman and Kottkamp 2004)

school education.[8] In *Becoming a Critically Reflective Teacher* (Brookfield 1995), for example, Stephen D. Brookfield identifies critical incidents—when classes don't go well; when students resist in an unusual way; when an assignment fails—as pedagogical occasions faculty might review in order, much as surgeons, to enhance practice. More generally, Karen F. Osterman and Robert B. Kottkamp outline the use of critical incidents in education in their *Reflective Practice for Educators*. In their review, Osterman and Kottkamp (2004) point to a six-part schema, what they call a case record format useful for analysis of critical incidents, including: problem, outcome desired, alternatives, strategies employed, results, and assessment of outcome. In sum, critical incident theory provides another lens through which we might view enhanced practice, and in our case, transfer of writing knowledge and practice.

Indeed, as we saw in chapter 3, a critical incident is certainly one way to describe what happened to Rick—a first-year student with an affection for all things scientific—as he experienced a misfit between his prior knowledge and new writing tasks. A physics and astrophysics major, Rick was working on a faculty research project in the physics laboratory, and was planning a research career in his major area. He professed:

> I am a physics major so I really like writing about things I think people should know about that is going on in the world of science. Sometimes it's a challenge to get my ideas across to somebody that is not a science or math type, but I enjoy teaching people about physics and the world around them.

Rick's combination of prior knowledge and motivation, however, didn't prove sufficient when he began the research project in the TFT class. He chose a topic with which he was not only familiar but also passionate, quantum mechanics, and his aim was to communicate the ways in which quantum mechanics benefits society. He therefore approached the research as an opportunity to share what he knew with others, rather than as an inquiry into a topic and a discovery of what might be significant. He also had difficulty making the information clear in his essay, which he understood as a rhetorical task: "The biggest challenge was making sure the language and content was easy enough for someone who is not a physics major to understand. It took a long time to explain it in simple terms, and I didn't want to talk down to the audience." In this context, Rick did understand the challenge of expressing the significance of his findings to his audience, which he determined as his fellow college students. But the draft he shared with his peers was confusing to them, not because of the language or information, as Rick had anticipated, but instead because of uncertainty about key points of the essay and what they as readers were being asked to do with this information.

As a self-identified novice, however, Rick reported that this experience taught him a valuable lesson about audience. "I tried to make it simple so . . . my classmates would understand it, but that just ended up messing up my paper, focusing more on the topic than on the research, which is what mattered. I explained too much instead of making it matter to them." Still, when the projects were returned, he admitted his surprise at the evaluation of the essay, but was not willing to entertain the idea that his bias or insider knowledge about quantum mechanics had prevented his inquiry-based research.

> After everyone got their papers back, I noticed that our grades were based more on following the traditional conventions of a research paper, and I didn't follow those as well as I could have. I don't really see the importance of following specific genre conventions perfectly.

In the next semester, however, these issues of genre and audience came together in a critical incident for Rick as he wrote his first lab report for chemistry. Ironically, Rick was particularly excited about this writing because, unlike the writing he had composed in the English class, this was writing in the desired context of science—in this case, the writing of a lab report. But, as it turned out, it was a lab report with a twist: the instructor specified that the report have a conclusion that would link it to "everyday life":

> We had to explain something interesting about the lab and how that relates to everyday life. I would say it is almost identical to the normal introduction one would write for a paper, trying to grab the reader's attention, while at the same time exploring what you will be talking about.

Aware of genre conventions and in spite of these directions for modification, Rick wrote a standard lab report. In fact, in his highlighting of the data, he made it *more* lab report-like rather than less: "I tried to have my lab report stick out from the others with better explanations of the data and the experiment." The chemistry instructor noticed, and not favorably: Rick's score was low, and he was more than disappointed. Eager to write science, he got a lower grade than he did on his work in the TFT class. It wasn't because he didn't know the content; rather it was because he hadn't followed the directions for writing that violated his own sense of what was important.

This episode constituted a critical incident for Rick. Dismayed, he went to talk to the teacher about the score. She explained that he indeed needed to write the lab report, not as the genre might strictly require, but as she had *adapted* it. Chastened, he did so in all the next assigned lab reports, and to good effect: "My lab reports were getting all the available points and they were solid too, very concise and factual, but the conclusions used a lot of good reflection in them to show that the experiments have implications on our lives." The ability to adapt to teacher directions in order to get a higher grade, as is common for savvy students, doesn't in and of itself constitute a critical incident: what makes it so here is Rick's response *and* the re-seeing Rick engages in afterwards. Put differently, he begins to see writing as synthetic and genres as flexible, and in the process he begins to develop a more capacious conception of writing, based in part on his expert-practice of tracing similarities and differences across his own past and present writing tasks.

This re-seeing operates at several units of analysis. On the first level, Rick articulates a new appreciation for the value of the assignment, especially the new conclusion, and the ways he is able to theorize it: "I did better on the conclusions when I started to think about the discourse community and what is expected in it. I remembered that from English 1102 [the TFT course], that discourse community dictates how you write, so I thought about it." On another level, while Rick understands that the genres in the lab courses were different from the TFT class, he is also able to map similarities across them:

> One similarity would be after reading an article in 1102 and writing a critique where we had to think about the article and what it meant. This is very similar to what we do in science: we read data and then try to explain what it means and how it came about. This seems to be fundamental to the understanding of anything really, and is done in almost every class.

This theorizing, of course, came after the fact of the critical incident, and one might argue that such theorizing is just a way of coming to terms with meeting the teacher's directions. But, as the term progressed Rick was able to use his new understanding of writing—located in the multiple concepts, borrowed from writing and science, of discourse communities *and* genres, and keyed to reading data and explaining them—remixed into a frame for one of his new assignments, a poster assignment. His analysis of how to approach it involved taking the terms from the TFT class and using them to frame the new task, as we saw in chapter 3:

> I have this poster I had to create for my chemistry class, which tells me what genre I have to use, and so I know how to write it, because a poster should be organized a certain way and look a certain way and it is written

to a specific audience in a scientific way. I wouldn't write it the same way I would write a research essay—I'm presenting the key points about this chemistry project, not writing a lot of paragraphs that include what other people say about it or whatever. The poster is just the highlights with illustrations, but it is right for its audience. It wasn't until I was making the poster that I realized I was thinking about the context I would present it in, which is like rhetorical situation, and that it was a genre. So I thought about those things and I think it helped. My poster was awesome.

Here we see Rick's thinking across tasks, genres, and discourse communities as he maps both similarities and differences across them. Moreover, as he creates the chemistry poster he draws on new prior knowledge, the prior knowledge he developed in his TFT class. This is a rhetorical knowledge keyed to three features of rhetorical situations generally: (1) an understanding of the genre in which he was composing and presenting, (2) the audience to whom he was presenting, and (3) the context in which they would receive his work. Despite the fact that this chemistry poster assignment was the first time he had composed in this genre, he was successful at creating it, at least in part because he drew on his prior knowledge in a way that allowed him to see where similarities provided a bridge and differences a point of articulation.[9] In sum, what we see here is Rick drawing on the prior knowledge he developed in the TFT class, as suggested in *HPL* (Bransford, Pellegrino, and Donovan 2000), and using it to theorize differences and similarities, in the process continuing to develop a theory of writing.

All this, of course, is not to say that Rick is an expert, but as many scholars in composition—Sommers and Saltz (2004) and Beaufort (2007), as well as psychologists like Marcia Baxter-Magolda (2001)—argue, students need the opportunity to be novices in order to develop toward expertise. This is exactly what works for Rick when college writing challenges, in both the TFT class and more particularly in chemistry, encourage him to think of himself as a novice and take up new concepts of writing and new practices. Moreover, the critical incident prompts Rick to develop a more capacious understanding of writing, one in which genre is flexible and the making of knowledge includes a dynamic application. Likewise, this new understanding of writing provides him with a framework he can use as he navigates new contexts and writing tasks, as he does with the chemistry poster.

If indeed some college students are, at least at the beginning of their postsecondary career, boundary guarders, and others boundary crossers, and if we want to continue using metaphors of travel to describe the experience of college writers, then we might say that Rick has moved beyond boundary crossing: as a college writer, he has taken up residence.

THE USES OF PRIOR KNOWLEDGE

Through the experiences of the students reported here, we are able to put a face on what transfer in composition as "an active, dynamic process" looks like: it shows students working with such prior knowledge in order to respond to new situations and to create their own new models of writing. As documented here, students are likely to begin college with attitudes about writing and about themselves as writers that shape their writing development, a point of departure, and they also begin in a context of absent prior knowledge, particularly in terms of conceptions of writing and models of non-fiction texts. Once in college, students tap their prior knowledge in one of two ways. In cases like Eugene's, students work within an assemblage model, grafting pieces of new information—often key terms or process strategies—onto prior understandings of writing that serve as a foundation to which they frequently return. Other students, like Alice, work within a remix model, blending elements of both prior knowledge and new knowledge with personal values into a revised model of writing. And still other students, like Rick, use a writing setback, what we call a critical incident, as a prompt to retheorize writing and to practice composing in new ways.

This line of research points in two promising directions: one pedagogical, one theoretical. This framework may be particularly useful in teaching situations; instructors may want, for example, to ask students about their absent prior knowledge and invite them to create a knowledge filling that absence. Put differently, if students understand there is an absence of knowledge that they will need—a perception that many of them don't seem to share—they may be more motivated to take up a challenge they have heretofore not understood. Likewise, defining remix as a way of integrating old and new, personal and academic knowledge and experience into a revised conception and practice of college composition may provide a mechanism to help students understand how writing development, from novice to expertise, works, and how they participate in their own development. Last, but not least, students might be alerted to writing situations that qualify as critical incidents; working with experiences like Rick's, they may begin to understand their own setbacks as opportunities. Indeed, we think that collecting experiences like Rick's (of course, with students' permission) to share and consider with students may be the most helpful exercise of all.

There is more research on student use of prior knowledge to conduct as well, as a quick review of Rick's experience suggests. The critical incident motivates Rick to rethink writing, as we saw, but as a science major, Rick understands, as he told us, that science not only thrives on error, but also progresses *on the basis of error*. For Rick, error was already an accepted part of the learning process. Rick was also well positioned to consider how to respond to the setback, given his work with and reception of the TFT theory. He could draw on both language and concepts—discourse community and genre, for example—to help him in three fundamental and related ways: (1) to make sense of the setback; (2) to learn from it; and (3) to articulate that learning so as to make it his own, using a remix combination of his language and the language of the TFT course.

Likewise, given his intellectual interests, Rick was particularly receptive to a setback, especially—and it's worth noting this—when it occurred in his preferred field, science. Rick identifies as a scientist, so he is motivated to do well. Additionally, failure in the context of science is critical to success. Without such a context, or even an understanding of the context as astute as Rick's, other students may look upon such a setback as a personal failure (and understandably so), which can prompt resistance instead of rethinking. Interestingly, failure was also a key to the success of Navarre Cleary's (2013) Doppel, who theorized his writing process as "crash and burn," as Cleary explains:

> In addition, Doppel's work as a researcher has taught him to embrace failure as part of the learning process, making it easier for him to be willing to freestyle without worrying about whether his writing is any good: "You try things. You go, 'Wow, that completely didn't work,' but then you have one level of experience. So you take the next step, and you go 'Okay, let's put some new parts together.' Then, after you've crashed and burned five times, you go, 'I think I have a handle on this now, and I know how to make it work.'"
>
> Applying this experimental process to his schoolwork allows Doppel to write a rough draft without expecting it to be perfect, "I will do very loose, almost bullet point drafts of the first time through, and then after that I'll start filling in the blanks, so I am doing more drafts. Whereas before when I would write a paper, the first draft really was the final draft. . . . Now, I'll . . . build it into the second one, and then into a third one." Borrowing from his experience as a researcher, he described this iterative revising as his "crash and burn" process. (677)

Doppel, of course, is a mature student, both chronologically and experientially: he understands failure as a part of the process and as an opportunity to "put some new parts together." In the case of Rick, a younger and yet more privileged student, failure was expected and welcomed as part of the culture of science where he felt at home. A general pattern, then, emerges: what we begin to see here is that we need to explore what difference a student's culture, major, and the intellectual tradition it represents makes in a student's use of prior knowledge. Likewise, we need to explore other instantiations of the assemblage use of prior knowledge, as well as differentiations in the remix model. And we need to explore the relationship between these differentiations and efficacy: surely some are more efficacious than others. And not least, we need to explore further what happens to students like Rick, who, through critical incidents or setbacks, begin to take up residence as college composers.

Notes

1   In this chapter, we draw upon two studies of transfer, the study reported in chapter 3, Liane Robertson's "The Significance of Course Content in the Transfer of Writing Knowledge from First-Year Composition to other Academic Writing Contexts" (Robertson 2011), as well as the parallel study focusing on reflection, conducted by Kara Taczak (2011): "Connecting the Dots: Does Reflection Foster Transfer?"

2   As noted in chapter 1, the travel metaphor in composition has been variously used and critiqued: for the former, see Gregory Clark (1998); for the latter, see Nedra Reynolds (2004).

3   According to *How People Learn* (Bransford, Pellegrino, and Donovan 2000), prior knowledge can function in three ways. But when the prior knowledge is a misfit, it may be because "correct" prior knowledge, or knowledge that is more related, isn't available, which leads us to conceptualize absent prior knowledge. Without naming it as such, Tinberg and Nadeau (2013) trace the same absence; for a similar argument in the context of materials science, see Krause et al. (2009).

4   For a discussion of the reading aspect in particular, see Jolliffe (2007). It's also fair to note that this situation—of a dearth of models of non-fiction texts in high school language arts classes—may change with the advent of the Common Core State Standards.

5   Rhetorical situation may be what Meyer and Land (2003, 2006) call a threshold concept: see chapter 5.

6   Alice's interest in "being direct" may be a more specific description of her voice, whose value she emphasized upon entering the TFT class.

7   Ironically, the function of such tests, according to testing advocates, is to help writers develop; here the FCAT seems to have hindered rather than helped, as Alice laments.

8   See, for example, Karen Simpson and Helen Cameron's "Sharing PDP Practice" (Simpson and Cameron 2012).

9   This ability to read across patterns—discerning similarities and differences—that we see Rick engaging in is a signature practice defining expertise, according to *How People Learn* (Bransford, Pellegrino, and Donovan 2000).

5

UPON REFLECTION

*What would students tell us after the fact—two months, two years,
twenty years—about their reflective habits? What proved to be most useful and why? How are we defining useful? Which habits of mind could
they transfer into the world?*

— Kathleen Blake Yancey

We opened this book, in part, by looking at McCarthy's (1987) Dave
and thinking about how we might help students like Dave make sense
of the multiple sites of writing in postsecondary education. Toward that
end, we began by reviewing and cross-referencing multiple definitions
of transfer, noting the different vocabularies employed in each, as well as
synthesizing empirical evidence demonstrating that students have transferred—that they have carried forward and used what they have learned
in FYC appropriately in new situations—what we have taught them. We
included in that review a consideration of writing process, of students'
need for a vocabulary, and of the utility of taking a novice stance. With
this as a context, we took up two fundamental questions related to first-
year composition. First, how do different forms of content influence
students' transfer of knowledge and practice? Second, how might reflection be used systematically to help students create a map of writing that
could function as a passport to various postsecondary sites of writing
and, more specifically, how might using course content and reflection
together help students develop a theory of writing facilitating transfer of
knowledge and practice?

Pursuing both questions in chapter 2, we defined expertise, calling
on the research reported in *How People Learn* (Bransford, Pellegrino,
and Donovan 2000), before looking at a continuum of curricular
approaches intending to support the transfer of writing knowledge and
practice. On one end is David Smit's (2004) position that transfer is difficult if not impossible; on the other end is Doug Brent's (2012) position
that students transfer tacitly, as a function of a generalized "rhetorical
situation." Between these poles, we defined and analyzed four models:

DOI: 10.7330/9780874219388.c005

the Downs and Wardle (2007) Writing about Writing model; the Dew (2003) variation of the WAW model; the Nowacek (2011) "agents of integration" model of concurrent transfer; and our own Teaching for Transfer (TFT) model.

With this as a background, chapter 3 reported on how three different FYC courses were helpful to students, or not, in completing their FYC course and continuing into a post-composition term. The first course we examined, the Expressivist course, linked well to values the students experienced in high school—expression and authorial voice, among them—but didn't provide a bridge to writing tasks in new contexts. The second course, the cultural studies and media writing course, presented material that was new and unfamiliar to students, but neither the material of the course nor the emphasis on writing process matched students' perceptions of the needs of their post-composition writing tasks. As a consequence, students did not use, adapt, or repurpose what they had learned in their FYC course, but rather defaulted—or, in our language, *leapfrogged* past FYC—to draw upon what they had learned in high school to complete the new post-composition writing tasks. The third course, Teaching for Transfer (TFT), used integration of key terms, writing-as-content, and systematic reflective practice—supporting students in creating a framework facilitating transfer—successfully for two of the three participating students we report on here.

And in chapter 4, we amplified and complicated our analysis by tracing what we call surprising findings: first, a *point of departure* that influences how students see themselves and writing more generally; second, the absent prior knowledge that can frustrate efforts to take up new tasks; third, two ways students' use prior knowledge, assemblage and remix; and fourth, critical incidents that have the potential to prompt a re-seeing of writing and revision and move to a conceptual model of writing. Throughout this process we emphasized the numerous situations where language plays a role in writing: as students move into college influenced by points of departure and absent prior knowledge; as they learn new writing knowledge and practice, especially in the TFT course; as they connect old and new writing knowledge and practice in an assemblage or remix model of adaptation; and as they encounter, make sense of, learn from, and articulate critical incidents.

Additionally, in this process we mapped a very different situation than the one Lucille McCarthy's (1987) Dave encountered, in part because of changes in the field, in part because of research on transfer, and in part because of the new curriculum we outline here. As documented by McCarthy, the model of composition Dave encountered was focused on a kind of generic discourse and, more particularly, on the structural elements of discourse:

> Learning the conventions of academic discourse was also the purpose of students' writing in Freshman Composition. Dr. Carter was less concerned with the content of the students' five essays than she was with their cohesiveness. She repeatedly stated that what would serve these students in their subsequent academic writing was the ability to write coherent prose with a thesis and subpoints, unified paragraphs, and explicitly connected sentences. In an interview she said, 'Ideas aren't going to do people much good if they can't find the means with which to communicate them . . . When these students are more advanced, and the ability to produce coherent prose is internalized, then they can concentrate on ideas. That's why I'm teaching the analytic paper with a certain way of developing the thesis that's generalizable to their future writing.' Dr. Carter's goal was, thus, to help students master conventions of prose which she believed were central to all academic discourse. (244)

In this class, then, students focus on the parts of writing in an effort to create coherent prose that is "generalizable to their future writing"; once they have mastered the parts-is-parts approach, they can "concentrate on ideas." In contrast—and not surprisingly, given the changes in how we understand composing now—all the courses we studied emphasized ideas; indeed, the popularity of themed courses across the country is based on the idea that themes, or ideas, are a centerpiece of a writing course. The TFT course shares this assumption, but with a twist: it too assumes that that *ideas matter*, but also that *specific ideas* in the form of key terms for composition are critical to students' writing development, and that weaving these terms throughout writing assignments *and* the accompanying (intentionally designed and integrated) reflection assignments begins to equip students to move appropriately into new writing contexts. Of course, by calling our curriculum a Teaching for Transfer (TFT) approach we signal our intention to make ways of transferring knowledge and practice in writing central to the course. At the same time, and given the complexity of transfer, we understand the ambition of this purpose.

We have several aims for this concluding chapter. First, we review some of what we think we have learned—what we're calling recurring themes—referencing both other transfer scholarship and our own study. Second, to help others interested in adopting and adapting our TFT curriculum, we briefly review the suggestions for teaching for transfer provided by *How People Learn* (Bransford, Pellegrino, and Donovan 2000) as a context for our suggestions for teaching the TFT course. In the process, we provide some of our own recommendations for teaching for transfer and address teaching issues specific to the TFT course. Third, we identify current research questions that we hope will advance the field.

RECURRING THEMES

One of the main themes that surfaced as a consequence of this study is what we have referred to as the *content of composition*. It might go by other names: Doug Brent (2012), for instance, refers to rhetorical education, which seems similar, but as we have noted, rhetorical education has deep historical roots, ancient via Aristotle, more recent in the education of women as documented by scholars like Suzanne Bordelon (2010). Likewise, a difference between Brent's understanding and ours is that what we are referring to when we say content of composition is the very specific knowledge *about* composing that the TFT course fosters, as anchored in key terms: for example, that writing occurs in a rhetorical situation, that writers compose in genres, and so forth. At the same time, we understand students can "invent" such content for themselves, as we noted in our discussion of Navarre Cleary's (2013) Doppel and in our discussion of Glen, who is particularly important here given our focus on the role that the FYC curriculum can play in facilitating transfer. Headed toward a career in media production, Glen learned—by reflecting on his failed meteorology assignment—that for writing in his major to be successful, he needed to consider the context in which the writing occurred. For Glen, who was not enrolled in the Teaching for Transfer course, the key term "context" is one he determined on his own; other students have done likewise. The hope of a TFT course, and others like it, is that we can create the course material, the assignments, and the structure that will help students transfer intentionally and thoughtfully. The evidence presented here suggests we can, and that when we do, students begin reading across rhetorical situations for similarities and differences and respond rhetorically to them.

A second theme speaks to the transition point between high school and college, and how FYC students make use of what they learned about writing in high school. Not all students move immediately from high school to college (although statistics from the US Labor Department indicate nearly two-thirds of high school graduates proceed directly into postsecondary education), and many of those who do go have already satisfied their FYC requirement. However, as we saw in the case of Navarre Cleary's (2013) Doppel, even those who don't go immediately to college draw on what they learned about writing in earlier educational contexts, in his case middle school. More specifically, however, what we also see is a beginning theory of students' use of prior knowledge. Drawing on Reiff and Bawarshi's (2011) research, Wardle's

Typology of Students Entering College Writing	
Type One	*Type Two*
Problem solving	Problem exploring
Boundary guarding	Boundary crossing
Assemblage conception	Remixed conception
of writing	of writing
	Openness to critical
	incidents?

(2012) notion of educational habitus, and our own empirical research, we see a contextually informed and procedurally detailed model of contrasting prototypical uses of prior knowledge. The first is exercised by a boundary guarding student, more interested in problem solution than problem exploration, and whose use of prior knowledge we characterize as assemblage, where new learning about writing is grafted into an unchanged basic structure already defining writing. The second is exercised by a boundary crossing student, interested in problem exploration, whose prior learning is integrated into new learning (remix) and whose conception of writing is often infused with individual values. It seems likely that there are gradients of this model—we might see the two versions as conceptual poles framing a continuum—but, in any event, the contours of it are intriguing for both research and teaching.

A third theme has to do with what we have referred to as concurrent transfer, a situation where students are writing in two contexts at the same time and borrow and/or share from one to the other or both. Again, we see several models of this, each with different virtues. The linked courses model, as outlined by Nowacek (2011)—and in its intention for students to share material across contexts—is one that is keyed in design to concurrent transfer. At the same time, most colleges don't offer such courses; even when they do, it's not clear that the writing curriculum, assuming there is one, is robust enough to support writers' development. A second model is what we might call the serendipity model, which is what most students experience: a situation where students are writing for different courses in the same term. Early in their careers, this set of courses would most likely include a writing course. A difficulty with trying to build on such a model, however, is its unpredictability— while serendipity can be fortuitous, it doesn't lend itself to a systematic approach—and yet some of the learning we reported here occurred precisely because of such an opportunity. How we might make better use of serendipity is a good question. A third model is likewise based on serendipity: one where students, like Carolina writing the fundraising letter, are writing for a purpose *outside* of school. Again, here it might be

Opportunities for Concurrent Transfer
/ to See Similarities and Difference

1. Linked classes
2. Serendipity across classes
3. Serendipity in/outside school
4. Structured co-curriculars
5. Composition in three genres

possible to build in a comparison—a reading across sites—that would prompt observations about similarities and differences. Baird and Dilger (2013) outline a fourth model: "double majors, internships, and apprenticeships, which are emerging as rich sites for transfer and/or the intellectual experimentation that supports it." In addition to these, there is a fifth model: the composition-in-three-genres assignment, which provides a good opportunity for concurrent transfer with the advantages of a systematic approach. Since students already have worked with the material, they can focus on how composing in different genres for various purposes and audiences means composing differentially, and how composing differentially is composing rhetorically. Accompanying this assignment, too, is a reflection that asks students to engage in precisely this kind of thinking about transfer, and to make what they have learned—their composing knowledge—explicit for themselves and thus available for future use.

A fourth theme has to do with vocabulary and concepts. Since the 1960s and 1970s, writing process and its related terms like drafting and revision have dominated the curriculum. However, other terms are now of considerable interest, among them rhetorical situation, context, and genre. Reiff and Bawarshi (2011) had hoped to discover that genre, which could provide a link between high school and college, was a salient term for first-year students, but found it had not taken hold in that way. Nowacek (2011) argues that genre provides a portal into transfer, and though it may be that genre contributes to such a portal, as Mary Soliday (2011) points out, genres in and of themselves aren't particularly helpful. What is helpful, as Soliday's study shows, is asking students to compose in real world genres—so-called "wild" genres—for real audiences. Genre, then, seems to offer promise as a key term, especially, or perhaps only, when it links to real world practice and purpose.

Our approach, of course, is founded on the idea that there are several key terms that facilitate transfer, and that's a fifth theme. We identified eleven such terms, integrated them into the course reiteratively, and asked students to work with them as they made them their own. Not surprisingly, some terms were more salient than others; rhetorical situation, audience, context, and genre seemed especially useful. Others were less so, but it's not clear why. One explanation suggests the less salient terms came closer to the end of the course, so students worked with them less often. Another proposes that they were terms that received less emphasis, as the TFT instructor's teaching journal indicated, just as the students most often used the terms that received the greatest emphasis.[1] What also impressed us, especially given our observations about students' assemblage and remix use of prior knowledge, is how important the *structure* connecting key terms is likely to be. Although we didn't explore that aspect of key terms, we think it is a useful area for exploration. We're interested, too, in current research on threshold concepts (e.g, Adler-Kassner, Majewski, and Koshnick 2012), which are based on a particular *kind* of key term. Overall, then, what we see are useful efforts to identify a set of key terms that build on and expand the process terms that have dominated the field, and that provide vocabulary for a framework students can use to facilitate transfer.

A sixth theme is the role that failure—which we call critical incidents or setbacks—plays in transfer. We didn't build failure into the course design, but we did build in challenge. The purpose of such challenge is to help students understand that challenges—or critical incidents, which seem to be part of the college writing trajectory for many students—prompt learning in ways that perhaps no other mechanism can. Interestingly, we found that students in the sciences seem particularly receptive to this approach to failure, and we speculate that it's because science itself (like some other fields, including computer science, engineering, and architecture) builds failure into the disciplinary model through an emphasis on experimentation, replication, and null hypotheses. Rick and Clay, both science majors, identify failure as a learning experience rather than a judgment, and they are able to make failure an opportunity for learning rather than defeat. Failure, in other words, is part of the learning model. Clay struggled in the research essay for his writing class, and Rick in his lab reports for a science class, but both students were interested in using these "negative" experiences to learn how to improve. In contrast, the non-science students didn't recognize failure as providing an opportunity to learn or improve. It may be that the more capacious understanding of failure comes from seeing oneself as part of a disciplinary community where failure is part of the tradition; perhaps in the humanities areas there is no sense of failure-as-opportunity, just failure as problem or meritless performance.

The seventh and final theme involves what we are learning from students about how transfer "works," especially for students who are successful. These students tend to theorize in ways that not only show us connections across writing sites, but also how the process functions for them. Thus, Clay employed disciplinary language to describe the role of context in writing—the new and unfamiliar—using the language of the familiar, actuarial science: "the context of a statistic is what matters, not the statistic itself." He also characterizes his emerging theory of writing as his "remodeled" theory. Rick provides another good example of this phenomenon. He deliberately uses a strategy from science in his writing, borrowing the RERUN heuristic to help him write conclusions:

> I tried to do the same thing in [ENC 1102] class, saying what we learned from the assignment, why we did the assignment, what the assignment meant. We didn't talk about the measurements of uncertainty but instead we talked about our problems in the assignment, and we talked about what we learned or are still wondering about after the assignment.

Likewise, Rick takes the practice of reflection from FYC and uses it in his science courses, a case of concurrent transfer that benefits both contexts, and what he theorizes as "360-degree transfer." In other words, the theorizing that students engage in provides us with new understandings of how transfer works for them, with new metaphors to describe it and new understandings for us to explore.

TEACHING FOR TRANSFER: SOME GENERAL MAXIMS

The researchers in *How People Learn* (*HPL*; Bransford, Pellegrino, and Donovan 2000) make four suggestions for teachers interested in helping students begin transferring knowledge and practice. They observe, first, that

> Students come to the classroom with preconceptions about how the world works. If their initial understanding is not engaged, they may fail to grasp the new concepts and information that are taught, or they may learn them for purposes of a test but revert to their preconceptions outside the classroom. (10)

In part, we saw this maxim in students' points of departure, but it's fair to note that we learned about these incrementally in the context of asking students about how they understood writing. A good question, then, is how to engage students more intentionally about their "preconceptions about how the world works" so as to help them "grasp new concepts and information," especially given that the TFT course includes several new fundamental concepts.

HPL also observes that

> To develop competence in an area of inquiry, students must: (a) have a deep foundation of factual knowledge, (b) understand facts and ideas in

the context of a conceptual framework, and (c) organize knowledge in ways that facilitate retrieval and application. (13)

As we've seen, the purpose of the TFT course is to help students develop their own "framework," one organizing what they have learned about writing through remixing prior knowledge, new theory, and new practice that will support their moving forward to new contexts, where through "retrieval and application" of prior knowledge they can write anew. Although we take the *HPL* point about frameworks—as well as Bartholomae's (1986) point about the need for students to "invent" the university—we see this task of creating frameworks somewhat differently, as students' actively *reinventing* their own university through the integration of their own writing practices, their new concepts, and their reflections.

A third observation pertains to metacognition:

> A "metacognitive" approach to instruction can help students learn to take control of their own learning by defining learning goals and monitoring their progress in achieving them. (Bransford, Pellegrino, and Donovan 2000, 13)

One of the distinctive features of the TFT course is its attention to metacognition. Reflection in the course is seen as a mechanism for review and planning, per Yancey (1998), as well as a twofold source of invention: for individual assignments *and* for students' development of a theory of writing.

And not least, the fourth observation in *HPL* speaks to the integration and content-specificity of metacognition:

> The teaching of metacognitive activities must be incorporated into the subject matter that students are learning (White and Frederickson 1998). These strategies are not generic across subjects, and attempts to teach them as generic can lead to failure to transfer. Teaching metacognitive strategies in context has been shown to improve understanding in physics (White and Frederickson 1998), written composition (Scardamalia et al. 1984), and heuristic methods for mathematical problem solving (Schoenfeld 1983, 1984, 1991). And metacognitive practices have been shown to increase the degree to which students transfer to new settings and events (Lin and Lehman, in press; Palincsar and Brown 1982; Scardamalia et al. 1984; Schoenfeld 1983, 1984, 1991). (Bransford, Pellegrino, and Donovan 2000, 15)

Interestingly, we see efficacy in this approach as well as need. On the one hand, the students whose accounts of writing in the Expressivist and media and culture classes were presented here echoed what we have seen in literature related to the efficacy of process pedagogy. In our language, these students understood the courses to focus on the *how* of writing, not the *what* of writing. In such courses, students identify process as the central goal of the course, and that is what they carry forward and use in new situations, much like the students in the Hilgers, Hussey, and Stitt-Bergh (1999) and the Jarratt et al. (2005) studies. Put simply: (1) we teach process; (2) students develop a process, one that is often elaborated in FYC and abbreviated in other settings; and (3) they transfer process.

On the other hand, and as we saw in our studies, the students in the TFT class have *much* more to draw on. When learning a content of composition and practicing it, they create a knowledge of composing practices, knowledge they then draw upon in the TFT course and in other courses. They learn; they practice; they theorize; they transfer. In some ways, our TFT approach provides one model for adapting Beaufort's (2007) advice to teach students through making the five domains explicit. In other ways, it's a revised model: we identify and provide the content for composition, and prompt students to use reflection to synthesize learning for the purpose of theorizing. The subject matter is thus composition itself, which, when combined with practice and reflection, facilitates transfer. In the language of *How People Learn*, "our teaching of metacognitive activities [is] incorporated into the subject matter that students are learning" (19).

TEACHING FOR TRANSFER: GENERAL
RECOMMENDATIONS, SPECIFIC OBSERVATIONS

Based on our TFT study, and the recommendations in *How People Learn* (Bransford, Pellegrino, and Donovan 2000), we can make six general suggestions for effective teaching for transfer.

1. Be explicit. Writing is a social practice; it's governed by conventions, so it changes over time. Writing requires both practice and knowledge, which is what a FYC course provides. These are very explicit lessons, and as the research on learning demonstrates, if we want students to learn them we do better to be straightforward in our teaching.

2. Build in expert practices. Describing practices is helpful; demonstrating them is better, in part because it shows what's expected, in part because it illustrates how what is expected can be accomplished.

3. Tap prior knowledge and concurrent knowledge. As explained in *HPL* and demonstrated by our students, prior knowledge is the base from which we all learn. Explaining what we think we know—moving from the tacit to the explicit—is a first step toward the remixing of prior

knowledge engaged in by successful students. In addition, since students' learning isn't static, it's important to include learning that is occurring at the same time a student is in a given class.

4. Include processes and link them to key terms and a framework. The composition field, we think, takes considerable pride in its success improving teaching process (although we share some of the reservations expressed by Matsuda (2003) and DeJoy (2004)), but processes, and they are plural, need to be connected to a framework located in key terms, in our case rhetorical situation, genre, discourse community, and so on.

5. Consistently ask students to create their own frameworks using prior knowledge. Learning doesn't occur in a linear way for most people; we tack, and reiterative assignments support such tacking by inviting students to revisit what they have learned in light of new information and experience. However, the learning also has to be mapped onto a larger framework lest it function as an intellectual GPS device.

6. Build in metacognition, verbal and visual, balancing big picture and small practices. The field has recognized the value of reflection for some time (Belanoff 2001; Yancey 1998, 2009b), though often it is focused exclusively on process. Given the success we see in supporting the transfer of process, there is every reason to expand our use of reflection, especially if it is integrated into conceptual center and assignment design, as we do in the TFT course.

Despite these general maxims and our research telling us that teaching for transfer can be successful, our teaching experience with the TFT course also tells us that success doesn't come easily. For one thing, this approach is very different when compared to more conventional approaches to composition; it is much more disciplinary in nature, a point we return to below. For another, as we saw in chapter 4, barriers to transfer like the point of departure and absent prior knowledge help us understand the ambition of what all of us who teach composition are trying to achieve. And for yet another, some of the historically successful students, like Marta, resist both learning theoretically and theorizing writing in any sophisticated or knowledgeable way. At the same time, transfer *can* be successfully achieved for students who are willing to learn, with instructors who are interested in guiding them through the foreign land that is writing theory.

SITUATING A TFT COURSE

Our goal for first-year composition, like the field's collective goal, is to help writers develop and prepare students for the writing they will do in other college courses. Our Teaching for Transfer course was thus designed to build on what we as a field know about the conditions in which transfer is more likely to occur, as well as tap the research on learning presented in volumes like *How People Learn* (Bransford, Pellegrino, and Donovan 2000). Likewise, it was designed with an eye on the outcomes established by the Council of Writing Program Administrators, which are the same outcomes contextualizing the Florida State University First-Year Composition Program, where the course was developed, piloted, and taught during the research and afterward. Given this context, the course is both familiar and unfamiliar: admittedly, somewhat of a departure from more conventional approaches, but also available for use within very familiar institutional settings.

One of the tenets of the FSU program that was important to maintain was the inclusion of a research essay assignment in the course, not only to provide the students in our course with this valuable experience, but also because the type of analytical research writing we encouraged in our course helped teach some of the key terms. The terms "critical analysis" and "knowledge" were discussed in the context of assessing common research sources, for example, and the terms "audience" and "genre" were reiterated in the research unit as students analyzed the genres represented by their sources and the audiences for which they were intended. "Discourse community" was discussed in the context of requiring academic journals as sources, and "reflection" begins to take shape as a tool for evaluating sources and their value in a written research assignment.

The research essay assignment was most successful because of the way it occurs in the sequence of the TFT course: it reiterates the source-based analysis included in the earlier assignment and supplies the foundation for the composition-in-three-genres assignment that follows. In addition, it provides a link between research students may have conducted in high school (which for our students was often writing to report more than analyze) and the analytical-style research writing they were experiencing in their college courses. The familiarity of this genre, or the expectation of this genre as part of a college writing class, helped students understand that there might be more to college writing than what they learned in high school, and it provided a connection to the writing they expected to do in other courses, if they weren't already so engaged. Writing about research analytically helped most of our students understand that college-level writing required more than good format and style, and it signaled to them that there might be much more to learn about writing. While we didn't study student response to this assignment, our anecdotal observation is that working on it helped students understand they were preparing to write in a new environment, college, and it gave them the confidence to do so.

Before students begin the research essay assignment in the TFT course, they write a source-based analysis, using evidence from sources provided (the course readings for this first unit) and engaging in analytical writing about those sources. In effect, students begin creating the prior knowledge they can draw upon when they are asked, in the next unit, to conduct research targeted to their finding sources they will write with. It also teaches them that the literary analysis they learned to do in high school is not necessarily the only type, or always the appropriate type, of analysis. They learn that what's important is not the deeper meaning of what a writer says in a piece of literature, but the way the writer reaches an audience or what the rhetorical situation was for that writer. The first assignment thus acts as a familiar experience for the writing, just as research experience in high school might be familiar in students' search for sources. Students feel at ease, in fact, when this is pointed out to them during the research essay assignment; they realize they already know how to write analytically so they only need to find good sources, and that the instructor and the experts at the school's library will assist them in their success.

The analytical writing students complete in the first assignment is also challenging in two ways: (1) students are just beginning to grasp the concepts, especially rhetorical situation, when they are expected to write about them, and (2) the assignment requires students to think theoretically about writing, typically for the first time. We speak to the first challenge by informing students of the assignment goals and the larger picture: they are advised to grapple with the concepts of genre, audience, and rhetorical situation using evidence and analysis from the course readings. We assure students that at this point in the course *engaging* with the concepts is more important than *fully understanding* them, that engaging is one means of developing understanding, and that concepts are often learned by writing about them. Even students who don't quite grasp rhetorical situation—and there are many of them at the beginning—can offer insights about the sources that work toward their understanding of it. When we assure students that an incomplete understanding of concepts is acceptable, they are more willing to engage with the material and less concerned about creating a correct definition.

The second challenge is addressed in the same way: we ask students to identify the concepts, look for examples within the sources, and then write about how they think the author uses those concepts in each source. When the assignment is turned in, we see that students show various levels of understanding of the key terms, but the goal of the assignment is to incorporate evidence from sources and analyze those sources in their article. They are able to do this without as firm a grasp on the concepts as they will have later in the semester, and they feel more confident about completing the assignment if that is made clear to them.

These key terms become clearer to students in the third unit of the course, when they are asked to create genres based on various audiences and information they determine from their research essay topic. The concepts from the first unit are linked to the third unit through the reflection activities in the research essay unit. While students are focused on researching and analyzing sources, the reflection exercises throughout this unit require their consideration of (1) genre, in the types of sources they found; (2) audience, for each source and for their own research essay; and (3) rhetorical situation, in considering the exigence for the research and making their own knowledge, both through their own research and through reflection and writing. By the time they reach the third unit, the composition-in-three-genres, students have worked with several key terms—those from unit one are mentioned above, and, from unit two, "discourse community," "critical analysis," and "knowledge"—while they have continued to explore "reflection" as a key term in both theory and practice.

The composition-in-three-genres project is a turning point for many students in understanding the key terms for the course and beginning to appreciate the ways their knowledge about writing is situated in context. For this composition-in-three-genres assignment, students draw on the second assignment, focused on their topics of individual interest, which is then repurposed for the new genres. Put simply, they work with this material in a new way. Students appreciate that they can use the information they've just researched; they won't be distracted by searching for new material while designing a strategy for presenting this researched information to a real-world audience in a coherent composition.

The purpose of the third assignment is also to help students *enact* key terms, and the rhetorical choices—which genres will work for which audience, for example, and what the purpose of the writing might be— help solidify the key terms and the ways they can be used to help conceptualize a writing task. The keys to students' understanding of this aspect of the assignment are the smaller tasks—proposal, rationale, and reflection—since here the choices made about genre, audience, and rhetorical situation provide a better index to students' understanding of the writing concepts than the degree of production of each finished genre. And in this process, the project serves to illustrate "exigence" and "discourse community" in a real-world scenario where students see their work in the first two units as leading to a potential real-world purpose. The project also introduces the terms "context" and "circulation," and it reiterates "composing" in a new way. Not least, we emphasize the importance of coherence in composition: all three genres should link toward the identified outcome in the proposal and in the rhetorical strategy employed. This should be fully explained in the rationale and reflection, although some students sometimes shift strategy as they work and gain a better understanding of the key terms in action, an outcome we welcome.

The reiteration and sequencing we've mentioned is critical to the success of the course. We believe that through this sequence we gain students' trust, and they gain confidence, which together ensure that they'll follow our design of the course. We find it helpful to be clear and deliberate with students in explaining the course goals, and we ask for their trust throughout the course, especially since what is being asked of students is so different from what has been asked of them previously. When students understand the goal of the course and the role of the assignments in reaching that larger goal, they are more likely to trust the process of instruction. Moreover, by the time students reach the third unit of the course and begin the composition-in-three-genres project, they are able to understand the purpose of the sequenced iteration and where each unit or key term fits within the course. Enacting the concepts they've been learning often prompts a "lightbulb" or "aha" moment for students as they realize they know how to approach writing for a situation they constructed and that has meaning or purpose for them and for others beyond—and in addition to—academic meaning and purpose.

At this point in the course, as we saw with Clay, students appreciate the value of the course content to their writing, so they are open to returning to the mostly theoretical material of the fourth and final unit. In fact, they are often eager to take advantage of the opportunity to make sense of what they've learned by reflecting further. Students have been developing a theory of writing all semester, through regular prompted writing and reflection assignments, but this last assignment asks them to flex the reflection muscles they've developed as they work toward a cumulative theory of writing. While the assignment calls for students to look back at their writing from the semester and engage in reflective theory, students are also asked to consider writing they will do in the future, in their majors, for example. In this way, students are encouraged to continue thinking in terms of transfer as they complete the course.

THE IMPORTANCE OF RELEVANCE

Tying in student interests or writing genres from students' majors is helpful in the final unit because it helps forecast the future writing students will do as they leave the composition course and helps them think of what they have learned in the context of future use. But as important to students is relevance to their lives, and course material related to students' interests can be included from the start of the course. The course readings, while designed to illustrate how writers work with the key terms we study and represent in different genres of writing, can also be chosen for their relevance to students. For example, "Letter from Birmingham Jail" by Martin Luther King, Jr., which is chosen for its consideration of audience and use of rhetorical situation, may not seem relevant to the lives of students today; it may feel too much like a part of someone else's history. The themes of social injustice about which Dr. King writes, however, resonate with students who connect these issues of the Civil Rights Era to the injustices they see today. While the focus of the course work is on key terms and their role in composition, the reading material resonates as students explore the author's use of the concepts to achieve a goal in a written piece. In other words, the combination of the concepts of composition, as well as the concepts of the article itself, make texts like King's a good choice for a TFT course.

Another observation that has resonated with us over the years is a difference among types of students—those who self-identify as writers and those who don't—in their willingness to embrace writing theory and study key terms about writing. Put as a proposition: theory is what science majors expect in a college course generally, as Rick and Clay demonstrated; it is not what self-identified writers expect in first-year composition. The disciplinary influence that the developing scientists in our research exhibited—the willingness or preference for theory—made it easier for them to experience the course as a learning opportunity. Many other students who were not science majors, but who were also not confident in their writing ability, were also willing to embrace the theory in the writing class, mostly because they wanted to improve or saw a need for improvement in their writing. The few who remained closed to the idea of theory, like Marta, were writers who were good enough to excel in FYC without changing their methods or mindset. These students "invented the university," as Bartholomae (1986) suggests, but in reverse. Perceiving that they are competent writers—a perception authorized by their successful performance in writing—such students saw college writing as an exercise in what they had *already* learned. Consequently, they were able to shape new university writing tasks to fit with what they were already doing and knew how to do—often successfully, especially when the assignments were very similar one to the next.

WHAT WE NEED TO KNOW

It is probably no surprise that our study of the TFT course and its effects has raised a number of issues that we believe merit additional exploration. Here we highlight six of those issues.

How can challenge and failure facilitate transfer? How does self-identifying as a writer complicate our approach? Although students like Emma and Marta do not encounter sufficient challenge, or failure, to motivate change during the time of the study, we are interested in how challenge and failure can provide this motivation. One question here, then, relates to how much challenge should be designed into a curriculum; alternatively, how much challenge a student might take on when deciding how to respond to assigned writing tasks. Were we to build into the course a consideration of concurrent writing activity—i.e., writing tasks that students are working on *as* they take FYC—what might those comparisons help students see in terms of patterns of similarity and difference, especially where they faced challenges?

We think the situation is a bit more complicated than this. We were impressed by the science students' willingness to engage with failure. Is there a way to engage all students in seeing failure so capaciously, not as a mark of incompetence, but rather as a site of invention? And we think there's yet another wrinkle. As indicated above, we think a student's self-identification as a writer may also play into the reaction to failure/ challenge and the ability to use such a situation for learning. Put as questions: How does the perception of self-as-writer influence the ability to transfer? How does the perception of failure as opportunity influence transfer? How might these factors work together? Might it be the case that writers who make use of failure, for example, are then more inclined to self-identify as writers?

How might the model of assemblage and remix, when shared with students, help them understand how they can take control of their development as writers? As we indicated in chapter 4, we hadn't designed a focus on prior knowledge into the study reported here, but in the course of the study we found that prior knowledge was not only a foundation for learning, but also a *continuing* context for learning. And students, we found, were either trying to graft enough new "bits" of knowledge and practice onto a persistent structure of prior key terms to meet teacher expectations—which substituted for a conceptual framework like rhetorical situation—or engaged in a kind of remix that supported writer development. We are continuing our research with students to see how useful, and in what ways, sharing these metaphors with students might be. We wonder if all students might benefit, and if so, how.

How might the TFT course be adapted to support differing populations of students? For many college students, getting by as Marta and Emma did is not possible. Marta and Emma were each well prepared for college and had worked on their writing in both academic and extracurricular settings; they did not struggle with writing, nor did they seem to struggle with the transition to college from high school, at least during the year of our study. But other students are not so fortunate, and populations different from those typical at an institution like FSU might not respond as well to our course design.[2] Since the conclusion of the study we have offered the TFT course on two other campuses, each quite different and each with different populations. Perhaps not surprisingly, it has not engaged students in precisely the same way it did at FSU, though the fundamental aspects of it seem very similar. Further research among these populations is underway, but initial indications are that the course can be adapted to new contexts and student populations. To ensure such adaptation, though, some shifts might be suggested, principally to increase relevance to students and to ensure maximum engagement with the material. For example, one population of students we worked with in 2012 did not necessarily expect to finish college, although they were currently enrolled in school at the time of this writing. They have jobs, families, and other obligations they know might conflict with learning, and indeed those obligations do so constantly. A combination of factors—absenteeism, failure to submit assignments or complete readings, and willingness to earn passing grades rather than excellent grades—prevents these students from engaging fully, but they are reacting to life realities. Because the nature of the TFT course is reiterative and sequenced, missing classes and assignments poses a challenge to its structure that might result in different findings. Accordingly, adjustments to course material in the interest of relevance, and to reading and writing assignments in relation to the time students have available to devote to them, have helped tailor the course to this population, but ongoing research will tell us more about how well it transfers between institutional contexts.

How might concurrent writing activity be tapped to help students develop expertise? Impressed by students' accounts of differences among writing tasks, such as Rick's account of the differences between the research project and a poster assignment in chemistry, we wonder what might be gained by linking a TFT course to one course in another discipline or by including it in a multidisciplinary cohort. Would adaptation to such a cohort compromise writing content? Would the explicit comparison among writing tasks that such linkage would make available foster students' ability to see, like experts, patterns of similarity and difference across tasks and thus enhance their theories of writing? Which leads to a larger question: how do we best research the idea of content and transfer, or reflection in transfer, in a study of longer duration, with more participants, and over a wider range of academic courses? What would it take for all students to be able to transfer like Rick, who observed that the conclusion in his lab report was like the reflection in his writing class? And would that ability to transfer stick with students who were successful in an immediate context, or does that knowledge decline without regular use, like knowledge of a foreign language that isn't regularly practiced?

How do we engage instructors in teaching this more explicit and content-driven TFT course? While we know the Teaching for Transfer course is successful in fostering transfer, and we are currently exploring how it can be successfully adapted to different contexts of teaching and learning, we also know its "delivery" might pose a challenge. A large percentage of those teaching FYC in this country are contingent faculty or teaching assistants without the training in rhetoric and composition that was advantageous for us in teaching the course successfully. How to provide sufficient information to enable these instructors to feel confident in teaching a TFT course is thus a key factor in helping students transfer knowledge and practice. We might begin with questions like the ones we share here, since we would then engage as teacher-researchers together. Likewise, just as prior knowledge created a barrier for some of the students in our studies, long-held beliefs and attitudes about writing courses might also prove a barrier to improving the way college writing is taught. A myriad of factors—among them, the minimal academic value associated with first-year writing for full-time faculty; its perception as a course from which a test score can exempt a "good" student writer, held by students, parents, and high school principals and perpetuated by college administrators and testing services; and the growing trend of taking composition courses while still enrolled in high school—all contribute to the diminished respect for the first-year writing classroom as a place where innovation is needed and should be sought. Although, as we make plain here, more exploration is needed to support the claim that students would fare better in college if they engaged in a writing course that teaches for transfer, we have enough research in the field, as we saw in chapters 1 and 2, to know that such transfer isn't just possible; it exists. Our hope is that the research reported here will contribute to that effort.

How do we engage members of the field in taking up teaching for transfer? Interestingly, we believe another source of resistance to a TFT approach is located in the field itself, as suggested in Geoff Sirc's (2012) comment on the idea of including composition scholarship in a composition course: "Let me add, in sad disbelief, that some [in the field] actually have their undergraduate students read composition scholarship. Oh, my people, my people!" (516). Given our field's history, Sirc is, no doubt, not alone in his dismay. Over the recent life of the field, regardless of the date (1949 and 1963 both compete for the honor), we have been, as Fulkerson (2005) notes, able to agree on process only; agreement on approach and content continues to elude us. Instead of being content-informed, our courses, in Joe Harris's (1996) well-known formation, are a teaching subject. Even Anne Beaufort (2007), who identifies subject matter knowledge as one of five necessary domains, doesn't identify what the content for FYC might be. What we in the field do instead in FYC is identify content relevant to the interest of the instructor, in the belief that the teacher's interest and knowledge base will motivate students. As Harris explains regarding the theme-based writing program at Duke University:

> But in fact our versions of Writing 20 are far from the same. On the contrary, the success of our approach rests in large part, I think, on the sense of our faculty that they and not the program own their courses. Why should one expect a writing course taught by an epidemiologist or an architect to follow the same template as one designed by a historian or a political scientist? And so students in the various sections of Writing 20 often end up reading and writing very different sorts of texts, considering very different kinds of problems, and talking about their work in very different ways. (Harris 2006, 160–61)

As we saw in the Expressivist and media and culture themed classes, however, such an instructor-centered approach can disappoint. If we are correct in this claim, and if faculty members want to adopt a TFT approach, it might be important to find a way to make the interest of a faculty member (of whatever rank) and the content of TFT work together.

IN SUM: REDUX

Research on transfer continues to expand, as we saw in chapters 1 and 2. Likewise, we see efforts focused on transfer across the country. The 2012 Conference on College Composition and Communication's gateway theme, for example, included transfer. The Elon University research seminar on "Critical Transitions: Writing and the Question of Transfer," which has invited approximately forty scholars researching transfer to meet for one week each year and collaborate on research projects about writing and transfer, also reflects the growing interest in transfer (Critical Transitions: Writing and the Question of Transfer 2011). And in the fall of 2012, a special issue of *Composition Forum* on transfer was published. What has not been determined yet, despite this activity, is the role transfer will play in future FYC curricula, or in a revision of our curricular design for the teaching of college writing. What can be asked now, however, is whether we *should* be teaching for transfer in the writing classroom—in spite of the elements that conspire to make it more difficult—and whether we have any research showing us *how to go about it.*

The answer to both questions, we believe, is yes.

Notes

1   The key term *context* provides a contradiction to this generalization, and it's useful to think about why that might be. As indicated in chapter 2, "context" is not introduced early in the course: students work with it later in the semester, but they remember and use it to frame new writing situations, as we saw with Clay. We're not entirely sure as to why this is. It's possibly because, as a term that students have heard before, context is available for use (and indeed, transfer) in a way expressions like rhetorical situation are not. Consequently, while it may not be repeated in class as often as other terms like genre or audience that are used every week, context resonates because it's heard elsewhere (e.g., popular culture). In addition, and perhaps more important, context receives intense attention later on in the semester in the composition-in-three-genres assignment. In this situation, students gravitate toward it because it's familiar and because it solidifies in one term what they're learning to think about for that project. Put another way, it seems to be a term with lightbulb-moment potential.

2   As a research institution, Florida State University enrolls students that are often very well prepared; it has a retention rate of over 90% and a graduation rate of 76%. At the same time, many students are underprepared, working class or poor, and/or first-generation college students, as indicated by a Pell Grant (which is a measure of poverty) recipient rate of 23%. About 23% of students are students of color (according to the records; not all students so self-identify); FSU graduates more African Americans than any other research institution in the country.

APPENDIX A

TEACHING FOR TRANSFER: COURSE POLICIES AND SYLLABUS
ENC 1102: Writing in Context

First-Year Composition Mission Statement

First-year composition courses at FSU teach writing as a recursive and frequently collaborative process of invention, drafting, and revising. Writing is both personal and social, and students should learn how to write for a variety of purposes and audiences. Since writing is a process of making meaning and communicating, FYC teachers respond to the content of students' writing as well as to surface errors. Students should expect frequent written and oral response on the content of their writing from their teacher and peers. Classes rely heavily on a workshop format. Instruction emphasizes the connection between writing, reading, and critical thinking; students should give thoughtful, reasoned responses to the readings. Both reading and writing are the subjects of class discussions and workshops, and students are expected to be active participants of the classroom community. Learning from each other will be a large part of the classroom experience.

Course Outcomes

You will engage in daily writing activities, discussions, reflection, and collaboration designed to realize the following outcomes:

- Read and write in multiple genres and across several media
- Explore and analyze, in writing and reading, a variety of genres and rhetorical situations
- Understand that composing is a process that uses different genres, communicating through different media to various audiences
- Recognize and practice key terms when engaged in writing situations in and beyond this course
- Demonstrate ability to define key terms discussed in the course
- Develop a theory of writing

DOI: 10.7330/9780874219388.c006

Required Texts

1. PDFs you will need to print from our Blackboard site, found under "Course Library"

2. *The McGraw-Hill Handbook*, 3rd Edition, by Maimon, Peritz, and Yancey

Writing Requirements

All of the formal written assignments below, including all drafts for each, must be turned in to pass the course.

- Four Major Assignments: three major essays and one multi-genre project and reflection assignment, including multiple drafts and revisions for each assignment
- 8–10 exploratory writing journals
- Two individual writing conferences with instructor (to be scheduled)
- Thoughtful, active, and responsible engagement in class discussion, preparation for class, and in-class informal writing

In-class Writing

Regular, in-class work will focus on writing as a way of making meaning of text, as a means of understanding our thought process, and a way to expand and organize ideas. In-class writing will also be used as a planning tool for research, incorporating an inquiry-based approach into research topic development. Reflections, collaborative writing, and other in-class work will help students think through their research process and the rhetorical issues that bear consideration in the development of a research essay. Students will also write responses to selected readings as a way of reflecting on the various community contexts we will explore.

Conferences and Workshops

Student conferences will be used to help develop research topics and methodology and to organize research and determine writing strategies. Students will collaborate in the form of brainstorming topics, addressing issues in research, obtaining feedback to develop rhetorically sound strategies, and working on the writing process. Throughout the semester, students will become familiar with collaborating as a rhetorical tool, much as they might experience in different academic disciplines or workplace situations. By the time they engage in the collaborative segment of the third essay, students will be comfortable working in teams.

Journals

Exploratory journals written in class or as homework assignments will relate to a reading assignment or class discussion topic. All journals must be posted on the class Blackboard site by their deadline (schedule to follow). Journals should demonstrate the depth of students' critical thinking process; they might tell stories to illustrate ideas, raise contradictory positions, or explore ideas that are not easily resolved. Journals will be shared in class regularly; in fact, all class writing is considered public writing, so students should be sure to consider topics and content they are comfortable sharing with others.

Drafts, Revisions, and Final Papers

Students are responsible for bringing multiple copies of drafts to class on days a workshop is scheduled. This aspect of class preparedness is part of overall class participation. All drafts and revisions must be typed (MLA format, one-inch margins). Since students have access to a number of computer labs around campus, or own computers, technological setbacks/difficulties will not be accepted as an excuse for missed deadlines. All written work must include students' name, course and instructor details, and the date at the top of the first page.

Course Grading

Evaluation of work in this course is based on not only the writing students produce, but also the process in which they engage. Student work will receive detailed evaluation in the form of comments and suggestions on drafts, feedback to guide revision work, instructor conferences designed to address specific areas of writing, opportunities to generate ideas and feedback in class, and extensive written responses on final submissions.

Active participation in class discussion, journals, conferences, workshops, and preparedness for class all factor into the final course grade and will be an integral part of the work for each of the four papers. Drafts of papers will be graded on completeness and submission by deadline, the development of ideas, coherence and organization, and appropriateness to the assignment.

Specific grade allocation is as follows:

Journals/in-class writing/preparation for class: 15%

Source-based article on genre and audience: 20%

Inquiry-based essay: 25%

Composition in three genres assignment: 25%

Reflection-in-presentation: 15%

Specific Policies:

Attendance

This course adheres to the first-year composition policy, which states that an excess of four absences is grounds for failure. Students should always indicate, ahead of time when possible, if a missed class is anticipated so they can stay abreast of class work and assignments. Save the four allowable absences for illness or emergencies that will happen unexpectedly. Students who are late to class/leave class early more than three times will be charged an absence. Not showing up for a scheduled conference, which takes the place of a class meeting, counts as an absence as well. Part of the overall course grade is based on contribution to class discussions and in-class writing, which requires participation and therefore attendance in all classes.

First-Year Composition Course Drop Policy

This course is NOT eligible to be dropped in accordance with the "Drop Policy" adopted by the Faculty Senate in Spring 2004. The Undergraduate Studies Dean will not consider drop requests for a first-year composition course unless there are extraordinary and extenuating circumstances utterly beyond the student's control (e.g., death of a parent or sibling, illness requiring hospitalization, etc.). The Faculty Senate specifically eliminated first-year composition courses from the University Drop Policy because of the overriding requirement that first-year composition be completed during students' initial enrollment at FSU.

Civility

Neither disruptive language nor inappropriate behavior will be tolerated in this class. Disruptive language includes, but is not limited to, violent and/or belligerent and/or insulting remarks, including sexist, racist, homophobic or anti-ethnic slurs, bigotry, and disparaging commentary, either spoken or written (offensive slang included).

Disruptive behavior includes the use of cell phones, pagers, or any other form of electronic communication during class discussion. Disruptive behavior also includes talking while the instructor or another member of the class is speaking or engaged in relevant conversation. This classroom functions on the premise of respect, and students will be asked to leave the classroom for any behavior that violates this premise.

Plagiarism

Plagiarism is grounds for suspension from the university and failure in this course. It will not be tolerated. Any instance of plagiarism must be reported to the Director of First-Year Writing and the Director of Undergraduate Studies. Plagiarism is a counterproductive, non-writing behavior that is unacceptable in a course intended to aid the growth of individual writers.

Plagiarism is included among the violations defined in the Academic Honor Code, section b, paragraph two, as follows: "Regarding academic assignments, violations of the Academic Honor Code shall include representing another's work or any part thereof, be it published or unpublished, as one's own." A plagiarism education assignment that further explains this issue will be administered in all first-year writing courses during the second week of class. Each student will be responsible for completing the assignment and asking questions regarding any parts they do not fully understand.

Resources for Writers:

Reading/Writing Center (RWC)

The Reading/Writing Center, located in Williams 222-C, is devoted to individualized instruction in reading and writing and serves Florida State University students at all levels and from all majors. Its clients include a cross-section of the campus: first-year students writing for composition class, upper level students writing term papers, seniors composing letters of applications for jobs and graduate schools, graduate students working on theses and dissertations, multilingual students mastering English, and a variety of others. The RWC serves mostly walk-in tutoring appointments, however it also offers three different courses for credit that specifically target reading, undergraduate-level writing, and graduate-level writing.

The tutors in the RWC, all graduate students in English with training and experience in teaching composition, use a process-centered approach to help students at any stage of writing: from generating ideas to drafting, organizing, and revising. While the RWC does not provide editing or proofreading services, its tutors can help writers develop those strategies. Its approach to tutoring is to provide guidance to help students grow as writers, readers, and critical thinkers by developing strategies to help writers in many situations.

RWC at Strozier Library

A satellite RWC location at Strozier Library provides tutoring to students where they congregate most often, and where writing and research can co-develop. This location includes more evening hours to align with student needs. Late-night tutoring is also offered at this location during peak times in the semester, when students are up late writing midterm or final papers.

The Strozier location serves only walk-in appointments on a first-come, first-served basis, but students can sign up in advance the same day they want an appointment at the tutoring area. Hours vary by semester, but are updated on both the RWC website and the Strozier Library website at the start of each semester.

Digital Studio

The Digital Studio provides support to students working individually or in groups on a variety of digital projects, such as designing a website, developing an electronic portfolio for a class, creating a blog, selecting images for a visual essay, adding voiceover to a presentation, or writing a script for a podcast. Tutors who staff the Digital Studio can help students brainstorm essay ideas, provide feedback on the content and design of a digital project, or facilitate collaboration for group projects and presentations.

Students can use the Digital Studio to work on their own to complete class assignments or to improve overall capabilities in digital communication without a tutoring appointment if a workstation is available. However, tutor availability and workspace are limited so appointments are recommended.

Gordon Rule

In order to fulfill the Gordon Rule "W" Designation (writing) credit, the student must earn a "C-" or better in the course. In order to receive a "C-" or better in the course the student must earn at least a "C-" on the required writing assignments. If the student does not earn a "C-" or better on the required writing assignments, the student will not earn an overall grade of "C-" or better in the course, no matter how well the student performs in the remaining portion of the course.

Florida State University stipulates that students must write 7,000 words in ENC 1101 and 1102 (around 3,500 per class).

ADA

Students with disabilities needing academic accommodations should, in the FIRST WEEK OF CLASS, 1) register with and provide documentation to the Student Disability Resource Center (SDRC) and 2) bring a letter to the instructor from SDRC indicating the need for academic accommodations. This and all other class materials are available in alternative format upon request.

APPENDIX B

Teaching for Transfer: Overview of Major Assignments

Assignment	Description	Key Terms	Purpose
Source-based Article	A source-based article, in which the student goes beyond summarizing to analyze/make connections between the concepts of genre, audience and rhetorical situation, and begin to develop a theory of writing.	Genre, Audience, Rhetorical Situation, and Reflection	To have students begin to theorize about key terms and writing; to deliberately model inquiry or exploration of writing concepts; to begin to understand and practice reflection.
Inquiry-based Essay	Students analyze information from sources they researched and intentionally explore the role of genres in presenting the research as well as the audiences for their topics.	Exigence, Critical Analysis, Discourse Community, and Knowledge	To have students engage in inquiry-based research while practicing their understanding of eight of the key terms.
Composition in Three Genres	Students create a composition that strategically identifies three different genres to communicate to a targeted audience about the research topic explored in the second major assignment.	Context, Composing, and Circulation	To have students put their understanding of the key terms into practice, and specifically develop a composition that considers various contexts for composing.
Reflection-in-Presentation	The reflection-in-presentation asks students to identify key terms they believe are most important to their writing practices and to theorize about that choice. In other words, it asks students to create their theory of writing, using the idea of their own "made knowledge" about writing and the idea of reflection as both theory and practice.	Knowledge and Reflection (reiterated specifically in this unit)	To write their final iteration of their theory of writing; to consider theory about learning; to reflect on the concepts and knowledge made throughout the course.

DOI: 10.7330/9780874219388.c007

APPENDIX C

Major Assignment #1: Source-Based Article on Genre,
Audience, and Rhetorical Situation

Potential Sources for Study

- Lloyd Bitzer, "Rhetorical Situation"
- Kathleen Blake Yancey, "On Reflection"
- Billy Collins, "Commencement Address at Choate-Rosemary Hall"
- Martin Luther King, Jr. "Letter From Birmingham Jail"
- Nora Ephron, "A Few Words About Breasts"
- Gloria Anzaldua, "How to Tame a Wild Tongue"
- Al Gore, Jr. (w/ William Clinton), "White House Climate Change Action Plan"
- *The McGraw-Hill Handbook*, 3rd Edition, Chapter 1 (Writing Today), Chapter 2 (Understanding Assignments), Chapter 3 (Planning and Shaping), and Chapter 7 (Reading, Thinking, Writing).

For this assignment, you will **write a 6–8 page source-based article**, in which you will go beyond summarizing to **analyze and make connections between the concepts of genre, audience, and rhetorical situation**, and begin to **develop a theory of writing**. You will choose four of the assigned sources (which represent a variety of genres) listed above, from which you will incorporate evidence to support your ideas about these key concepts and reflect on a possible theory of writing.

You must first define the key terms *audience, genre*, and *rhetorical situation* and investigate their relationships within the context of all sources in order to determine the connections between them. You will closely analyze the sources you choose to write about in your article, looking at how each writer uses genre, handles the rhetorical situation, and reaches an audience. As you develop your article you will incorporate

DOI: 10.7330/9780874219388.c008

both the rhetorical strategies we will explore in class and your understanding of *audience, genre,* and *rhetorical situation.*

At the same time you are developing your article, **you will also create a 2–3 page reflection piece in which you begin to develop your theory of writing**, considering the concepts of genre, audience, and rhetorical situation and how they connect.

Week One: *Course Introduction, Overview of Major Assignments*

READING DUE:
Billy Collins; M-H Handbook Ch. 1

WRITING DUE:
Journal #1—What is Writing?
Reflection on Key Terms

Week Two: *Genre, Rhetorical Situation*

READING DUE:
Nora Ephron or Gloria Anzaldua; Martin Luther King; M-H Handbook Ch. 2

WRITING DUE:
Journal #2—Genre and Audience
Journal #3—Rhetorical Situation

Week Three: *Rhetorical Situation, Audience*

READING DUE:
Lloyd Bitzer; M-H Handbook Ch. 7

WRITING DUE:
Draft #1 of Major Assignment #1

Week Four: *Workshop, Reflection*

READING DUE:
Kathleen Yancey, "On Reflection"; M-H Handbook Ch. 3

WRITING DUE:
Draft #2 of Major Assignment #1

FINAL—Major Assignment #1; Reflection
Intro to Essay Two

Major Assignment #2: Inquiry-Based Research Essay

Potential Sources for Study

- Al Gore, TED lecture on climate change
- Paul Auster, "Why Write"

- Henry Jenkins, "Survivor Spoilers"
- Nora Ephron, "The Boston Photographs"
- Steven Johnson, "Where Good Ideas Come From" (excerpt from book and video)
- Nicholas Carr, "Is Google Making Us Stupid?"
- The *McGraw-Hill Handbook*, 3rd Edition, Chapter 15 (Understanding Research), Chapter 16 (Finding and Managing Sources), Chapter 18 (Evaluating Sources), Chapter 21 (Working with Sources and Avoiding Plagiarism), Chapter 22 (Writing the Paper), and Chapter 23 (MLA Citation Style)
- Sample student research essays

For this assignment you will **write a 7–10 page research essay**. The objective in developing this **inquiry-based research essay** is not, perhaps, like other research essays with which you may be familiar. In an inquiry-based essay, the development of a research question is the cornerstone of the essay, providing a guideline for you to follow your research wherever the information takes you. You are investigating and possibly raising additional questions rather than providing a definitive answer or arguing for one side or another. Therefore, the careful formulation of a solid research question about your topic is crucial to ensure your inquiry will be effective.

Once your research question is finalized, you will conduct extensive inquiry into the potential implications and significance of your research question. You will **seek connections between the information you discover during your research and the potential significance** to your topic, identified audiences, and further inquiry. Your thorough research of multiple sources, and full analysis of your findings, will be the foundation from which you develop your essay. Your sources should be used as evidence to support, contradict, or expand on your ideas, and your essay must include extensive analysis around the question you explore.

The following types of research must be incorporated into your essay:

- Field notes about an observation that you conduct
- An interview conducted by you with a subject relevant to your research
- At least 4 academic sources
- At least 3 popular media sources relevant to your topic

Throughout the research process, you will write several short assignments in various genres. These genre assignments are designed to keep your research focused, to have you reflect on the research process and your sources so that you might better analyze them, and to help you present strong ideas in your essay. Each genre assignment is designed to help you through various stages of your research.

Writing Genre #1: Research Topic **Reflection**

This reflection will be based on your topic exploration and initial research. You'll reflect on what may have inspired the desire for further inquiry, including how you came up with the question, why it might be important, and how you plan to explore the question in your research. If you can't decide on a single question at this point, write about the top three you have in mind. We'll work together on narrowing your focus into one final research question, and we'll evaluate examples of strong research questions.

Writing Genre #2: Research **Proposal** *(1–2 typed, single-spaced pages)*

The proposal should identify the specific, final research question that you determine based on your initial exploration/research. Your proposal should discuss the same ideas as the topic reflection, but should be a more finely tuned presentation of the question your research will explore. Be sure to consider audience at this stage, specifically who might be interested in such an essay and for what type of publication it might be appropriate.

NOTE: This assignment is the **last chance to change your research question**. Once your proposal has been approved, the question you propose is final.

Writing Genre #3: **Report** *on Research in Progress (1–2 typed, single-spaced pages)*

In this report you will provide an update on your research in progress. You should provide the following information:

- Discuss the sources you have found so far and analyze their credibility
- Provide details about each source: how was each found, what makes each viable, and how you imagine each one effectively supporting your ideas
- Which source do you think will work best in your essay?
- Identify a source you found while conducting your research but have discarded, and explain why you are excluding it
- Discuss a source you are considering using, but about which you are still unsure, and explain your uncertainty
- Identify what's missing in your research, and speculate about information you are still seeking from additional sources

Writing Genre #4: **Post-Essay Reflection**

In this reflection, you will explore the process of researching and incorporating sources into your essay. Your reflection will provide an opportunity for you to think through the connections between your sources, how you presented them to your audience in your essay, and for what purpose. Fully analyze the rhetorical strategies you have employed. **Discuss how those strategies and the process of writing your research essay have contributed to the further development of your theory of writing**.

Week 5:   *Research, Critical Analysis, Exigence*

READING DUE:
Henry Jenkins; Nora Ephron; Steven Johnson
Student Essay Samples

WRITING DUE:
Journal #4—Knowledge
Research Topic Brainstorm
Writing Genre #1—Research Topic Reflection
Journal #5—Research Question Brainstorm

Week 6:   *Critical Analysis, Knowledge, Exigence*

READING DUE:
Paul Auster; Al Gore; M-H Handbook, Ch. 15 and Ch. 16

WRITING DUE:
Final Research Question
Individual Conferences

DUE AT CONFERENCE: Research Proposal

Week 7:   *Individual Conferences (cont.)*

READING & POSTING DUE:
Nicholas Carr; M-H Handbook Ch. 18 and Ch. 20
Journal #6—Research progress
MLA Citation

READING DUE:
M-H Handbook Ch. 21 and Ch. 23

WRITING DUE:
Writing Genre #3—Research Report
Draft #1 of Major Assignment #2

Week 8:   *Discourse Community*

READING DUE:
Sample Student Essays

WRITING DUE:
Journal #7—Context
Works Cited Draft
Workshop Day

WRITING DUE:
Draft #2 of Major Assignment #2

Week 9:   *Workshop, Revision*

WRITING DUE:
Draft #3 of Major Assignment #2
Journal #8—Reflection on Drafts

FINAL—Major Assignment #2 Due
Writing Genre #4—Post-Essay Reflection

MAJOR ASSIGNMENT #3: COMPOSITION IN THREE GENRES

Potential Sources for Study

- George Clooney interview, *Esquire,* May 2009
- Photo essay, "The Death of Dr. Martin Luther King Jr."
- Kathleen Yancey, "Made Not Only in Words: Composition in a New Key"
- Excerpt from *An Inconvenient Truth* documentary film
- Al Gore, "Nobel Peace Prize Acceptance Speech"
- Michael Jackson Obituary from the *LA Times*
- Steven Johnson Blog
- Bruce Springsteen interview on *60 Minutes* – aired on January 9, 2009
- *The McGraw-Hill Handbook,* 3rd Edition, Chapter 4 (Drafting), Chapter 5 (Revising), Chapter 6 (Designing Texts), Chapter 14 (Multimedia Writing), and selections from Part 5 (Writing Beyond College)

For this assignment you will move from researching and analyzing your topic, as you did in the Research Essay, to creating a composition which uses three different genres to communicate to a targeted audience about that same topic. You will use your previous research, along with new sources, to inform your creative strategy and help you make the rhetorical choices necessary to create an effective composition. These three genres are up to you to decide upon, based on your analysis of the rhetorical situation and the way in which you respond to it.

In this assignment, you will be relating your topic to audience even further, incorporating additional evidence, presenting new arguments, and considering audience expectations. You will first strategically target a specific audience(s), then develop key messages to communicate to that audience—based on knowledge of your topic gained from developing the research essay—and finally create three genres designed to communicate those messages to your audience(s). You will also write a rationale to communicate the connections between genres and your strategies for choosing them, and you will write a reflection that will consider the effect of these choices on your audience.

This assignment requires you to engage your critical thinking, rhetorical awareness, and reflection capabilities in order to most effectively communicate with your specified audience. Your strategy will determine the choices you make in communicating to your audience, how you present the research, and what you create to convey your message. The composition will include:

- **Three genres** of communication created for your audience(s)
- A **rationale** for your composition (3–4 pages) that orients your reader to the purpose of your work and its significance to your audience
- A **reflection** (3–4 pages) that outlines the process from audience strategy to final composition, exploring the rhetorical choices you made in creating this project
- A **works cited page** – minimum of five sources (three from Essay #2 may count here) appropriate to the audience you define in your audience strategy

Potential Genres:

You may use any genres you feel are appropriate to your audience. The strategy you develop will guide you in choosing the genres you want to create. Communicating effectively to your audience by choosing genres best suited to conveying your message will determine the potential effect of your composition. You may choose one genre from each of the following areas:

- newspaper article/magazine article
- memoir/personal essay
- obituary
- advertising campaign
- photo essay
- website/blog
- short-feature video
- musical composition
- academic journal article or case study
- brochure
- speech
- multimedia presentation
- Other genres you think of, **with instructor approval**

Just as you did for the research essay, for this composition project you will engage in a series of short writing assignments designed to help you focus your thinking about audience, message, and outcome before you begin the composition.

Short Assignment #1: Potential Genres Proposal

Through a series of journal entries and in-class activities, you will explore various genres that might be appropriate to your project, and write a proposal outlining the ones you're thinking about using in your composition. This proposal is designed to help you explore several possible genres and then narrow in on a strategy for the three specific genres (besides the rationale and reflection) you will ultimately use in your project. You should also consider your audience strategy as you write this.

Short Assignment #2: Audience Strategy

This strategy will be developed based on your research essay and your genres proposal. The audience strategy is the blueprint or foundation of your composition, so it is critical to develop a strategy with the end effect in mind. Planning in advance about how you will communicate your ideas to an audience will ensure its success; poor planning will result in a less-than-effective final project.

Short Assignment #3: Research Sources Report

In this report you will provide an update on your research sources, explaining which sources you will carry over from your research essay and why they make sense for your composition project. You will also report on the relevance of at least two additional sources you will use to support your project. Rather than finding additional sources about the topic itself, these sources may be about communicating your researched information to your identified audience.

Short Assignment #4: Reflection on Your Composition

In this reflection, you will analyze the process of moving from your research essay to your composition project, as well as think through questions that involve the key terms. Think about what rhetorical choices you have made, and consider the following questions: 1) Audience—what barriers in communicating to your audience(s) did you encounter? How did you overcome these barriers? 2) Process—how was the composing process different from your research essay? 3) Genre—why did you choose the three genres that you did? How did the genre affect the audience choice? 4) Reflection—what rhetorical practices did you find yourself using? Were they effective in the way you presented them? 5) Discourse Communities—how was your original discourse community affected in new genres?

Week 9   *(cont):*
                   Intro to Assignment Three

Week 10:   *Genre Exploration, Composing, Reflection—(Re)define genre*

                   READING DUE:
                   Clooney interview—Esquire; Springsteen interview

                   WRITING DUE:
                   Journal #8—Genre Exploration
                   Context, Circulation

                   READING DUE:
                   Kathleen Yancey, "Composition in a New Key"; Martin Luther King Jr., Photo Essay

                   WRITING DUE:
                   Short Assignment #1—Potential Genres Proposal

Week 11:   *Audience, Reflection—(Re)define audience*

                   READING DUE:
                   Los Angeles Times, Jackson Obituary; M-H Handbook Ch. 4 and Ch. 5

                   WRITING DUE:
                   Journal #9—Composing in Context
                   Revision Techniques

                   READING DUE:
                   Steven Johnson Blog; *Inconvenient Truth* Excerpt; Al Gore, Jr., "Nobel Peace Prize Acceptance Speech"

                   WRITING DUE:
                   Short Assignment #2—Audience Strategy

Week 12:   *Individual Conferences*

                   READING DUE:
                   M-H Handbook Ch. 6 and Ch. 14, selections from Part 5

                   WRITING DUE:
                   Short Assignment #3—Report on Sources due at conference

Week 13:   *Project Work Day*

                   WRITING DUE:
                   Update on Project

Week 14:   *FINAL PROJECT—Major Assignment #3 Due*
Intro to Reflection Assignment

READING DUE:
How People Learn, Chapter 2, "How Experts Differ from
Novices"

WRITING DUE:
Short Assignment #4—Reflection on your Composition

MAJOR ASSIGNMENT #4: REFLECTION-IN-PRESENTATION

Potential Sources For Study

*   *How People Learn*, Chapter 2, "How Experts differ from Novices"
*   *How People Learn*, Chapter 3, "Learning and Transfer"

Reflection allows us the **opportunity to process knowledge and then apply that knowledge.** Through reflection, we can **come to an understanding** and **interpret** what we have learned. This semester, on several occasions, we have used reflection in this way; in this final assignment you will return to this definition of reflection.

You have also been **developing your theory of writing** and what your theory of writing means in terms of **its relationship to your writing**—i.e., you have been exploring whether you enact your theory of writing in your own composition. As a result of this, you have had the opportunity to create a knowledge base of writing and its practices. In this final reflection, you will be returning to your theory to discuss several questions, including (but not limited to):

*   Define your theory of writing.
*   What was your theory of writing coming into ENC 1102? How has your theory of writing evolved with each piece of composing?
*   What has contributed to your theory of writing the most?
*   What is the relationship between your theory of writing and how you create(d) knowledge?
*   How might your theory of writing be applied to other writing situations both inside and outside the classroom?

For each of these questions you will need **to support your ideas with your previous writing** in this course and, **through these examples, interpret what you have learned.** You will create a compelling argument for whatever you decide to write for this, supported by evidence and analysis of the work completed in class this semester.

You will **choose a genre to work in**—letter, email, essay, journal entry, or any genre you may desire that is approved by the instructor—that you feel best represents your goals for your reflection and then explain why you chose that genre. In turn, you will also describe how your chosen genre affects the outcome (the final product) of your reflection.

This final reflection is an opportunity for you to demonstrate your increased knowledge in writing—the practices of writing, the key terms, and any specific skills you've acquired. **Think of this piece as another move in the evolution of your theory of writing**, and a chance for you to fully explore yourself as a writer and maker of knowledge.

Week 15:	*Theory of Writing, Reflection—your key terms*
	READING DUE: *How People Learn*, Chapter 3, "Learning and Transfer"
	WRITING DUE: Journal #10—"The Unveiling of a Writer"
Week 16:	*Finals Week* Reflection-in-Presentation Due

APPENDIX D

The Significance of Course Content in the Transfer of Writing Knowledge from First-Year Composition to other Academic Writing Contexts

The following set of interview questions were used for all study participants. Additional discussion often stemmed from these prepared questions.

Interview 1.1: (Fall Semester 2009, late September)

1. Please list all writing courses taken in high school and any college courses taken, including current classes. Did you take ENC 1101 at FSU or elsewhere, or did you get credit for it another way?

2. How would you describe your process of writing for a school assignment? Please describe all that goes into that process, from the time you receive the assignment to the time you submit the final product. Include as much detail around the writing process as possible, even details such as whether you listen to music or eat a certain snack while you're writing.

3. Do you think about what you're going to write, or plan your writing in advance?

4. Do you just start writing to see what comes out?

5. Do you revise your writing? If so, describe the process—what does revising include?

6. How would you describe yourself as a writer right now?

7. What kind of writing do you like to do most? What topics do you like to write about (be specific and list as many as possible)? Do you prefer to choose what you write about, or do you prefer it when a teacher gives you a specific topic? Why?

8. What kind of writing represents your best work, both in class and outside of school writing? Which of your previous classes have helped you do your best work? Why? Are there any other aspects of your life that help you with any writing you do? If so, what are they?

DOI: 10.7330/9780874219388.c009

9. Have you ever written in a journal or diary? Do you keep one regularly? If so, why do you journal write and how often do you journal write?

10. Have you ever been assigned reflection writing in a class? If so, which class(es)? If so, how did you enjoy reflection writing compared to other types of writing? If you were asked to write a reflection about your first week at college, what would you write about? How would you approach such an assignment?

11. How is ENC 1102 different or similar to any of the writing classes you have taken in the past? What have you learned in ENC 1102 that was completely new to you or that you did not learn in any previous classes? What have you improved upon in ENC 1102 that you may have already been familiar with from previous writing classes?

12. What kind of writer are you? Describe yourself as a writer.

Interview 1.2: (Fall Semester 2009, late October)

1. Tell me about the last major assignment in your writing class—was it clear and easy to understand? What made it clear? Or how did you clarify if not clear? Did expectations for the assignment become more or less clear as you progressed? Why or why not?

2. What was your topic? How was the topic chosen? Did you develop a main point about your topic right away? How did you reach the point of developing a main point or thesis?

3. Did you consider audience when writing this assignment? If so, who were your audiences? How did you establish that this was the audience you wanted to target? Or did you write without a specific audience in mind?

4. What was the primary purpose for writing this essay? Did you identify any additional purposes for writing?

5. What experience, if any, have you had in the past with conducting research or writing using research sources? If you had past experience with research, where did that take place and did anything from that experience apply to this assignment? What, specifically?

6. How did you plan this essay? Did you just start writing, or did you plan what to write before you started? What specific tools, if any, did you use to plan your approach? Were these tools you have learned previously, or did you use planning methods you learned in this course, or a combination of both? How do you usually plan something you're going to write?

7. How did you develop an approach to this essay? How did you decide on the content? Was there a requirement you followed? Did the research or course readings help you decide? Did you decide content first and then do research?

8. What were the biggest challenges for you in completing this assignment? What strategies did you use to meet those challenges? How did they work for you? Have you discovered anything since that might have helped you better meet any of the challenges in this assignment? If so, please explain what you've discovered that might have helped.

9. What was most challenging specifically about the revision process for this essay? What did you do to make the revision process work for you? Did you reflect during the process about what was working or not? Did you learn anything during the revision process?

10. Looking back on the course of preparing this assignment, what experience did you draw upon most? What was most valuable in helping you complete this assignment? (PROBE: either from this class or from some other experience, did you draw on something you've done previously?)

11. After completing the assignment, did you reflect on the process? Did you discover anything either during that reflection, or that you think of now, that you might use in future? If so, what did you discover and how do you think you'll use it in future writing?

Interview 1.3: (Fall Semester 2009, mid-December)

1. Was there a theme to your 1102 course? How would you summarize what the course was about?

2. Tell me about your major assignments in 1102—what were they about? What did they require of you?

3. Did each assignment build on the last one? Did you take anything from the first assignment and use what you learned in a later assignment, for example? What did you apply from one assignment to another?

4. Did you learn any particular writing strategies? What were they? (i.e., did you learn ways to plan writing, or to think about your writing . . . strategies that helped you get started, add more of something, or improve something in your assignment?)

5. Tell me about the writing process for each assignment? Were they the same, or different? How did the instructor get you started, or how did you get started on your own? What were the steps you took to complete the assignment? What was the hardest part of that process? What was the best part? Why?

6. What was your favorite assignment from this class? What made it your favorite? What did you take away/learn from that assignment?

7. Did you apply what you learned from that assignment to another assignment—in this class or any other? Tell me about that.

8. What specifically helped you about doing X (i.e., multiple drafts or other specific strategies)?

9. What is your theory about writing? (PROBE: If you had to create a theory of writing, what would you say?)

10. What does writing mean to you? In college, or elsewhere . . . is it the same for every situation? Are there things you do or think about in every writing situation?

11. What does it take to be successful at writing? How would you advise someone else if they asked you what it takes to be successful at writing (not as a professional writer, but just doing the writing you need to do in school/work/life)?

12. Think for a minute about your 1102 class . . . what prepared you to take that class from high school or a previous college class? Did you bring any knowledge with you from previous experiences that you used specifically in 1102?

13. Did you learn anything in 1102 that you might use throughout college . . . about writing, the writing process, or any specific strategies/tools for writing or improving your writing? What do you take from that experience? Have you had any situation so far this semester that reminded you of anything you learned in 1102, or in which you used something you learned in 1102?

14. What are the most important elements you learned in 1102 that you will use in writing for other classes, do you think? In what situations do you think your knowledge and practices taken from 1102 will be useful?

Interview 2.1 (Spring Semester 2010, mid-January)

1. Tell me about the courses you're taking this semester: what kind of writing is expected of you? What assignments will you have to write? List all—from smaller assignments to major writing assignments. (Look at syllabi provided for courses to discuss/probe about writing expectations).

2. What genres of writing will you be engaging in, based on the list you've just provided? Can you categorize the writing? Please list as many as you can think of.

3. How would you describe the kinds of writing, beyond the category you listed above? What do you imagine will be involved in the writing (PROBE: analysis, summarizing, description, research, etc)?

4. What is the purpose of writing in each assignment? What's the point of it and why do you think it is asked of you?

5. How do you plan to approach each of these assignments? What do you think you'll need to do to complete them successfully?

6. What strategies will you use to write these assignments? (PROBE: Do you have a process you use to get ready to write? Do you make a plan? What will you do for each?)

7. Are any of these assignments new types of writing for you? Are there any you haven't been asked to write in your academic experience as yet? Which ones?

8. How will you approach new, unfamiliar types of writing? What will you do to figure out the best way to write these? What specific things will you focus on?

9. What did you learn from your ENC 1102 course that you might apply to the writing you have to do this semester—either the types of writing you've done before or the ones that are less familiar or new. What will you bring from your 1102 course to these assignments?

10. What are the similarities between the writing you are being asked to do this semester, and the writing you did in ENC 1102? And differences?

11. How would you describe your approach to doing something you've never done before in college? (PROBE: Are there courses you have taken or are taking that ask you to do something different than anything you've experienced? Do you have a way of dealing with a new situation that works for you? What is your way of dealing with new situations in terms of writing? How do you make sure you'll be successful at an assignment that is not like something you've ever done before?)

12. How did your experience in ENC 1102 help you with writing in new situations?

13. What about other courses you've had in which writing was something that was required? Did you learn anything about writing from any other courses that help you to write in new situations? What exactly did you learn that is helpful?

14. Is there something you've learned in the past about writing that does not help, or that you find is inappropriate or inaccurate to writing in your courses this semester? If so, what is it (explanation in detail)?

15. Follow up if yes: What do you do with that information? Is it something you use only in certain situations, or something you think you'll never use again?

16. Is there one thing about writing, some writing tool or strategy, or just a thought about writing, that you find works for you all the time? (If yes: what is it? Where did you learn it? Why does it work?)

Interview 2.2 (Spring Semester 2010, early March)

1. Tell me again about the courses you're taking this semester: did you expect to be writing in each course, and was that expectation accurate?

Did you end up writing more than you thought you would? Or less? Please explain in as much detail as possible.

2. What kinds of writing did you do? How would you categorize the writing (i.e., lab reports, essays, etc) you've been doing in each of your courses? Please list as many types or categories as you can think of.

3. How would you describe the kinds of writing, beyond the category you listed above? What was involved in the writing (i.e., analysis, summarizing, description, etc)?

4. What was the purpose of writing in each course? What role did writing play in each? What did writing do for you in each course?

5. For each course, how did you come up with ideas for the writing? Were you given explicit instructions? Did you have to generate your own ideas or topics? Were the writing requirements specialized? Describe in detail for each.

6. Think back to when you began to write the assignments for each course—what did you think about to be successful at the assignments? What "rules" or prior knowledge about writing did you use in writing these assignments?

7. What process did you use in writing these assignments? Did you plan it out, did you write more than one draft, did you get feedback from a friend? Was there a specific process you followed usually, or did it depend on the writing task? Did you reflect at all? Describe your process.

8. How did you figure out what was going to make your writing successful for each assignment? What was your strategy for each writing situation?

9. What made your strategy work for each situation? What made you think or know it would work? How successful was it, looking back? What would have been more successful do you think?

10. Think back to your ENC 1102 course . . . Did you use anything you learned in your ENC 1102 course to complete the writing assignments for these courses? Did you do anything in the same way you did in 1102? What did you use and did it work well? Or did you use something that didn't work well? Please explain.

11. Did you use anything you learned somewhere other than ENC 1102 in completing these assignments? If so, what did you use and where did you learn it?

12. How would you describe the similarities between writing in ENC 1102 and the writing you did this semester? And how would you describe the differences? Please answer in as much specific detail as possible, making as many comparisons as you can think of.

13. Do you think anything you learned in ENC 1102 transferred to any of the writing situations you were in this semester? If so, what transferred?

14. How did it transfer? Did you transfer it deliberately, or are there things that transferred unconsciously?

15. Did you approach writing any differently, or do anything differently, this semester than you have in the past? What did you learn about writing from these courses?

16. What do you think students need to do to be successful at writing in any course at FSU? What would you tell a fellow student if you were asked what makes writing good in college? If you could advise yourself as an incoming freshman, what advice would you give yourself about writing, or learning writing, before you started college courses?

Interview 2.3 (Spring Semester 2010, end of April)

1. What did you do best this semester in terms of writing? What was your best work and why?

2. (WITH PARTICULAR ASSIGNMENT IDENTIFIED) What did the assignment ask you to do? How did you do that? What made it successful?

3. Where did you learn this writing strategy/approach?

4. (IF NECESSARY) Can you say more about where that came from . . . did you apply that from some other time it worked well for you? What made it appropriate this time, or what made you think it would work well here?

5. Thinking across all your writing that you've done so far at FSU, how does it all connect? How is it related? (PROBE: Would you say it's all related, or that each writing experience builds off the last? If yes, in what ways? Or is each writing experience random, or new, with no connection to the past?)

6. Think back to when you began to write the assignments for each course—what did you think about to be successful at the assignments? What rules or prior knowledge about writing did you use in writing these assignments?

7. How do you characterize good writing?

8. What makes writing successful for each situation?

9. What makes writing successful in college, in your experience so far? What strategies or approaches will you use to remain successful or to improve at it?

10. What worked best for you in your 1102 course? What was most successful for you in your writing in that course? Is there anything you take

from your ENC 1102 course that you use in writing today? Are there any elements you would recommend a future 1102 student make the most of?

11. Other than actual writing techniques, what would you say are the most important elements about writing that you consider in order to make it work well in any situation?

12. How will you use writing in your future life? Will your approach to writing always be the same or will it vary? What do you know about writing now that you would transfer to future writing you'll do?

Connecting the Dots: Does Reflection Foster Transfer?

Interview #1 (End of Fall Semester 2009):

1. To you—what is writing? How does it (if it does) differ from what you believe is "good" writing? What type of author represents your definition of good writing? Would you consider yourself to be a good writer based on your definition? Where do you use writing most? Walking into ENC 1102—what did you believe was involved in writing? How has this evolved in the past semester?

2. What previous knowledge (regardless of what class it came from) did you use in this class?

3. What is your theory of writing? What assignments helped you to define your theory of writing? Did any assignments contradict with your theory of writing or take away from your understanding of your theory of writing?

4. What readings stick out most to you? What readings did you feel helped you understand your own writing? What readings helped you understand your assignments?

5. How was this class different or the same as other writing classes you have taken? Which type of writing class do you believe is better for you to learn in?

6. Define reflection. What did you think reflection was before ENC 1102? Do you believe you reflected before? Based on your definition, where might reflection be useful and where might you use it? Do you believe you will use reflection for a class or another purpose again?

7. What reflective assignments were most helpful to you in this course and in developing your theory of writing? Do you believe reflective assignments are important in your understanding of yourself as a writer, composer, and thinker? Which of the reflective assignments did you enjoy

the most? The least? Why do you believe reflection was such a major element in this course?

8. What are your key terms for writing? Are they similar to your ENC 1102's key terms? How do they differ? Do you see overlap from ENC 1102's key terms to the other times you wrote this semester—which could have been in another class or for your own leisure?

9. What is one thing you are taking away from ENC 1102?

10. If you had to give advice to an incoming student taking ENC 1102— what would it be?

Interview #2 (Second week of classes, Spring 2010)

1. Discuss your overall reaction to the class now that you have had a chance to be away from it for a bit.

2. Think through all of the assignments—the readings, reflections, writings, etc. What stands out to you as most useful? Least useful?

3. Remind me of your theory of writing? How has it evolved since the beginning of Fall 2009?

4. Define reflection.

5. What key terms do you remember from ENC 1102 that you believe are important for you to use in other places that you write?

6. Did you use any of the practices you learned in ENC 1102 during your Christmas break—i.e., did you do any sort of writing (email, text, letter, etc) that you found yourself recalling something you learned in ENC 1102?

7. What is one thing you are taking away from ENC 1102?

8. If you had to give advice to an incoming student taking ENC 1102— what would it be?

Interview #3 (Week 13, Spring 2010)

1. Talk to me about the writing you have done this semester. What has been your process?

2. How has the process changed since ENC 1102?

3. What type of writer are you? Are you an expert or a novice and why?

4. What do you believe is most important in writing?

5. Do you believe that writing—the practice of it as well as the practices involved—can be important to your success in other classes and/or other writing situations? Be specific.

6. Discuss your overall reaction to the class now that you have had a chance to be away from it for a bit.

7. Remind me of your theory of writing? How has your theory writing progressed so far?

8. Do you see your theory of writing as something that is important to how you approach writing right now? In other words do you believe you are enacting your theory of writing?

9. Define reflection.

10. Do you find yourself using reflection in other classes? How?

11. What key terms do you remember from ENC 1102 that you believe are important for you to use in other places that you write? Do you believe you are using these key terms in the writing you are doing right now?

12. What is the most important aspect about writing that you learned in ENC 1102?

Interview #4 (Week 16, Spring 2010)

1. Create a set of key terms for writing. What would they be? And why did you choose the ones that you did?

2. I'm going to say some words, and I want you to please define them with the first thing that comes to your mind (could be a couple words or could be a complete sentence)—

    Rhetoric:
    Audience:
    Discourse Community:
    Rhetorical Situation:
    Exigence:
    Genre:
    Context:
    Composing:
    Writing:
    Reflection:
    Knowledge:
    Transfer:

3. Out of these words, which do you believe are most important in writing?

4. Which do you believe you think about when writing? Why?

5. If you were to going to teach someone what writing is—how would you do it and how would you go about explaining it to them?

6. Do you believe that by taking ENC 1102 (with Liane) you have helped build a foundation that will bring you a successful college career? Why or why not?

7. What makes you the most apprehensive in terms of writing?

8. What makes the writing process a little easier for you?

9. Walk me through your theory of writing. What does it mean to you now as a writer and as a student?

10. What role does reflection play in learning for you?

11. Do you see a connection between reflective activities (and/or reflection) and the development of your theory of writing?

12. Did at anytime you find yourself reflecting outside the walls of academia? When? Explain.

13. What do you believe was the most important practice of writing you learned so far in your academic career?

Email Exit Survey

1. Use three words to describe your theory of writing. Are these the same as what you would call your key terms for writing? Can you define these terms (in your own words)?

2. What is your theory of writing? How has it changed, progressed, and/or morphed since taking ENC 1102?

3. Do you believe a theory of writing is important to have? Explain. Have you enacted your theory of writing this semester? If so, how can you tell?

4. What did you learn in ENC 1102 that you have carried forward to right now? Give an example.

5. Describe and define reflection as you understand it to incoming FSU students.

6. Use two or three words to describe why you think you were asked to use reflection so much.

7. Reflection, according to Kathleen Yancey, allows you to become an agent of your learning and is rhetorical. What does this mean to you and would you agree with her assessment of reflection?

8. What does it mean to be a competent writer? Do you believe this connects to literacy?

9. Transfer is the ability to take knowledge learned in one area and apply it in another area. Do you believe you learned how to transfer writing knowledge from ENC 1102 to other writing situations you encountered this semester? Why or why not?

10. Please do a quick reflection on your participation in this study.

REFERENCES

Adler-Kassner, Linda, John Majewski, and Damian Koshnick. 2012. "The Value of Troublesome Knowledge." *Composition Forum* 26. compositionforum.com/issue/26/troublesome -knowledge-threshold.php.

Applebee, Arthur, and Judith Langer. 2009. "What's Happening in the Teaching of Writing?" *English Journal* 98 (5): 18–28.

Applebee, Arthur, and Judith Langer. 2011. "A Snapshot of Writing Instruction in Middle Schools and High Schools." *English Journal* 100 (6): 14–27.

Bacon, Nora. 1999. "The Trouble with Transfer: Lessons from a Study of Community Service Writing." *Michigan Journal of Community Service Learning* 6: 53–62.

Baird, Neil, and Bradley Dilger. 2013. "Writing Transfer and the First Generation Transfer Student." Paper presented at Critical Transitions: Writing and the Question of Transfer session 1.2.

Bakhtin, M. M. 1986. *Speech Genres and Other Late Essays*. Austin: University of Texas Press.

Bartholomae, David. 1986. "Inventing the University." In Rose, Mike, *When a Writer Can't Write: Studies in Writer's Block and Other Composing-Process Problems*, 134–166. New York: Guilford.

Baxter-Magolda, Marcia B. 2001. *Making Their Own Way: Narratives for Transforming Higher Education to Promote Self-Development*. Sterling, VA: Stylus.

Beach, King. 2003. "Consequential Transitions: A Developmental View of Knowledge Propagation through Social Organizations." In Tuomi-Gröhn, Terttu and Yrjö Engeström, *Between School and Work: New Perspectives on Transfer and Boundary-crossing*, 39–61. Bingley, UK: Emerald Group.

Beaufort, Anne. 1999. *Writing in the Real World: Making the Transition from School to Work*. New York: Teachers College Press.

Beaufort, Anne. 2007. *College Writing and Beyond: A New Framework for University Writing Instruction*. Logan: Utah State UP.

Beaufort, Anne. 2009. "All Talk, No Action? Or, Does Transfer Really Happen after Reflective Practice?" Paper presented at the *Conference on College Composition and Communication*, San Francisco, CA.

Beaufort, Anne. 2012. "College Writing and Beyond: Five Years Later." *Composition Forum* 26. http://compositionforum.com/issue/26/college-writing-beyond.php

Belanoff, Pat. 2001. "Silence: Reflection, Literacy, Learning, and Teaching." *College Composition and Communication* 52 (3): 399–428. http://dx.doi.org/10.2307/358625.

Bergmann, Linda S., and Janet S. Zepernick. 2007. "Disciplinarity and Transference: Students' Perceptions of Learning to Write." *WPA: Writing Program Administration* 31 (1/2): 124–49.

Beyer, Catharine Hoffman, Andrew T. Fisher, and Gerald M. Gilmore. 2007. *Inside the Undergraduate Experience, the University of Washington's Study of Undergraduate Learning*. Bolton, MA: Anker Publishing.

Bordelon, Suzanne. 2010. "Composing Women's Civic Identities during the Progressive Era: College Commencement Addresses as Overlooked Rhetorical Sites." *College Composition and Communication* 61 (3): 510–33.

Bransford, John D., James W. Pellegrino, and M. Suzanne Donovan, eds. 2000. *How People Learn: Brain, Mind, Experience, and School: Expanded Edition*. Washington, DC: National Academy Press.

DOI: 10.7330/9780874219388.c010

Brent, Doug. 2012. "Crossing Boundaries: Co-op Students Relearning to Write." *College Composition and Communication* 63 (4): 558–92.

Britton, James, T. Burgess, N. Martin, A. McLeod, and N. Rosen. 1979. *The Development of Writing Abilities 11–18.* New York: MacMillan.

Brookfield, Stephen D. 1995. *Becoming a Critically Reflective Teacher.* San Francisco, CA: Jossey-Bass.

Bunn, Michael. 2013. "Motivation and Connection: Teaching Reading (and Writing) in the Composition Classroom." *College Composition and Communication* 64 (3): 496–517.

Carroll, Lee Ann. 2002. *Rehearsing New Roles: How College Students Develop as Writers.* Carbondale, IL: Southern Illinois UP.

Clark, Gregory. 1998. "Writing as Travel, or Rhetoric on the Road." *College Composition and Communication* 49 (1): 9–23. http://dx.doi.org/10.2307/358557.

Council of Writing Program Administrators. 2000, 2008. "WPA Outcomes Statement for First-Year Composition." http://wpacouncil.org/positions/outcomes.html.

Critical Transitions: Writing and the Question of Transfer. 2011. Elon University. http://www.elon.edu/eweb/academics/teaching/ers/writing_transfer/default.xhtml

Davis, Matt. 2012. *Rhetorical Composing: A Multimodal, Multimedia Model of Literacy.* PhD diss., Florida State University.

DeJoy, Nancy C. 2004. *Process This: Undergraduate Writing in Composition Studies.* Logan: Utah State UP.

Denecker, Christine. 2013. "Transitioning Writers across the Composition Threshold." *Composition Studies* 41 (1): 27–51.

Detterman, Douglas K., and Robert J. Sternberg, eds. 1993. *Transfer on Trial: Intelligence, Cognition, and Instruction.* Norwood, NJ: Able.

Dew, Debra. 2003. "Language Matters: Rhetoric and Writing I as Content Course." *WPA: Writing Program Administration* 26 (3): 87–104.

Donnelly, Michael. 2006. "What's the Content of Composition?" CompFAQ. *CompPile.* http://compfaqs.org/ContentofComposition/HomePage

Donahue, Christiane. 2012. "Transfer, Portability, Generalization: (How) Does Composition Expertise 'Carry'?" In *Exploring Composition Studies,* edited by Kelly Ritter and Paul Kei Matsuda, 145–66. Logan: Utah State UP.

Downs, Douglas, and Elizabeth Wardle. 2007. "Teaching About Writing, Righting Misconceptions: (Re)Envisioning 'First-Year Composition' as 'Introduction to Writing Studies.'." *College Composition and Communication* 58 (4): 552–84.

Downs, Douglas, and Elizabeth Wardle. 2012. "Reimagining the Nature of FYC Trends in Writing-about-Writing Pedagogies." In *Exploring Composition Studies,* edited by Kelly Ritter and Paul Kei Matsuda, 123–44. Logan: Utah State UP.

Driscoll, Dana, and Jennifer Wells. 2012. "Beyond Knowledge and Skills: Writing Transfer and the Role of Student Dispositions in and beyond the Writing Classroom." *Composition Forum* 26. http://compositionforum.com/issue/26/beyond-knowledge-skills.php

English Department. 2011/2012. "English Department Resources: First Year Composition." *Florida State University.* http://wr.english.fsu.edu/First-Year-Composition

Faigley, Lester, Roger Cherry, David Jolliffe, and Anna Skinner. 1985. *Assessing Writers' Knowledge and Processes of Composing.* Norwood, NJ: Ablex.

Freire, Paulo. 2000. *Pedagogy of the Oppressed. Thirtieth Anniversary Edition.* New York: Continuum.

Fulkerson, Richard. 2005. "Composition at the Turn of the Twenty-First Century." *College Composition and Communication* 56 (4): 654–87.

Gawande, Atul. 2002. *Complications: A Surgeon's Notes on an Imperfect Science.* New York: Holt/Picador.

Hansen, Kristine, Suzanne Reeve, Richard Sudweeks, Gary L. Hatch, Jennifer Gonzalez, Patricia Esplin, and William S. Bradshaw. 2004. "An Argument for Changing Institutional

Policy and Granting A.P. Credit in English: An Empirical Study of College Sophomores' Writing." *WPA: Writing Program Administration* 28: 29–54.

Harris, Joseph. 1996. *A Teaching Subject: Composition since 1966.* New York: Prentice Hall.

Harris, Joseph. 2006. "Undisciplined Writing." In *Delivering College Composition: The Fifth Canon,* ed. Kathleen Blake Yancey, 155–67. Portsmouth: Boynton/Cook.

Harvard College Writing Program. 2010. *Harvard University.* Web.

Haverford College Writing Program. 2013. Haverford College. Web.

Hawk, Byron. 2007. *A Counter History of Composition: Toward Methodologies of Complexity.* Pittsburg. University of Pittsburg Press.

Hilgers, Thomas, Edna Hussey, and Monica Stitt-Bergh. 1999. "'As You're Writing, You Have These Epiphanies': What College Students Say about Writing and Learning in Their Majors." *Written Communication* 16 (3): 317–53. http://dx.doi.org/10.1177/074 1088399016003003.

Jarratt, Susan, Katherine Mack, Alexandra Sartor, and Shevaun Watson. 2005. "Retrospective Writing Histories." Paper presented at the Writing Research in the Making Conference, Santa Barbara, CA.

Jarratt, Susan, Katherine Mack, Alexandra Sartor, and Shevaun Watson. 2008. "Pedagogical Memory and the Transferability of Writing Knowledge: an Interview-Based Study of Juniors and Seniors at a Research University." Paper presented at the Writing Research across Borders Conference, Santa Barbara, CA. Web.

Jolliffe, David A. 2007. "Review Essay: Learning to Read as Continuing Education." *College Composition and Communication* 58 (3): 470–94.

Kaufer, David, and Richard Young. 1993. "Writing in the Content Areas: Some Theoretical Complexities." In Odell, Lee *Theory and Practice in the Teaching of Writing: Rethinking the Discipline,* 71–104. Carbondale: Southern Illinois UP.

Krause, Steve, Jacquelyn Kelly, James Corkins, and Amaneh Tasooji. 2009. "The Role of Prior Knowledge on the Origin and Repair of Misconceptions in an Introductory Class on Materials Science and Engineering." 2009 REES (Research in Engineering Education Symposium) Conference Proceedings, Palm Cove, QLD, Australia.

Lenhart, Amanda, Sousan Arafeh, Aaron Smith, and Alexandra Macgill. 2008. "Writing, Technology, and Teens." Pew Internet & American Life Project. Accessed January 13, 2012. http://www.pewinternet.org/Reports/2008/Writing-Technology-and-Teens.aspx.

Matsuda, Paul Kei. 2003. "Process and Post-process: A Discursive History." *Journal of Second Language Writing* 12 (1): 65–83. http://dx.doi.org/10.1016/S1060-3743(02)00127-3.

McCarthy, Lucille. 1987. "A Stranger in Strange Lands: A College Student Writing across the Curriculum." *Research in the Teaching of English* 21 (3): 233–65.

Meyer, Jan H.F., and Ray Land. 2006. *Overcoming Barriers to Student Understanding.* London: Routledge.

Meyer, Jan H.F., and Ray Land. 2003. *"Threshold Concepts and Troublesome Knowledge: Linkages to ways of Thinking and Practising within the Disciplines."* Enhancing Teaching-Learning Environments in Undergraduate Courses Project, Occasional Report 4. University of Edinburgh.

Miles, Libby, Michael Pennell, Kim Hensley Owens, Jeremiah Dyehouse, Helen O'Grady, Nedra Reynolds, Robert Schwegler, and Linda Shamoon. 2008. "Commenting on Douglas Downs and Elizabeth Wardle's 'Teaching about Writing, Righting Misconceptions.'" *College Composition and Communication* 59 (3): 503–11.

Miller, Carolyn. 1984. "Genre as Social Action." *Quarterly Journal of Speech* 70 (2): 151–67. http://dx.doi.org/10.1080/00335638409383686.

Moffett, James. 1968. *Teaching the Universe of Discourse.* Boston: Houghton Mifflin.

Moore, Jessie. 2012. "Mapping the Questions: The State of Writing-Related Transfer Research." *Composition Forum* 26, http://compositionforum.com/issue/26/map-questions -transfer-research.php.

Navarre Cleary, Michelle. 2013. "Flowing and Freestyling: Learning from Adult Students about Process Knowledge Transfer." *College Composition and Communication* 64 (4): 661–87.

Nowacek, Rebecca S. 2011. *Agents of Integration: Understanding Transfer as a Rhetorical Act.* Carbondale, IL: Southern Illinois UP.

Osterman, Karen F., and Robert B. Kottkamp. 2004. *Reflective Practice for Educators.* 2nd ed. Newbury Park, CA: Corwin.

Palinscar, Annemarie Sullivan, and Ann L. Brown. 1982. "Reciprocal Teaching of Comprehension Monitoring Activities." *Cognition and Instruction* 1: 117–75.

Perkins, David N., and Gavriel Salomon. 1992. "Transfer of Learning." In *International Encyclopedia of Education,* 2nd ed., 2–13. Oxford: Pergamon Press.

Perry, William. 1976. *Forms of Intelligence and Ethical Development in the College Years: A Scheme.* New York: Holt, Rinehart, and Winston.

Petraglia, Joseph. 1995. "General Writing Skills Instruction and Its Discontents." In *Reconceiving Writing, Rethinking Writing Instruction,* by Joseph Petraglia, xi–xvii. Mahweh: Lawrence Erlbaum.

Prather, Dirk C. 1971. "Trial and Error versus Errorless Learning: Training, Transfer, and Stress." *American Journal of Psychology* 84 (3): 377–86. http://dx.doi.org/10.2307/1420469.

Prior, Paul. 1991. "Contextualizing Writing and Response in a Graduate Seminar." *Written Communication* 8 (3): 267–310. http://dx.doi.org/10.1177/0741088391008003001.

Pytlik, Betsy P., and Sarah Liggett. 2002. *Preparing College Teachers of Writing: Histories, Theories Programs, Practices.* New York: Oxford.

Reiff, Mary Jo, and Anis Bawarshi. 2011. "Tracing Discursive Resources: How Students Use Prior Genre Knowledge to Negotiate New Writing Contexts in First-Year Composition." *Written Communication* 28 (3): 312–37. http://dx.doi.org/10.1177/0741088311410183.

Reynolds, Nedra. 2004. *Geographies of Writing: Inhabiting Places and Encountering Difference.* Carbondale, IL: Southern Illinois UP.

Ritter, Kelly, and Paul Kei Matsuda, eds. 2012. *Exploring Composition Studies: Sites, Issues and Perspectives.* Logan: Utah State UP.

Robertson, Liane, Kara Taczak, and Kathleen Blake Yancey. 2012. "Notes toward a Theory of Prior Knowledge and Its Role in College Composers' Transfer of Knowledge and Practice." *Composition Forum.* http://compositionforum.com/issue/26/prior-knowledge-transfer.php

Robertson, Liane. 2011. "The Significance of Course Content in the Transfer of Writing Knowledge from First-Year Composition to other Academic Writing Contexts." PhD diss., Florida State University.

Robinson, Tracy Ann, and Vicki Tolar Burton. 2009. "The Writer's Personal Profile: Student Self Assessment and Goal Setting at Start of Term." *Across the Disciplines* 6. http://wac.colostate.edu/atd/assessment/robinson_burton.cfm

Roozen, Kevin. 2009. "From Journals to Journalism: Tracing Trajectories of Literate Development." *College Composition and Communication* 60.3: 541–72.

Russell, David R. 1995. "Activity Theory and Its Implications for Writing Instruction." In Petraglia, Joseph, *Reconceiving Writing, Rethinking Writing Instruction,* 51–79. Mahweh: Lawrence Erlbaum.

Russell, David R., and Arturo Yañez. 2002. "'Big Picture People Rarely Become Historians': Genre Systems and the Contradictions of General Education." In Bazerman, Charles and David Russell, *Writing Selves/Writing Societies: Research From Activity Perspectives.* Fort Collins, CO: The WAC Clearinghouse and Mind, Culture and Activity. http://wac.colostate.edu/books/selves_societies/russell/

Scherff, Lisa, and Carolyn Piazza. 2005. "The More Things Change, the More They Stay the Same: A Survey of High School Students' Writing Experiences." *Research in the Teaching of English* 39 (3): 271–304.

Simpson, Karen, and Helen Cameron. 2012. "Sharing PDP Practice: University of Edinburgh Medical School." Presentation at the Higher Education Academy, UK. http://www.docstoc.com/docs/112968064/Sharing-PDP-Practice-University-of-Edinburgh-Medical-School

Sirc, Geoffrey. 2012. "Review Essay: Resisting Entropy." *College Composition and Communication* 63 (3): 507–19.

Smit, David. 2004. "Transfer." In *The End of Composition Studies*, 119–37. Carbondale: Southern Illinois UP.

Soliday, Mary. 2011. *Everyday Genres: Writing Assignments Across the Disciplines*. Carbondale, IL: Southern Illinois UP.

Sommers, Jeff. 1988. "Behind the Paper: Using the Student-Teacher Memo." *College Composition and Communication* 39 (1): 77–80. http://dx.doi.org/10.2307/357824.

Sommers, Jeff. 2011. "Reflection Revisited: The Class Collage." *Journal of Basic Writing* 30 (1): 99–129.

Sommers, Nancy, and Laura Saltz. 2004. "The Novice as Expert: Writing the Freshman Year." *College Composition and Communication* 56 (1): 124–49. http://dx.doi.org/10.2307/4140684.

Stanford Study of Writing. 2008. http://ssw.stanford.edu/research/paul_rogers.php.

Taczak, Kara. 2011. "Connecting the Dots: Does Reflection Foster Transfer?" PhD diss., Florida State University.

Thaiss, Chris, and Terry Myers Zawacki. 2006. *Engaged Writers and Dynamic Disciplines: Research on the Academic Writing Life*. Portsmouth: Boynton/Cook.

Tinberg, Howard, and Jean-Paul Nadeau. 2011. "Contesting the Space between High School and College in the Era of Dual-Enrollment." *College Composition and Communication* 62 (4): 704–25.

Tinberg, Howard, and Jean-Paul Nadeau. 2013. "What Happens When High School Students Write in a College Course? A Study of Dual Credit." *English Journal* 102 (5): 35–42.

Thorndike, Edward L., and Robert S. Woodworth. 1901. "The Influence of Improvement in One Mental Function upon the Efficiency of Other Functions." *Psychological Review* 8 (3): 247–61. http://dx.doi.org/10.1037/h0074898.

Tuomi-Gröhn, Terttu, and Yrgo Engeström, eds. 2003. *Between School and Work: New Perspectives on Transfer and Boundary-crossing*. New York: Pergamon.

Vander Lei, Elizabeth, and bonnie lenore kyburz, eds. 2005. *Negotiating Religious Faith in the Composition Classroom*. Portsmouth: Boynton/Cook.

Wardle, Elizabeth. 2007. "Understanding 'Transfer' from FYC: Preliminary Results of a Longitudinal Study." *WPA: Writing Program Administration* 31 (1–2): 65–85.

Wardle, Elizabeth. 2009. "'Mutt Genres' and the Goal of FYC: Can We Help Students Write the Genres of the University?" *College Composition and Communication* 60 (4): 765–89.

Wardle, Elizabeth. 2012. "Creative Repurposing for Expansive Learning: Considering 'Problem-Exploring' and 'Answer-Getting' Dispositions in Individuals and Fields." Introduction. *Composition Forum* 26. http://compositionforum.com/issue/26/creative-repurposing.php.

White, Barbara Y., and John R. Frederickson. 1998. "Inquiry, Modeling, and Metacognition: Making Science Accessible to All Students." *Cognition and Instruction* 16 (1): 90–91.

Yancey, Kathleen Blake. 1998. *Reflection in the Writing Classroom*. Logan: Utah State UP.

Yancey, Kathleen Blake. 2004. "Made Not Only in Words: Composition in a New Key." *College Composition and Communication* 56 (2): 297–328. http://dx.doi.org/10.2307/4140651.

Yancey, Kathleen Blake. 2006. "Delivering College Composition into the Future." In Yancey, Kathleen Blake, *Delivering College Composition: The Fifth Canon*, 199–209. Portsmouth: Boynton/Cook.

Yancey, Kathleen Blake. 2009a. "Re-designing Graduate Education in Composition and Rhetoric: The Use of Remix as Concept, Material, and Method." *Computers and Composition* 26 (1): 4–12. http://dx.doi.org/10.1016/j.compcom.2008.11.004.

Yancey, Kathleen Blake. 2009b. "Reflection and Electronic Portfolios: Inventing the Self and Reinventing the University." In *Electronic Portfolios 2.0: Emergent Research on Implementation and Impact*, ed. Darren Cambridge, Barbara Cambridge, and Kathleen Blake Yancey, 5–17. Washington, DC: Stylus.

Yancey, Kathleen Blake. 2013. "The (Designed) Influence of Culture on Eportfolio Practice." In *International Perspectives on Teaching English in a Globalised World*, ed. Lou Ann Reid, et al. Routledge: 266–78.

ABOUT THE AUTHORS

KATHLEEN BLAKE YANCEY is Kellogg W. Hunt Professor of English and Distinguished Research Professor at Florida State University. She has served as the elected leader of several scholarly organizations, including the National Council of Teachers of English (NCTE), the Conference of College Composition and Communication (CCCC), and the Council of Writing Program Administrators (CWPA). Codirector of the Inter/National Coalition for Electronic Portfolio Research and editor of *College Composition and Communication*, Yancey has authored or co-authored over seventy articles and book chapters, and authored, edited, or co-edited eleven scholarly books—including *Portfolios in the Writing Classroom, Reflection in the Writing Classroom*, and *Delivering College Composition*. Among her current projects is *The Way We Were: Everyday Writing in the 20th Century United States*.

LIANE ROBERTSON is Assistant Professor of English at William Paterson University of New Jersey, where she also serves as the assistant director of the writing and rhetoric program. For the past several years her publications and research have primarily focused on transfer and the content of writing courses, specifically the role content plays in fostering the transfer of writing knowledge and practice across multiple contexts. She is currently conducting a multi-institutional research study comparing content across various sites of writing, exploring further the potential for selected content to effect transfer. Robertson is also involved in research on writing assessment. Her latest writing project centers on threshold concepts in writing.

KARA TACZAK is on the writing faculty at the University of Denver, where she teaches first-year composition and advises first-year students. Her research centers on the intersection of reflection and transfer of knowledge and practice. Taczak's current research project seeks to determine how reflective practices encourage and/or support the transfer of writing knowledge and practice from FYC to other academic writing sites. As an Elon Research Seminar participant, she is also a member of a multi-institutional research study comparing content across multiple sites of writing. Taczak's publications have appeared in *Composition Forum, Teaching English in the Two-Year College*, and *ATD: Across the Disciplines*.

INDEX

absence of prior knowledge, 104, 108, 110, 112

academic writing, 1, 2, 17, 30, 36n2, 43, 45, 47, 65, 128n1, 131, 169

activity-based perception of transfer, 8, 10

Adler-Kassner, Linda, viii, 59n1, 135

Advanced Placement (AP), 18, 20, 63, 77, 88, 106, 112, 116–117

agency: writer's, 5, 41–42, 98

Agents of Integration model, 35, 38, 42, 53–55, 130

AP. *See* Advanced Placement

Applebee, Arthur, 13, 108–109

assemblage model of prior knowledge, 5, 35, 104, 112, 114–116, 126–128, 130, 133, 135, 145. *See also* prior knowledge

Bacon, Nora, iv, 20–21, 36n5, 36n12, 59n1

Bartholomae, David, 1, 137, 144

Bawarshi, Anis, 9, 14–15, 17, 27, 34, 101, 106, 112, 133, 134

Beach, King, 9, 32, 50, 54

Beaufort, Anne, 3, 6, 28–32, 34, 36n12, 44, 49, 51, 60, 63, 125, 138, 148

Bergmann, Linda S., 25–27, 44, 85, 100

biology: writing in, 28–29, 43, 50, 61, 67

blogger (blogging), 21, 40, 70, 72, 111, 155, 163–164, 166

blogging. *See* blogger

boundary crossers (crossing), 14–15, 27, 33, 106, 125–126, 133

boundary crossing. *See* boundary crossers

boundary guarders (guarding), 14–15, 27, 106, 125, 133

boundary guarding. *See* boundary guarders

Bourdieu, Pierre, 10–11

brainstorming, 16, 71–72, 151, 162

Bransford, John D., 13, 35, 38–39, 41, 63, 79, 82, 90, 93, 97, 104, 121, 125, 128n3, 128n8, 129, 131, 136–138, 140

Brent, Doug, 9, 35, 38, 44, 45–48, 59n3, 79, 87, 110, 129, 132

Carroll, Lee Ann, 19–20, 88

CCC. *See College Composition and Communication*

CCCC. *See* Conference on College Composition and Communication

chemistry: writing in, 67, 82, 97–98, 123–125, 147

circulation, 57, 73, 74, 143, 157, 166

College Composition and Communication (CCC), 49

community of practice, 121

composing: practices, 76, 84, 107, 117, 118–120, 125, 126, 138; process(es), 94, 107, 118–120, 125, 150, 165; understanding of, 131–132, 134, 157

composition: content of. *See* content; curricula, 3–6, 34, 40; curricular models of, 31, 38, 56, 63; field of, 1, 3, 10, 11, 44; teaching of, 1, 3, 18

composition-in-three-genres, 58, 93, 134, 140, 142–143, 149n1, 157

Composition Forum, viii, 10, 149

conceptions: of writing, 23, 25, 49, 53, 104, 117, 126

conceptual framework (conceptual model; of writing knowledge and practice), 30–31, 57, 67, 73, 83, 116, 130, 137, 146

conceptualization of transfer, 8, 10

conceptual model. *See* conceptual framework

concurrent transfer, 20–21, 27, 36n11, 54, 102n13, 130, 133–134, 136

Conference on College Composition and Communication (CCCC), vii, viii, 3, 13, 36n3, 149

content: absence of, 52, 77, 81, 83, 85, 87–88; context-specific, 49, 77, 83; in first-year composition, 3–5, 31, 35, 42, 56, 60–61, 64–65, 67, 76, 81–82, 87–88, 99, 132, 138, 147–148; indiscernible, 77–78, 80, 82–83, 85, 87–88; language as, 42, 52–53; reflection as, 5, 63, 129; rhetoric as, 38, 42, 52–53; role of, 2–3, 31–32, 60–61, 63, 67, 87, 147; specific, 3, 5, 52–53, 60, 76, 83, 90, 101, 137; and transfer, 3, 5, 31, 33, 42, 49, 56–57, 60, 63–65, 73, 129, 138, 147; writing as, 32, 42, 49, 52–53, 83, 85, 130

context, 1, 3, 8, 18, 21, 22, 28, 33, 43, 45, 49, 50, 55, 61–63, 65–69, 78, 79, 85, 88, 91, 95, 97, 103–105, 108–111, 117, 118, 122, 123, 125–127, 128n3, 130, 132, 134, 136, 137, 140, 142, 146, 149n1,

DATE DUE